MYSTIC SEAPORT LIBRARY
DUPLICATE

THE FLIGHT FROM THE FLAG

U.S.S. Kearsarge on Roncador Reef, February, 1894.
From the collection of Franklin D. Roosevelt. *Reproduced by permission of the President.*

THE FLIGHT FROM THE FLAG

THE CONTINUING EFFECT
OF THE CIVIL WAR
UPON THE AMERICAN
CARRYING TRADE

By GEORGE W. DALZELL

CHAPEL HILL
THE UNIVERSITY OF NORTH CAROLINA PRESS
1940

COPYRIGHT, 1940, BY
THE UNIVERSITY OF NORTH CAROLINA PRESS

PRINTED IN THE UNITED STATES OF AMERICA
VAN REES PRESS, NEW YORK
PJ

To
W. T. SMITH
ἀρχοὺς αὖ νηῶν ἐρέω, νῆάς τε προπάσας

PREFACE

THE TWO GENERAL works which have dealt with the Confederate cruisers are J. Thomas Scharf's *History of the Confederate States Navy* (1887), a book of 824 pages, of which one short chapter relates to these ships; and James Russell Soley's *The Blockade and the Cruisers* (1883), a brief, closely condensed, and scholarly treatise, chiefly devoted to the blockade. These authors are concerned primarily with the military aspects of the activities of the raiders and do not deal with their economic effects.

The original sources of the present study are the *Official Records of the Union and Confederate Navies,* which have been published by the government; the diplomatic and consular reports available in the National Archives in Washington; the Case and Counter-Case for the United States and the Case for Great Britain before the Geneva Arbitration, the Tribunal's decision, and the reports of the American agent, in fourteen volumes; the decisions of the American and British courts in litigation resulting from the construction and operation of the cruisers and other vessels; the proceedings before the two claims courts set up to distribute the Geneva award; the memoirs of various officers and seamen, chiefly Confederate; and the press of the period. All of these have been consulted. The English press clippings have been collected in nine large scrapbooks in the Library of Congress, a set of books which I discovered after spending laborious days searching the files of the same newspapers, in which the absence of display type and of any method of distinguishing important news in the journals of the time makes a search of their columns trying to the eyes and to the patience of the investigator. The American and Anglo-Chinese papers cited are in the files of the Library of Congress.

The accounts of the Sumter and the Nashville are based on the naval records and on the manuscript consular reports in the National Archives (a place where every facility and convenience is at the student's disposal with a minimum of red tape), on contemporary newspapers, and, in the case of the Sumter, on the memoirs of her commander.

I should say somewhere, and it may as well be here, that before destroying a prize the commander of the captor always had her valued by a board of officers designated for the purpose. I have made no use of those figures because they were determined by inexperienced appraisers who were more interested in establishing a basis for hoped-for prize money than in making an accurate appraisal.

For the first section of Chapter IV ("Ways and Means"), reliance has been placed upon *Anglo-American Relations, 1861-1865*, by Brougham Villiers and W. H. Chesson; *Europe and the American Civil War*, by Donaldson Jordan and Edwin J. Pratt; *Great Britain and the American Civil War*, by E. D. Adams; *Diplomatic History of the Southern Confederacy*, by J. M. Callahan; *The Confederate States of America*, by John Christopher Schwab; and *King Cotton Diplomacy*, by Frank L. Owsley. On the external financing of the Confederacy I have examined the records of the Confederate Treasury in the National Archives and those of the State Department in the Library of Congress, under the guidance of the definitive studies of Professors Schwab and Owsley.

During the preparation of this book Mr. Burton J. Hendrick's *Statesmen of the Lost Cause* (1939) has appeared, dealing in part with the subject of Confederate finance, from the same sources, thus adding another name to my schedule of creditors. I have cited some of the English judicial decisions. Historians have seemed curiously reluctant to avail themselves of the court records.

The sources for the Florida and her auxiliaries are the naval records, Terry Sinclair's reminiscences, Commander Preble's defense of his conduct at Mobile, contemporary newspapers, and the evidence presented to the Geneva Tribunal.

Five men on the Alabama wrote books, Semmes, Kell, Arthur Sinclair, Fullam, and an anonymous seaman. These are listed in the bibliography at the end of this study. No one essaying to write the story of that ship can avoid leaning heavily on the writings of Semmes—not so much upon his discursive memoirs as upon his journals and reports. May I say to Mr. W. Adolphe Roberts, in case he is listening in, that from motives of self-preservation I refrained from reading his admirable *Semmes of the Alabama* (1938) until the manuscript of the present book had been completed. I then read it and made two corrections in my draft, for which, as well as for the pleasure of reading a good book, I make him my acknowledgment. The same comment applies to Mr. Burton J. Hendrick's *Statesmen of the Lost Cause* (1939). One of the most gratifying circumstances in the preparation of my book for the press has been that I have not found it necessary to make any substantial revisions in the light of Mr. Hendrick's mature and scholarly work.

One of the most readable books on the subject is entitled *The Cruise of the Alabama by One of her Crew* (1886), by "P. D. Haywood." No saltier sailor's yarn was ever put on paper. It is full of action, horseplay, fun, and gore. The author knows his berth deck and exhibits neither reticence nor compunction. He tells the story of the ship from beginning to end from the viewpoint of the seaman. The author's name is a pseudonym. Unfortunately the book contains internal evidence that it is a work of fiction. It is of interest as a clever literary hoax, probably by a person who never saw the Alabama. It is a pity that this racy book cannot be used as source material.

There is another spurious book on the Alabama. After her destruction, Semmes placed his journals at the disposal of a firm of London publishers. To catch a quick profit they brought out a highly embroidered redaction in two volumes.

Semmes fiercely repudiated the book, saying "I did not write a word of it."

Commander Bulloch's work on *The Secret Service of the Confederate States in Europe* is indispensable to the student of the Alabama case and of the general subject of Confederate naval operations in Europe.

The Case and Counter-Case before the arbitral tribunal are, of course, voluminous on the Alabama, her origin, activities, and prizes.

For the battle off Cherbourg, we have the official reports of the opposing commanders. They agree in the main. In nonessential points each contains some inaccuracies. Shortly after the engagement, Frederick M. Edge, an English inquirer, collected all the information he could assemble by interviewing numerous survivors, and published it in a pamphlet. Memoirs of officers and men on both ships are cited in the bibliography. Among the many stories of the battle subsequently published, there are succinct professional accounts by Professor Soley, Engineer Frank M. Bennett, and Captain Knox. These are valuable because written with technical knowledge. As for the Georgia and the Rappahannock, I have relied on the naval records and Midshipman Morgan's lively recollections. Similarly for the Tallahassee we have the official records and the account given by her commander, John Taylor Wood, in one of the series of historical articles published by the *Century Magazine*.

For the story of the Shenandoah and the whalers, Alexander Starbuck's monumental *History of the American Whale Fishery* must remain the point of departure for any examination of the subject to which it relates. I have been favored with an opportunity to examine a microfilm of the log book of the Shenandoah, which is in the possession of the North Carolina Historical Commission. My text represents a collation of the log book with the accounts of Whittle and Hunt of the cruiser's staff, with Waddell's own story, which is reproduced in the naval records, and with the official orders, and the evidence adduced at Geneva. Among the voluminous and conflicting accounts of the doings of the Shenandoah at Melbourne, a useful guide is "The Shenandoah Incident" (*Victoria Historical Magazine*, Vol. XI, No. 2), by Ernest Scott, Professor of History in the University of Melbourne.

To critical historians who may be aggrieved by the sketchy account of the Geneva Arbitration in Chapter XI, I plead in confession and avoidance that this is a book about certain phases of the merchant marine, not about an arbitral tribunal. The chapter is inserted to round out the tale and is a premium which comes with the book gratis. The analogy of the gift horse is appropriate. In the great library of books and pamphlets relating to the "Alabama claims," one of the clearest and simplest statements I know is that of Caleb Cushing in his little book *The Treaty of Washington*. I do not pretend to have read *verbatim et literatim* the one hundred and fifty volumes of proceedings before the claims courts—no one ever did except the judges who were paid for doing so. I have consulted them for verifications and corrections. There are innumerable controversial pamphlets, articles, and debates in various languages bearing on these claims. I have examined a gross or two of them.

The development and decline of the Merchant Marine, briefly described in Chapter XII, has been the subject of a number of studies, one of the most thorough being that of Winthrop L. Marvin, *The American Merchant Marine* (1902). Others are cited in the bibliography. For the history of government aids to shipping, the comprehensive work of Grosvenor M. Jones, *Government Aid to Merchant Shipping* (1916), is basic. The economic studies and other publications of the U. S. Maritime Commission are required reading for any investigation of the present condition of the merchant service.

Chapter XIII contains, I hope, the only propaganda in the book. I saved it up for that chapter. In the Preface to a story we all read in childhood, *Tom Brown's School Days*, the author remarks that he has been reproached for "too much preaching." He comments, "Why, my whole object in writing at all was to get the chance of preaching. When a man comes to my time of life and has his bread to make and very little time to spare is it likely that he will spend almost the whole of his yearly vacation in writing a story just to amuse people? I think not. At any rate, I wouldn't do so myself." The preparation of the present volume consumed rather more time than my yearly vacation, if any. In all other respects I echo the sentiments of Thomas Hughes. If any reader wishes to exercise his constitutional privilege of answering back, I suggest a method of treatment which has often afforded me relief. Let him rewrite the objectionable parts for himself.

For help on particular points thanks are due Mr. George R. Paschal of the Maritime Commission; Captain Dudley W. Knox, U.S.N., historian of the Navy; Mr. Harold H. Martin of the Department of State; Mr. Grosvenor M. Jones, of the Department of Commerce; Professor James Truslow Adams; Mr. Burton J. Hendrick; Mr. R. E. Devendorf. None of these gentlemen is to blame for the work as a whole or for any of the opinions expressed. That belongs to me.

I have made raids and captured prizes without resistance in the Libraries of Congress, the Department of State, the Navy Department, and the Carnegie Peace Endowment. I have already said and wish to repeat a word of sincere tribute to the National Archives.

Credit for the illustrations is indicated where they appear. President Roosevelt graciously permitted the frontispiece to be reproduced from his collection. The Office of Naval Records and Library has a liberal policy in permitting the use of its great store of pictures. The Chamber of Commerce of Gloucester, Massachusetts, and the estate of the late E. H. R. Green went to trouble to furnish illustrations which have been used.

In case anyone cares, I have a Yankee background which

has become pretty well obscured by a non-political residence of many years in Washington, where statesmen come and go. I have no conscious emotional reaction to the Civil War except impartial grief.

G. W. D.

Washington, D. C.
June, 1940

CONTENTS

	PREFACE	vii
I.	BACKGROUNDS, DOMESTIC AND FOREIGN	1
II.	THE SUMTER	30
III.	THE NASHVILLE	64
IV.	WAYS AND MEANS	72
V.	THE FLORIDA AND HER OFFSPRING	95
VI.	THE ALABAMA AND THE TUSCALOOSA	128
VII.	CHERBOURG, JUNE 19, 1864	158
VIII.	THE GEORGIA AND THE RAPPAHANNOCK	174
IX.	THE TALLAHASSEE AND THE CHICKAMAUGA	182
X.	THE SHENANDOAH AND THE WHALERS	198
XI.	GENEVA	231
XII.	THE FLIGHT FROM THE FLAG	237
XIII.	THE LESSON	263
	BIBLIOGRAPHY	275
	INDEX	279

ILLUSTRATIONS

U.S.S. Kearsarge on Roncador Reef, February, 1894, From the collection of President Franklin D. Roosevelt	*Frontispiece*
	FACING PAGE
King Cotton Bound, or The Modern Prometheus. From *Punch* (London), November 2, 1861	20
John Bull's Neutrality—A Distinction with a Difference. From *Harper's Weekly*, November 1, 1862	21
Raphael Semmes, Captain Commanding C. S. C. Sumter. From the Office of the U. S. Naval Records and Library	32
The Sumter Running the Blockade of Pass-à-l'Outre, June 30, 1861. From a lithograph in Semmes' *Memoirs*.	33
The Sumter Firing on the Brigantine Joseph Parke, of Boston. From *Harper's Weekly*, February 1, 1862	68
The Nashville and the Tuscarora at Southampton, England. From *Harper's Weekly*, February 15, 1862	69
Prospectus of the Erlanger Loan, page one. From the National Archives	76
Prospectus of the Erlanger Loan, page two. From the National Archives	77
Nassau, New Providence, in the Bahamas. From *Harper's Weekly*, September 3, 1864	102
The Pirate Tacony Burning Merchant Vessels and Fishing Craft. From *Harper's Weekly*, July 11, 1863	102
Destruction of the Clipper Ship Jacob Bell by the Florida. From *Harper's Weekly*, March 21, 1863	103

ILLUSTRATIONS

FACING PAGE

Gloucester Harbor and Part of the Fishing Fleet during the Civil War Period. From a photograph exhibited at the Centennial Exhibition in Philadelphia in 1876 — 112

The Revenue Cutter Caleb Cushing, blown up by Read and Other Pirates Who Had seized her. From *Harper's Weekly*, July 11, 1863 — 113

The Sinking of the Alabama off Cherbourg. From *Harper's Weekly*, July 23, 1864 — 170

The Gun That Sank the Alabama. From the Office of the U. S. Naval Records and Library — 171

The Rappahannock in the Harbor at Calais. From *Harper's Weekly*, January 16, 1864 — 178

The Florida and the Rappahannock. From *Harper's Weekly*, August 6, 1864 — 179

C. S. C. Tallahassee. From the Office of the U. S. Naval Records and Library — 196

C.S.C. Shenandoah. From the Office of the U. S. Naval Records and Library — 197

The Whaling Ship Charles W. Morgan. From the Estate of Edward H. R. Green — 230

A Still Bigger Claimant. From *Punch* (London) — 231

THE FLIGHT FROM THE FLAG

Men fight and lose the battle and the thing they fought for comes about in spite of their defeat. And it turns out to be not what they meant and other men have to fight for the same thing under a new name.   —William Morris

CHAPTER I

BACKGROUNDS, DOMESTIC AND FOREIGN

A course more promising than a wild dedication of yourselves to unpathed waters, undreamed shores.—Shakespeare, *The Winter's Tale*, Act IV, scene 4

I

THE NAVAL PHASE of the American Civil War presents a contrast to the operations on land. The Confederate armies moved unevenly to the peak of their offensive at Gettysburg, midway the conflict, and thereafter receded, with many fluctuations, to the end. The major naval objectives on each side were pursued steadily to the close of hostilities.

Naval policy, according to the official modern declaration of the United States, is "To maintain the Navy in sufficient strength to support the national policies and commerce and to guard the continental and overseas possessions of the United States." This presupposes the existence of a hostile fleet to dispute the command of the sea. The only hostile force on the high seas during the Civil War consisted of the Confederate cruisers. These contested the policy above formulated in one point only, the destruction of enemy merchant ships.

From the beginning of the war the opposing commands realized that the issue might be decided by the destruction of the enemy's seaborne commerce, which was of capital importance to both belligerents. The voluntary embargo which the southern planters and brokers placed upon the exportation of cotton throughout the first year of the war and the governmental regulations which were soon imposed, together with the spontaneous crop limitation and burning of stocks, in order to force British intervention by starving the Lancashire textile mills, lasted until the Federal blockade had attained some degree of effectiveness. The purposes of the blockade were aided by the increasing difficulty of transporting goods across the war-ridden country to and from the ports and by the reluctance of planters and merchants to risk blockade-running. Thus the basis of Confederate credit was sapped, and the way to replenishing the essential resources was barred, first by Confederate policy and then by United States gunboats and the conditions of war. By the time the Richmond administration got around to setting up absolute cotton control and purchase, and to operating its own blockade-runners, in order to establish the Confederate position abroad, the currency inflation, the decline of the internal bonds with which the cotton growers were paid, and the military reverses nullified an effort which, if adopted earlier, might have accomplished the foreign alliance upon which the hopes of the South depended. The South at first impoverished itself; then the North completed the work. Thus the war was lost and won as much by attrition as by marching men.

The hope of the Southern leaders was that an alliance with England could be forced by using cotton as a lever, and with France, by playing upon the cotton shortage and upon Franco-Mexican relations. The frustration of these plans deprived the South of its strongest weapon, while at the same time it forged two others, one on each side, i.e., British exasperation against the United States, expressing itself in indirect aid to the Confederacy; and Southern resentment against England for maintaining official neutrality, a resentment evidenced by the continuous disparagement of the English in the Southern press and culminating in the expulsion of British consuls by the Confederate government.

On the Confederate side the lack of a battle fleet precluded a military contest of the blockade of Southern ports and precluded also the establishment of a blockade against the North. The Confederacy had but one type of weapon against enemy commerce—predatory cruisers. These made a contribution to the Southern cause out of all proportion to their number. Had the South triumphed, they would have been entitled to share the honor. On the other hand, they contributed nothing to the defeat. There were some eighteen cruisers in all, only eight of which achieved consequential results; yet the damage done by these few vessels was continuous throughout the war, and the effects are still operating to the disadvantage of the united nation.

Our purpose here is to review briefly the work of the cruisers and then indicate the nature of the permanent consequences. No attempt is made to write the naval history of the war. The entire subject of the blockade and of the coastal and river operations is beyond the scope of this inquiry. So is the foreign construction of combat vessels, as distinguished from commerce destroyers. The long tiresome tale of the "Alabama Claims" after the war is summarized in a few pages. The story of the American merchant marine and fishery is involved only to the extent necessary to exhibit the relation of the cruisers to it. The subject is narrow; the ramifications are broad; and the end is not yet.

A preliminary glance at the sailing areas of United States ships will give an idea of the problem which confronted the Confederate cruisers. American vessels were in every sea. The embargo and the blockade confined coastal movements of cotton to outlaw ships of foreign flags. In all other commodities American vessels were minding the maxim, "Ships were made to sail the sea and not rot by the wall." The North Atlantic lanes were traversed by packet and cargo ships. The route to the Baltic lay by way of Havana for sugar; thence to Riga and Swedish ports for return cargoes of iron and Russian hemp, with a detour to the Azores on the way home for oranges and wines. In the Mediterranean run, eastbound ships carried molasses, sugar, rum, and Honduran logwood (for coloring wines) to Levantine, Greek, Italian, and French ports, in exchange for figs, lemons, oranges, currants, nuts, raisins, olive oil, and wines for the American market. The

China and East India traders via the Cape of Good Hope were sailing eastward with buffalo hides, jute, linseed, shellac, for return affreightment of tea, coffee, saltpeter, and sometimes sugar, and with fabrics loaded at Calcutta and Bombay. Then there was a brisk trade with Rio de Janeiro and the Plate, taking out lumber and supplies, returning with Argentine hides and Brazilian coffee.

The California clippers were carrying prospectors and their supplies around the Horn or to the Isthmus, returning (as the cruisers fondly hoped) with gold and silver, though the Confederacy never caught one of these "treasure ships." There were also voyages westward to Manila with general merchandise and back with sugar. American ships did a lively freight business between Europe and the east coast of South America and considerable port-to-port carrying in the Indian Ocean.

The best prospect of all for the cruisers, albeit the most likely to provoke pursuit, was the great West Indian trade. Rum, sugar, molasses, logwood, bananas, and other Caribbean and Central American products moved north for American consumption and for transshipment to Europe. Southbound the ships carried lumber, Yankee notions, dried codfish, and vast quantities of ice. The trade in ice extended much farther than the West Indies; shiploads of it were carried to India where English officers acquired a taste for chilled drinks and the Hindus cried fraud when the ice melted.

Next to the West Indian lanes the best hunting ground was the ocean belt between the bulge of Africa and the easternmost point of Brazil. This zone, fifteen hundred miles wide, was traversed by all ships bound to and from the Pacific and Indian oceans around either cape. This belt was somewhat narrowed by the trade winds north of the equatorial calm belt. These steady easterlies blew the shipping westward off the African coast towards that of Brazil, so that vessels bound to or from the Cape of Good Hope as well as those around the Horn were likely to be found in the Brazilian side of this lane.

Since the opening of the Suez and Panama canals has rerouted a large part of this trade, it is difficult to realize how much shipping was formerly to be encountered in this stretch of sea.

Thus American merchantmen might be found in every ocean trade route. The American carrying trade had steadily expanded, in pace with the growing prosperity of the country, in the golden era from 1846 to the outbreak of the war. In these fifteen years, the development of the West, the discovery of gold in California, Colorado, and Australia with the consequent rise in commodity prices, the new free trade policy of England, and the opening of treaty ports in China and Japan had increased the foreign commerce of the United States 300 per cent. American ships were carrying seven-tenths of the cargoes. They also were employed in a substantial business between foreign ports. In addition, there were the cod and mackerel fisheries off the Grand Banks and the whaling industry in the North Atlantic, the South Pacific, the Sea of Okhotsk, and the Arctic Ocean beyond Bering Strait.

In relation to the national economy as a whole, carriage by sea during the three decades preceding the Civil War occupied the position of a major industry. Its importance was due in part to discreet tariff legislation; more to the enterprise and ingenuity of American builders in the design and construction of soft wood ships; to the unrivaled skill and hardihood of the Yankee sailor of the sail; and to the sound business sense of the owners, masters, and supercargoes of the ships.

In planning depredations upon this far-flung commerce, the cruising radius of the naval vessels had to be taken into account with reference to the proximity of ports where fuel, supplies, and repairs could be procured—meaning, in effect, British colonial ports.

The Confederate Navy Department had its hands full with the blockade and the coastal and river operations. As there were never more than three first class cruisers afloat at one time to cover the vast extent of potential operations, the strategy was largely left to the initiative of the individual commanding officers, who for want of communications could not follow a concerted plan. Thus it happened that in May, 1863, three ships, the Alabama, the Florida, and the Georgia, were hunting in the same waters off the coast of Brazil, all at the same time, sometimes sighting one another.

The ocean is wide and lonely, the sea lanes broad. The horizon of the lookout is not more than thirty miles away. A slight variation in the course meant the difference between discovering a prize and missing her. One of the Confederate officers remarked to an unhappy Yankee master whose ship had just been destroyed, "Just think, Captain, if you had altered your course only a quarter of a point at daybreak we should never have seen you," to which the unlucky skipper replied, "That shows how little you know about it. I did alter my course a quarter of a point at daybreak and that's how I come in this fix."

It all adds up to the fact that the problem facing the Confederate commanders was one of great magnitude and complexity, with many unpredictable elements. There was one factor that they did not have to consider—the danger of retaliation. After the capture of three or four Southern ships by United States naval vessels at the beginning of the war, the South had no merchant marine against which reprisals could be made.

II

Before embarking it will be prudent to pack a light ditty bag of definitions.

The expression "American Merchant Marine" means the fleet of American vessels engaged in foreign and coastal commerce. As commonly used it does not apply to the fishing and whaling fleets although these are governed by substantially the same rules that apply to coastal traders. To be entitled to the status of an American vessel, a ship must be wholly American owned. If she is to be used in the coasting trade she must also be American built. Foreign trade is open to the ships of all nations, whereas only American vessels may engage in coasting trade. From 1789 to 1914 all American ships, wherever trading, had to be both owned and built in this country.

The officers of American ships have always been required to be citizens of the United States. Until 1936 there was no effective rule governing the citizenship of crews. Aliens could be, and constantly were, employed. Today, 75 per cent of the personnel of American ships must be American nationals. On passenger ships subsidized by the Maritime Commission, 90 per cent of the crew must be citizens, and on cargo ships 100 per cent.

"Tonnage" is a tricky word for a landsman because it has at least six meanings and is often used indiscriminately without explanation. In origin it was a measure of volume only. Ships were measured by the number of tuns of wine or grain they could carry, the wine tun and the grain tun being of different sizes. With the discovery of America and the expansion of ocean trade, it became necessary to standardize the tun. After a long history of changes in measurement, the modern standard was adopted by England in 1854 and by the United States in 1864. The number of cubic feet of enclosed space in a ship divided by 100 is her gross register tonnage. This is the figure used for comparing the size of vessels. It is a measure of volume and not of weight. The word "ton" meaning an avoirdupois weight, is also in common use with reference to ships to express their cargo capacity and displacement of water. To avoid confusion, ton is not used to mean weight in the following pages unless so indicated. The tonnage of naval vessels is determined by a method peculiar to the Navy.

The word "ship" is used in the generic sense to designate any seagoing craft. It is also a technical term meaning a square-rigged vessel with three masts. A bark has three masts with square sails on the fore and main, and with a fore-and-aft or schooner sail on the mizzen. A brig is a square-rigged two-master. A schooner has fore-and-aft (leg o' mutton) sails on all masts, a rig invented by a Gloucester fisherman. A clipper is a large full-rigged ship of a highly refined model, especially designed for speed. The remarkable performance of the clippers was due as much to skill in handling as to perfection of lines. In the art of sailing, American masters attained a superiority unapproached by those of any other nation. We shall have occasion to note how, in the end, this very quality brought misfortune to the merchant marine. But before that we shall accompany boarding crews from the cruisers to the decks of craft of all the types above mentioned.

Freight is money paid for carrying goods. It does not mean the goods themselves. A ship carries a cargo of goods for a freight.

Pratique is the right of a ship to use the facilities of a port and have free intercourse with shore. Naval vessels of friendly powers enjoy this right reciprocally. Union ships were entitled to it in British ports. Southern commanders argued that the exercise of pratique by the United States Navy warranted Confederate vessels in claiming and receiving equal privileges, notwithstanding the neutrality rules and the incapacity of the South to reciprocate. The argument was largely forensic, since Confederate ships got whatever they required through the complacency of officials in ports where the Southern cruisers spent money for supplies and repairs.

War, said the Supreme Court in 1863, is "that state in which a nation prosecutes its right by force."

Neutrality, like international friendship, is not a state of mind or feeling. It is merely an official status which permits certain acts and forbids others.

Belligerency is a term about which the international lawyers continue to debate. The Supreme Court, holding that the conflict between the states was a "public war," in a five to four decision, from which the above definition of war is quoted, put it thus: "The parties belligerent in a public war are independent nations. But it is not necessary to constitute war that both parties should be acknowledged as independent nations or sovereign states. A war may exist where one of the belligerents claims sovereign rights against the other.... It is not necessary that the independence of the revolted province or state be acknowledged in order to constitute it a party belligerent in a war according to the law of nations. Foreign nations acknowledge it as a war by a declaration of neutrality. The condition of neutrality cannot exist unless there be two belligerent states."[1] For our needs, it will be sufficient if we say (with a deprecatory nod to the text writers) that where a foreign nation recognizes an insurrectionary group as belligerent, the meaning is that the insurgent organization is to be treated as an independent nation for the purpose of prosecuting the war but not for other purposes such as commercial and diplomatic relationships and pratique. If the rebellion succeeds, belligerency blossoms into independent nationality. If it fails, the belligerent status terminates and the insurgents recur to their former allegiance. No foreign nation recognized the nationality of the Confederacy. Most of them, including the United States, conceded its belligerency.

A number of consequences flow from the existence of a state of belligerency. One is that the captives of each belligerent are entitled to be treated as prisoners of war instead of as criminals. Another is the right to take prizes. A prize is property taken at sea and subject to capture by the rules of war. Enemy-owned merchant vessels and enemy-owned cargo are good prize. Neutral cargo in an enemy-owned ship is not, unless it is contraband. An attempt to define contraband would lead us into a maze of technicalities from which we are happily relieved, for few questions of contraband arose out of the activities of the Confederate cruisers.

A privateer is a privately-owned armed vessel which carries a letter of marque from a belligerent government authorizing the ship to prey upon enemy commerce by taking prizes for the profit of her owner. This sort of adventuring enriched many

[1] The Prize Cases, 2 Black 635. Decided March 10, 1863.

bold spirits in the Revolution and the War of 1812. The Declaration of the Congress of Paris of 1856 provided that "Privateering is and remains abolished." Neither the United States nor, of course, the Confederacy was a party to that declaration, and when the United States tried to come under its wing in 1861, the British government refused consent unless an exception were made of the existing war, thus leaving it open to the belligerent governments to issue letters of marque, a privilege designed for the sole benefit of the Confederacy since the South had no merchant ships and the only prospective victims of privateering were United States vessels. A number of Confederate privateers took the sea early in the war. Their story has been admirably told by William Morrison Robinson, Jr., in *The Confederate Privateers*. Owing to the difficulty of realizing on their prizes and the greater profits of blockade-running, Confederate privateering never assumed considerable dimensions. A threat of privateering by authority of the Federal government in 1862 will be mentioned in its place. The threat, which was intended for its effect upon Great Britain, was not carried out.

The Confederate cruisers were not privateers. They were naval vessels owned and operated by a belligerent government.

On April 19, 1861, the Lincoln administration made an attempt by proclamation, to clothe private and public belligerent ships of the Confederacy with the character of pirates and there were a few prosecutions. As soon as it was discovered that the Confederacy was in a position to retaliate by hanging any sailor of the Federal Navy who fell into their hands, the pretense of piracy was abandoned (February 3, 1862). Thereafter captives on both sides received the status of prisoners of war, whether taken on sea or land. The Northern press continued to refer to the cruisers as pirates. The Secretary of the Navy also used the designation. When in a literary vein, he characterized them as "Algerine corsairs" and "piratical British wolves."

III

For our purposes the legalities of the position of the Confederate cruisers can be stated briefly, bearing in mind that the rules of public international law are merely the rubrics in the high church ritual of preponderant power.

The principal European powers early accorded belligerent status to the South and issued proclamations of neutrality. The British declaration was proclaimed on May 14, 1861, being precipitated by Lincoln's proclamation of blockade on April 19 and by the fact that there were English-owned goods worth upwards of five million dollars afloat on the Mississippi in the war zone. It was important to clothe these cargoes with neutral character, immune from interference by either party to the war. Since a nation does not blockade its own ports, England took the position that President Lincoln had acknowledged the belligerency of the Confederacy and that foreign governments were warranted in following suit. In 1863 the Supreme Court upheld this reasoning. The other maritime nations followed England's lead.

Curiously, the British proclamation, which was issued the day before the formal presentation of the declaration of blockade to the Foreign Office in behalf of the United States, was regarded by the Lincoln administration and throughout the North as unfriendly. The fact is that it was proposed to the Cabinet by the pro-Union members to enable England to acknowledge the validity of the blockade, and was accepted by the other ministers as setting up a valuable precedent for use in future when England might herself wish to rely upon an ineffective blockade, as she did in the opening days of the World War in 1914.

Under international law, the private citizens of a neutral state may (at their own risk) furnish munitions and supplies to either belligerent for the use of its armies, invest in its obligations, supply it with money, enlist in its service. The neutral government itself may not do any of these things and may restrict the right of its nationals to do so, as the United States and other powers have often done.

In the first thirty years of national life, Congress passed six neutrality laws. The last of those (1818) was a codification which remained unchanged, except for some implementing amendments, for upwards of a century. During this period the United States was a neutral in six major international European wars and countless civil conflicts.

On November 4, 1939, President Roosevelt approved a neutrality statute which lays down no new rules with respect to foreign enlistments. It contains no restriction upon the building of warships for belligerents in American shipyards; these are governed by the principles of international law and by a statute of 1917, which forbids the arming and equipping of belligerent vessels in American yards. The new act relates to international trade. No American goods, whether munitions or other commodities, sold to belligerent governments or their nationals, may be transported in American ships. Consignments to belligerent governments must be paid for and title must be transferred before shipment in foreign bottoms. Merchandise other than munitions may be sold to citizens of belligerent nations in the usual course of trade but must not be shipped in American bottoms. American vessels may not carry passengers to belligerent ports, nor may Americans (with some exceptions) travel to any destination on belligerent merchantmen. The President is empowered to define danger zones which American ships are forbidden to enter. American merchant vessels may not be armed except with small arms. No transaction in the securities of belligerent nations may occur in this country. Atlantic ports south of Gibraltar, those of the Bay of Fundy, the Pacific and Indian oceans, the China, Tasman, and Arabian seas, and Bay of Bengal are excepted from the restrictions applicable to belligerent ports. As of June 30, 1940, areas barred by proclamation are the Northeast Atlantic and the Mediterranean Sea.

The British Foreign Enlistment Act in force during the Civil War forbade British subjects to enlist on belligerent vessels of war within the realm. In this it was similar to the American statute, enacted in 1818 and revised in 1917.

Each neutral government may make its own rules (unless restrained by treaty) with respect to the purposes for which belligerent naval vessels may enter its ports, what they may do there, how long they may remain, subject to the overlying principle that the rules and practices adopted must not commit the neutral state to aiding one belligerent against the other and must not permit the use of a neutral port as a naval base. It may and does happen that the opportunity of visiting a port for repairs, fuel, and supplies, helps one belligerent and hurts the other. That is due to circumstances and the fortune of war. In the absence of a treaty or statute to the contrary, it does not involve a violation of neutrality. The neutrality statute of 1939 authorizes the President to restrict the use of American ports by foreign vessels.

Submarines were used during the Civil War. They did not become an effective weapon until the first World War, 1914-1918. Their use in that conflict resulted in the adoption in 1930 of the following rules by the United States, France, Great Britain, Italy and Japan:

"The following are accepted as established rules of International Law:

"1. In their action with regard to merchant ships, submarines must conform to the rules of International Law to which surface vessels are subject.

"2. In particular, except in the case of persistent refusal to stop on being duly summoned, or of active resistance to visit or search, a warship, whether surface vessel or submarine, may not sink or render incapable of navigation a merchant vessel without having first placed passengers, crew and ship's papers in a place of safety. For this purpose the ship's boats are not regarded as a place of safety unless the safety of the passengers and crew is assured, in the existing sea and weather conditions, by the proximity of land, or the presence of another vessel which is in a position to take them on board."

Germany has never agreed to be bound by these rules.

French and colonial British ports during the Civil War were by regulation open to belligerent naval vessels for only so long as was necessary to enable them to outfit to reach their next port. If opposing vessels came in, they were not permitted to leave within twenty-four hours of each other. The rules were not consistently enforced in France because French policy was subject to varying influences, and no clear pattern is discernible in it. Napoleon III had to be consulted personally about every decision. There was a cotton shortage in France in 1862; there was also a wheat shortage; the government had to consider both Southern and Northern sources of supply.

In 1863 the commodity situation improved, but two other factors entered the problem. First, the grandiose scheme of "Latin domination" below the Rio Grande had taken full possession of the Emperor's mind. Southern success was considered vital to this plan; but the Monroe Doctrine must not be flouted egregiously, and the North had to be placated in case the Union should prevail. Second, Prussia and Austria prepared for war with Denmark over the possession of the duchies of Schleswig and Holstein in order to get better outlets for seaborne commerce. French neutrality in the American war had to be adjusted to the interests of France in the European conflict. The policy fluctuated between conciliation and antagonism toward Prussia. When the Confederate cause began to decline in July, 1863, Napoleon III and Lord Palmerston were juggling all these balls in the air. United States Minister William L. Dayton and Confederate Commissioner John Slidell in Paris, Charles Francis Adams and James M. Mason in London found themselves alternately heeded and ignored. Dexterous mendacity was a diplomatic technique in which the French and the English were adept.

BACKGROUNDS, DOMESTIC AND FOREIGN 15

The American diplomats on both sides were inexperienced in it and never failed to react with hurt astonishment upon discovering that they had been duped.

In 1863 the Confederate cruiser Rappahannock, upon the angry insistence of the American Minister at Paris, was interned at Calais for the duration of the war.[1] In the same year, in spite of protests, the facilities at Brest were freely extended to the Florida for about six months. In the late autumn of 1863, while the Florida was enjoying these courtesies, the French government announced that Confederate cruisers entering the ports of the empire in future would be interned. Nevertheless the Florida was permitted to depart without objection. In June, 1864, when the Alabama came into Cherbourg and applied for permission to remain two months, action on the application was deferred, and the Confederates interpreted this as tantamount to a requirement to depart. The Emperor conspired to transfer Confederate naval construction from England to France, and when the scheme was exposed by Minister Dayton, expressed mortified ignorance of the project, halted the building of six ships, permitted three of them to be sold to Prussia, and let a fourth escape to sea as a Confederate warship at a time (February, 1865) when it was apparent that the Southern cause had failed.

Commander James D. Bulloch, the Confederate naval agent, sums up the French attitude thus: "It suited the Imperial policy, and appeared to be consistent with the designs upon Mexico, to extend a clandestine support to the South when the Confederate armies were still strong and exultant. It was neither prudent nor wise to maintain a doubtful or hesitating attitude toward the winning side when it became apparent that the prospect had changed, and that neither the Emperor Maximilian nor Mr. President Davis could probably maintain his position. *Voilà tout.*..."

To complete Bulloch's summary it should be added that the security of the imperial throne depended upon British

[1] See Chap. VIII, below.

support. Downing Street held veto power over the Quai d'Orsay, and exercised it to restrain Napoleon from implicating France in the American war.

Louis Napoleon himself summarized his ultimate position: "If the North is victorious I shall be happy. If the South is victorious I shall be delighted."

Throughout the war both belligerents complained that Great Britain was violating her neutrality in aid of the enemy. Her formal neutrality rules, which were promulgated January 31, 1862, to implement the previous proclamation, required every belligerent naval vessel to depart from a British or colonial port within twenty-four hours after arrival "except in case of stress of weather or of her requiring provisions or things necessary for the subsistence of her crew, or repairs." The supplies were to be only such as were required for immediate use or were necessary to take her to the nearest port of her country. There was a specific prohibition against using ports of the Bahamas as "stations or places of resort." The flexibility of these rules is apparent. The only regulation that was observed with any strictness was the one requiring the lapse of twenty-four hours between the departures of vessels of war.

At the beginning of the conflict English capitalists looked across the sea at the American scene. They thought about their trade in cotton, their profitable freights, their large investments in spindles. They pondered on the importance of these things to British industry and reflected with satisfaction that, while "the air of England was too free for a slave to breathe," Providence, ever well disposed towards the English, had favored the Southern states with a more salubrious climate. At first gratified by the high price commanded by their surplus stocks, the manufacturers soon realized that the shortage was confronting them with ruin. In 1860 England imported 2,580,000 bales of American cotton; in 1862, 72,000 bales. This diminution was attributed to the blockade, ineffectual as it was, rather than to the unofficial Southern embargo, crop limitation, and destruction which occurred before the exhaustion of the surplus stock. Grudgingly they paid the poor rates and contributed belated charity to support half a million idle operatives who went on relief in Lancashire, representing two million hungry mouths or four-fifths of the population of the county, when the stoppage of cotton had closed the mills. Punch reflected the attitude:

"We'll break your blockade, Cousin Jonathan, yet;
Yes, darn your old stockings, C.J., but we will,
And the cotton we'll have and to work we will set
Every Lancashire hand, every Manchester mill."

An advertisement in the *Manchester Guardian* reflected the sufferings of the mill owners: "TRAVEL: A gentleman whose son, aged 17, is thrown out of occupation by the Cotton Famine, would be glad to meet with one or two other young gentlemen to accompany his son on a Tour for five or six months in the Mediterranean or elsewhere. Address F, 127, at the Printers."

Then it appeared that Confederate commerce destroyers could make a contribution of great value to British interests which Britain could not obtain by any effort of her own. Every American vessel destroyed meant the substitution of several British ships for the prize and for the other American ships frightened off the sea by the capture. A group of Liverpool business men even built four steamers to trade to Southern ports after independence should be won, and, in the meantime, put them in the New York run where they turned a handsome profit by carrying Irish immigrants. Many of the young Irishmen enlisted in the Union Army, giving color to the Southern belief that the North was importing foreign mercenaries.

The British governing caste hoped, too, that the disintegration of the American Union might check the agitation for extension of suffrage in England, which was gaining impetus under the leadership of John Bright. He was continually citing the United States as an example of successful democracy. It was understood that the South had a landed gentry whose government would exemplify and perpetuate the virtues of aristocracy.

Early in the war the natural attitude of English capitalists, dictated by their own interests, was inflamed by the Trent affair in November, 1861.[1]

Reliable historians, including Professor E. D. Adams, a leading authority on Anglo-American relations during the Civil War, have expressed the opinion that Great Britain made a fairly good showing in the maintenance of official neutrality. Bearing in mind that the permissibility of warship construction remained debatable until 1871 (and indeed thereafter as a general principle), it may be said that the British official action kept reasonably well within the rules. The difficulty was that the paper work was not faithfully translated into deeds, especially in the Colonies, so that the principle was vitiated by the large number of exceptions in the practical application of it. Mr. Philip Guedalla has observed that neutrality has its subtleties. It has also its nuances. For the most part, the cunning and the emphasis were directed "benevolently," as the diplomatic phrase has it, in support of the Confederacy. In the Colonies the official rules were treated as scraps of paper. Then on September 5, 1862, came the direct American threat of war unless Britain should stop building Confederate ironclads, and British policy was again altered to mollify the North.

British opinion was far from unanimous. John Bright and Richard Cobden made antislavery speeches in the House of Commons. Henry Ward Beecher was heard and cheered. The idle cotton mill hands themselves, angered by the inadequacy and slowness of the relief measures, were favorable to the North because their former employers supported the South. At great mass meetings in London and Liverpool, promoted by Bright, throngs of workingmen acclaimed the Northern

[1] See Chap. III, below.

cause with self-disserving cheers. When Spurgeon prayed "God bless and strengthen the North," a vast congregation interjected "Amen." The middle class generally favored the North while many members of the ruling caste were active in aid of the Confederacy.

There was a division of sentiment within the Cabinet, where the South had only one outspoken champion. This was Gladstone, who subscribed for Confederate bonds and made speeches that were acutely embarrassing to the government and later to himself. Other ministers were not emotionally concerned with the trans-Atlantic struggle. On the balance they were generally favorable to the Southern cause. The variations of British policy, however, reflect the changing fortunes of the war rather than the sympathies of statesmen.

The more influential English newspapers favored the South. Propaganda was extensively used. The Union and Confederate governments subsidized newspapers and employed publicity agents.

English "intellectuals" (John Stuart Mill, Frederic Harrison, Edward Dicey, and F. J. Furnivall, for example) supported the North and organized a Union and Emancipation Society. They distributed some four hundred thousand pieces of pro-Northern literature and held five hundred public meetings.

A reaction of popular sentiment in favor of the North began in March, 1862, with Lincoln's change of front on slavery. He had been elected on a platform and in a campaign which coupled opposition to the extension of slavery with promises not to disturb the "peculiar institution" in states where it was already established. On March 6, 1862, he proposed to Congress the gradual manumission of slaves by purchase with funds to be contributed jointly by the Federal government and the slave states. The House of Representatives promptly passed a resolution declaring this to be the national policy. For the first time the United States had declared in favor of rooting out slavery. The effect at home was to bring Lincoln perilously near the edge of political disaster, for the new policy cost the Republicans thirty-one seats in the House of Representatives in the congressional election of 1862, thus reducing, though not extinguishing, the party majority.

The effect abroad was favorable to the United States. A modern English investigator, Brougham Villiers (Mr. Frederick J. Shaw), traces to this date a gradual shift in English sympathy from South to North.

The work of the Confederate cruisers themselves reacted to prevent the British intervention which the South so ardently desired. Great Britain had no wish to see the rapidly expanding Union Navy turn upon British shipping the same weapon which the cruisers were directing against that of the United States. The President of the British Board of Trade expressed this fear: "If two or three armed steamers, which a country with no pretensions to a navy can easily send upon the ocean armed with one or two guns, can almost clear the seas of the merchant ships of another nation, what might happen to this country with her extensive commerce over the seas if she went to war with some nation that availed herself of the use of a similar description of vessel?"

The United States was conscious of possessing this brake on English policy and followed it up. The Union Navy laid down the keels of a number of fast cruisers which were not completed until after the war. One of these, the U.S.S. Wampanoag, was the fastest ship afloat, steaming nearly 18 knots. Another, the Ammonosuc, was nearly as speedy. We shall later find these ships playing a significant part in the Anglo-American negotiations leading up to the Geneva arbitration.

The extension to the North American continent of the "balance of power," so important an element of Great Britain's foreign policy, was a pro-Southern factor in British official opinion. At the same time, the fact that the North controlled

KING COTTON BOUND:
Or, The Modern Prometheus.

From Punch (London), November 2, 1861.
Reproduced by permission of the proprietors of Punch.

JOHN BULL'S NEUTRALITY.—A DISTINCTION WITH A DIFFERENCE.

JOHN BULL (*solus*). "A few more Pirates afloat, and I'll *get all the carrying trade back into my hands.*"

From Harper's Weekly, *November 1, 1862.*

the movement of American wheat was kept in mind by those not vitally interested in cotton.

The course of the ministry was not governed by their prejudices or even by the economic interests of their political supporters. They acted upon the prospects of the war as reported by their military observers. Throughout the latter half of 1862 they regarded Southern victory as almost a *fait accompli*. Accordingly they prepared to recognize Confederate independence and connived at thinly veiled unofficial aid to the South. When Northern prospects improved in 1863, recognition was postponed and the enforcement of neutrality stiffened. The guiding principle of the ministry was to keep England out of the war. Sympathy for the South was to be restrained within that boundary. Seeming deviations from this policy were due to fortuitous circumstances, as in the Trent affair; or to misinformation, as in 1862, when several members of the Cabinet thought Southern victory was assured. Failure to perceive clearly the line of British policy kept the American minister and the Confederate commissioner in continuous anxiety.

The clue to the British policy of keeping out of the American war was the situation in Europe. Palmerston and his advisers were deeply distrustful of their putative friend and ally, Louis Napoleon, and, with all central Europe in actual or potential turmoil, the thing they were least ready to countenance was a diversion of British power to the prosecution of a war in America.

The sympathy of British officials for the South caused Confederate cruisers to be welcomed, feted, fueled, and supplied (though not openly munitioned) far beyond the limits prescribed in the official regulations. The purchases of the Confederates contributed to the prosperity of the ports they visited. The cruisers and the blockade-runners enriched Nassau, Bermuda, and Cape Town. When a cruiser came into port the United States Consul was an active person. It has been customary to deride the old consular service, filled as it was with political appointees. Let it be remembered for the men in the ports at which the cruisers called that in a delicate situation, confronted with foreign officials who were technically neutral and personally hostile, they acquitted themselves as creditably as any "career man" could do. Their insistent and incessant protests, which caused Captain Semmes of the Alabama to call them "gadflies," never involved their government in difficulty. After the war England was compelled to acknowledge the force of their efforts on behalf of their government.

With respect to the disposition of prizes taken by belligerent cruisers, neutrals made their own rules. They are now governed by the Hague Convention of 1907 "Concerning the Rights and Duties of Neutral Powers in Naval War," which permits a prize to be brought into a neutral port only under stress of weather or for unseaworthiness and requires its departure as soon as circumstances permit. In the Civil War no neutral allowed prizes to be brought in. "Adjudication in prize" is a judicial determination by the courts of the captor nation whether the captured ship was "good prize" or was neutral property not subject to seizure. The refusal of the neutral governments to harbor prizes, pending the outcome of the war, compelled the Confederate commanders to determine questions of prize law for themselves, a heavy responsibility, and to destroy their captures at sea, as the blockade precluded sending them into the Confederate courts and the cruisers could not man their numerous captures indefinitely with prize crews, that is, skeleton crews taken from the captor's own force. This operated grievously against the men of the Confederate cruisers, who enlisted for the sake of prize money and never got any. Prize money was paid from the proceeds of the sale of the captured ship and cargo, after condemnation by the prize court. It amounted to half the proceeds, or, if the capture was made in the face of superior force, to the whole. It was distributed among the captor's personnel ratably according to rank and seniority. A destroyed ship produced none.[1] The Confederate government protested ineffectually to the foreign ministries. The only souvenirs of the prizes were their chronometers, which were always kept. The men were promised that the Confederate government would appropriate money for destroyed ships. Needless to say, this was not done. Only one of the Confederate prizes, the Sea Bride, and the cargo of two others, the Tuscaloosa and the B. F. Hoxie, brought in any money, and this was not distributed. Small stores of currency found on prizes were appropriated to the operating cost of the captor.

In burning their prizes the Confederate cruisers were following the rule laid down by the United States Secretary of the Navy in his instructions to commanding officers during the War of 1812: "Destroy all you capture unless in some extraordinary case they clearly warrant an exception."

Occasionally a Confederate cruiser took a good prize that had neutral cargo on board. The practice was to take a "ransom bond" and let the ship go. The bond was an agreement signed by the master of the prize that the owner would pay the captor a sum of money. When the auxiliary cruiser Archer was captured at Portland, Maine,[2] she had on board $244,000 worth of these bonds. The bonded prizes went scot-free because the bonds were to mature in six months after the making of peace. As Lieutenant Sinclair of the Alabama remarked, when that time arrived the obligee government had vanished and the bonds were about as valuable as Confederate money. The Confederate commanders understood that in taking ransom bonds they were betting on the outcome of the cause. The good will of the nations in which the neutral cargoes were owned was more important to the South than a few prizes more or less.

On the cruiser Alabama her commander conducted what he called "The Confederate States Admiralty Court," in

[1] In the United States, by act of March 3, 1899, the distribution of prize money to captors was abolished. The entire proceeds of the prize are now the perquisite of the government.
[2] See p. 114, below.

which he acted as prosecutor, defense counsel, and judge. He did not invariably "try the whole cause and condemn you to death." His purpose was to make a record to support his action in condemning, bonding, or releasing captured property.

In determining the status of cargoes, the Confederate commanders attached great importance to notarial seals. American law required the ship's manifest, which disclosed the ownership of the goods, to be notarized before the beginning of the voyage, so as to prevent the substitution of false representations of ownership, manufactured after sailing. No doubt the formality of attaching a notarial certificate was sometimes omitted through carelessness. It was a small technicality. Over and over again, Confederate boarding officers found on the prizes uncertified manifests asserting neutral ownership. They treated all these as nugatory and fraudulent. They were fully justified in so doing. Sometimes the hastily prepared forgeries were crude and bungling. In a few instances the omission of the seal was probably accidental.

As captures succeeded one another, the Confederate cruisers became crowded with prisoners taken from the destroyed ships. The congestion was relieved by sending the prisoners into the nearest port on one of the prizes, which thereupon became a "cartel ship" of the Confederacy. The failure of the Confederacy, however, left no government to lay claim to the cartels, which reverted to their owners.

A field for research in the human-interest side of history is open to someone who will follow the adventures and trace the homecoming of the prisoners who were deposited in remote places. To sailors any port is home. Passengers and the families of officers who were sometimes placed on the cartels must have had interesting experiences.

The possibility of simplifying their problem by destroying the lives of the passengers and crews of their prizes did not occur to the Confederate commanders. That has been reserved for more enlightened warfare. From first to last, in the destruction of two hundred merchantmen, no life was lost as the result of that destruction. We shall find the commander of the cruiser Alabama permitting one of the most important captures of the entire war (the Ariel) to go free because he had no other means of saving her company. The only lives sacrificed by any cruiser were those of naval seamen lost in pitched battles with warships of the enemy.

When we come to the construction and equipment of vessels of war in neutral ports, we encounter the crux of the international controversy that arose. Publicists had long held (although both Great Britain and the United States had denied it) that naval vessels were on a different footing from arms, munitions, financial obligations, and personal services. The simplest way to state the rule for which the United States contended is to quote the principles that were laid down in the Treaty of Washington, entered into beween the United State and Great Britain in 1871 for the guidance of the arbitral tribunal that passed upon the claims arising out of the activities of the cruisers:

"A neutral government is bound—

"First, to use due diligence to prevent the fitting out, arming, or equipping, within its jurisdiction, of any vessel which it has reasonable ground to believe is intended to cruise or to carry on war against a Power with which it is at peace; and also to use like diligence to prevent the departure from the jurisdiction of any vessel intended to cruise or to carry on war as above, such vessel having been specially adapted, in whole or in part, within such jurisdiction to warlike use.

"Secondly, not to permit or suffer either belligerent to make use of its ports or waters as the base of naval operations against the other, or for the purpose of renewal or augmentation of military supplies or arms, or the recruitment of men.

"Thirdly, to exercise due diligence in its own ports and waters, and, as to all persons within its jurisdiction, to prevent any violation of the foregoing obligations and duties."

In the next sentence, Great Britain declined to admit that the foregoing rules state the law correctly but agreed as a gesture of friendship for the United States that the arbitrators should be governed by them. Notice that in the first and third clauses nothing is required except the exercise of "due diligence," while in the second, relating to naval bases, armament, munitions, and recruiting, the prohibition is absolute.

The treaty above quoted was made up in retrospect after long deliberation. In accepting it Great Britain was giving more weight to her possible future position than to legal principles. Whether it states correctly the rules that had previously existed is doubtful. In any case we must remember that no such neat definitions were before the many port officials, remote colonial governors, United States consuls, police magistrates, and miscellaneous officials who had to deal with the cruisers and their crews as occasion arose, in the light of their own prejudices, national interest, and judgment, and of the elastic British proclamation of neutrality. Indeed, it was the opinion of the law officers of the Crown and the legal advisers of the Confederate government that the construction, arming, and equipment of a belligerent naval vessel in a neutral nation were not obnoxious to international law but only to the British Foreign Enlistment Act, and therefore something for Great Britain to settle for herself.

The principles of the Treaty of Washington were subsequently embodied in an Act of Congress approved June 15, 1917, which implemented the rules with heavy penalties, thus importing the international rule into the law of the land.

In September, 1939, the President of the United States issued a proclamation for the guidance of Americans and belligerents substantially embodying these rules.

IV

In February, 1861, when the Confederate government was organized at Montgomery, with Stephen R. Mallory as Secretary of the Navy, he found the beginnings of a fleet. Each of the seceding states as it entered the Confederacy brought along a flotilla consisting of Federal vessels that had been seized in its waters. They were a miscellaneous lot of craft, revenue cutters, captured slavers, an ex-pirate, a few gunboats, a forfeited merchantman, and what not.

Then in May, 1861, the Confederate Congress authorized the issuance of letters of marque, and several privateers were commissioned. They had made a few captures when the closing of the ports by the blockade deprived them of opportunity to dispose of their prizes. As a privateer is operated for profit, letters of marque become dead letters when prizes cannot be realized upon. Privateering did not play an important part in the war.

The Confederate government requisitioned river steamers and armed them. It made extraordinary efforts to build ships by contract in its home ports on the rivers and bays, often frustrated by the capture of the port before the completion of the vessel. There were few materials except the trees standing in the forests. The two navy yards equipped for construction work fell into Union hands before the war was a year old. There was constant difficulty in arming ships, for the South was as destitute of gun factories and powder mills as of shipyards, and the available resources had to be devoted to equipping the army. The naval operations of the war in home waters consisted of contesting the blockade along the coast, and in coöperating with troop movements on the rivers. No "naval yardstick" could be devised to measure the heterogeneous collection of floating objects that made up the Confederate force afloat at any one time. It can only be said generally that it was far inferior to its adversary in strength. The remarkable fact is that the South managed to get together a respectable fleet at all, whereas the Federal Navy at the close of the war had twelve times as many ships as at the beginning.

Secretary Mallory had no difficulty in assembling officer personnel. More experienced officers tendered their services than he could find berths for. Most of them had been bred in the rough nature of the old navy. None of the higher officers of either navy was a graduate of the then much ridiculed seminary which the Reverend George Bancroft had set up at Annapolis in 1845 with the unheard-of idea of making boys into sailors by keeping them on shore. The old navy had no such nonsense. Midshipmen were appointed through political influence and put on ships. No official duties were assigned to them. There were but two requirements. Each boy was, first, to do whatever he was told and do it quickly; second, to keep a diary. The purpose of the diary, which was submitted to the commanding officer once a week, was to make certain that American naval officers knew how to spell.

Each ship carried a poor devil of an underpaid civilian schoolmaster, who was despised alike by officers, midshipmen, and crew. Whenever and wherever he could, he got a few midshipmen together and tried to give lessons in mathematics and navigation. One commander advised the youngsters to ignore the schoolmaster and devote their attention to dancing and French. The classes were always subject to interruption by an officer with an order to the boys, who thereupon scampered away. There were coaching schools at Boston, New York, and Norfolk, to which midshipmen were sent for six months' intensive "boning." After five years, more or less, they were ordered to report at the barroom of Barnum's Hotel in Baltimore, where they waited until summoned, one at a time, for examination before a board which was sitting in one of the rooms. After an hour during which the candidate's chief concern was to avoid showing that he knew more than the members of the board, he was warranted a passed midshipman, or rejected.

Somehow or other, this system bred seamen. The careers of Porter, Farragut, Foote, Winslow, Semmes, Buchanan, Tattnall, and many others testify to the fact.

This was the training of all the senior officers of the Union and Confederate navies. Some of the younger men had been at the Naval Academy.

The officers of the regular service, many of whom had done combat duty under the flag, had a difficult choice. They rationalized their predilections in various ways. Those who remained in the service fell back on their oaths. Those who joined the insurgents argued that the government with seven (later eleven) states subtracted from it was not the United States they had sworn to defend. This seems to beg the question. In the end each followed his personal bent, not without suffering.

The young men of the Class of 1861 at West Point were summoned to the chapel, where an oath of allegiance was tendered to them. A Southern boy wrote home to his mother: "I actually cried before I went over there, so you may conceive how I was bothered mentally. It was a solemn occasion for me."

Many others in the Army were bothered; Robert E. Lee for one, and George H. Thomas. In the Navy nearly seven hundred officers, slightly less than half of the active list, were from Southern states. Of these, three hundred and sixty remained in the service; the rest resigned. In the epic battle between the U.S.S. Kearsarge and the C.S.C. Alabama, the commanding officers of both ships were from the South and had been shipmates, messmates, and roommates.

CHAPTER II

THE SUMTER

Offshore where sea and skyline blend
In vain, the daylight dies;
The sullen shouldering swells attend
Night and our sacrifice.
—Kipling, *The Destroyers*

I

RAPHAEL SEMMES WAS born in Charles County, in southern Maryland, in 1809. He spent his boyhood in Washington, D.C., where he worked in his uncle's woodyard. At seventeen he received a midshipman's appointment from President John Quincy Adams. Warranted passed midshipman in 1832, he was appointed the next year to take charge of Navy chronometers. They became a hobby that stayed with him through life. Semmes moved through the slow course of promotion in the stagnating Navy, with plenty of leisure, which he devoted to studying law, and the usual leaves of absence, during one of which he went courting in Cincinnati and married Miss Anne Elizabeth Spencer. Two of their sons became midshipmen in the Confederate Navy.

As a lieutenant he saw active service in the Mexican War, at first aboard the brig Somers, a ship with an unhappy history; then in some hot work ashore, where he had occasion to comment favorably upon the intelligence and judgment of one of the army engineers, Captain Robert E. Lee.

In 1841, while stationed at Pensacola, he established a legal residence across the river and became a citizen of Alabama. The law studies which he continued during his early assignments were useful later in his innumerable contentions with United States consuls and foreign officials over the rights and immunities of the Confederate cruisers, their prisoners and their prizes.

In those days the Navy Department had charge of lighthouses. In 1856 Semmes, then a commander, was lighthouse inspector, and finally became a member of the Lighthouse Board with an office in the Department in Washington. He was vegetating there when the war broke out.

On February 14, 1861, Secretary Mallory sent a batch of telegrams to United States naval officers inviting them to come to Montgomery. Semmes had already made up his mind. He turned in his resignation and went at once to tender his services.

In later years Porter, who had known Semmes before the war, marveled at the reversal of form he exhibited at this time. He had been indolent, talkative, not reputed to be a very capable officer, an amateur of culture, mildly interested in the rating of chronometers, affecting an old world courtliness in Washington drawing rooms. He arrived in Montgomery a man of action, quick in decision, a thoroughly qualified seaman, vigorous, shrewd. Those who, like Porter, were astonished at the contrast, forgot the mettle Semmes had shown in the Mexican War.

Immediately after the attack on Fort Sumter Semmes asked to be detailed to the destruction of enemy commerce. It is not agreeable duty for an officer. The essential requirements are to attack the helpless and to run away from danger. If there is any glamor in war, it is not in this department. Nevertheless, the work is of fundamental importance. During the Civil War it was the most valuable service a Confederate naval officer could render. In the work of enhancing British interest in the success of the Southern cause, the contribution of the commerce destroyers was the elimination of American competition from the carrying trade.

Semmes had exceptional qualifications for this duty. He could conceive an audacious plan of action and carry it forward rapidly, without hesitation or compunction. The Northern press represented him as an inhuman ogre, a monster of sadistic cruelty. The picture is as erroneous as is the popular Southern conception of him as a hero. He was neither cruel nor heroic. He has left copious memoirs, which reflect his qualities and limitations. His writings exhibit a man in whom vanity and complacency compensated for unconscious doubts that come to light in his voluble self-justifications and long unnecessary arguments in support of the justice of the Southern cause. He even argued the case in his journal. In the disposition of prizes and prisoners he was as ruthless as the occasion required, and no more so. Toward this work he displayed none of the repugnance that often troubled his subordinates and the officers of other cruisers. He seems to have been relieved of that by a lack of imagination and by emotional sterility when his own interests were not engaged. Here perhaps lies the key to his psychological make-up. He echoed the sentiments appropriate to every situation as if he had read them in a book or heard them in church, not as if they sprang from any inner compulsion. The correct literary reaction is always ready. Indeed, he was much given to sententious moralizing, to the annoyance and amusement of his men, who had a song to the effect that the Old Man was saving his money to build a chapel where he could preach all day.

This predilection for concionary discourse came into play in arguments on legal questions with which Semmes was confronted in his ports of call during his cruises. Everywhere he was obstructed by the omnipresent United States consul. He argued at great length with all sorts of extraordinary officials in many ports, health officers, police chiefs, provincial governors, and others. He even wrote a long letter to the London *Times*.

Semmes was unpopular with his subordinates, toward whom he assumed an air of hauteur. It is more important for a commanding officer to be trusted than to be liked. Semmes commanded the fullest confidence. Officers who served with

Raphael Semmes, Captain Commanding C. S. C. Sumter.
Courtesy of the Office of the U. S. Naval Records and Library.

The Sumter Running the Blockade of Pass à l'Outre,
by the Enemy's Ship Brooklyn, on the 30th of June, 1861.
From a lithograph by A. Hoen & Co., Baltimore.

him on the Sumter were ready to join the Alabama. In contrast to Semmes, Lieutenant Kell, first officer on both ships, commanded the warm affection of the ward room and the forecastle.

The men nicknamed Semmes "Old Beeswax." It was not a term of playful fondness, merely a meaningless tag. His genuine devotion to the welfare of the crew did not atone for the angry curses he dispensed when irritated.

Semmes displayed greater animosity against the enemy than one usually associates with a professional military man, to whom war presents problems for solution rather than emotions to be satisfied. Perhaps the clue is to be found in the fact that he had not really a Southern background; that he had spent his life in the enemy navy; and that he was in need of perpetual bolstering of his position.

He was a fastidious man, ahead of his time in matters of sanitation and hygiene. He carried two surgeons, was careful of the health of his crew, required two changes of clothing every day when in tropical waters. He fed the best grub he could get, with the usual ration of grog. He boasted that he never lost a man or a prisoner through sickness. All his precautions could not prevent outbreaks of scurvy during long intervals between ports, when "salt horse" (corned beef or salt pork) was the ship's staple diet and everyone on board had the sensation of being perpetually hungry. The supplies taken from the prizes replenished the ship's larder without introducing variety into the food. The disease broke out on the Sumter. The officers and men who survived the Alabama on the last day of her life were full of scurvy. We know today that this condition will appear among a crew deprived of vitamin C for a fortnight if the men are working hard or get wet or cold. Limes or lemons, if the ship has a supply, will stop it.

Semmes' personal behavior was circumspect. There are no agreeable scandals to embellish the tale. He was no Nelson any way you take him. He was, in fact, a good deal of a prig.

In appearance he was below medium height; had a greying moustache; the eyes of a fanatic.

Thus much has been said in a fragmentary attempt to interpret the ablest and most eminent of the commerce destroyers. It would have been difficult to find a man whose qualities, including his deficiencies, were so exactly suited to the work for which he solicited employment.

II

Until cruisers could be obtained abroad, the Confederacy had no armed vessels with which to inaugurate an attack upon Northern commerce except the few small privateers that operated under letters of marque. A survey of vessels in Southern ports that could be requisitioned or seized for the purpose showed none that was adequate. Bulloch, who was in a position to know, thought there were not more than three to choose from. Semmes was allowed to select the least unsuitable of these, a packet steamer named the Habana that plied between New Orleans and Cuba and happened to be caught in the Confederate port. She was a screw steamer built in Philadelphia in 1859, 184 feet long, barkentine rigged, with a propeller that could not be hoisted and formed a drag on the ship when under sail. Her speed under steam was 9 knots. Semmes was placed in command April 18, 1861, and began the work of converting her into a warship in the hope of getting to sea before New Orleans should be blockaded. Passenger cabins had to be cleared away; the main deck strengthened to support the armament; magazines and enlarged bunkers installed; and many alterations made in structure and design. The work proceeded with heartbreaking slowness. She was armed with an 8-inch pivot gun between the fore and main masts and four 24-pound howitzers in broadside. These were ordered from Norfolk. In the disorganized condition of the railroads, Semmes had to send an officer to search for them. He found them at various points along the route where they had been thrown from freight cars in order to accommodate army supplies. At the end of two months she was ready for work with a complement of twenty-one officers, seventy-two seamen, and twelve marines. Most of the officers were "Old Navy" men. Ten of them afterwards served on the Alabama. The hands were picked from a large number of unemployed seamen of miscellaneous nationality in New Orleans, inexperienced in navy work but amenable. With this relatively large personnel there was little room on the Sumter for the accommodation of prisoners.

Semmes was supplied with only $10,000 for wages and expenses. He expected to live on his prizes. The Sumter's equipment, like that of all the cruisers, included a box of the flags of all nations, to be used for purposes of disguise.

When the Sumter was ready for sea on June 18, new troubles began. The port pilots, mostly Union men, refused to serve until compelled to do so. The blockade had become effective by the arrival off the delta of four Union vessels headed by the swift and powerful first-class screw sloop Brooklyn. Had the Brooklyn been able to get over the bar she would have entered the Mississippi and closed the river above the passes. Owing to her draft she had to stand off. There was a weary delay of twelve days, with two false starts, until, on Sunday morning June 30, 1861, while the Sumter was waiting inside the Pass-à-L'Outre, the Brooklyn was observed to leave her berth in chase of a blockade-runner. Semmes consulted his officers. One of them, who had served recently on the Brooklyn, said that there was no chance of getting away, for under steam the Union vessel was nearly half as fast again as the Sumter. Semmes decided to try it anyhow. His pilot took the Sumter out of the pass, over the bar, and departed, leaving the Sumter fairly at sea, with an enemy ship of superior force and speed about four miles in the offing.

As soon as the Brooklyn saw the Sumter, she abandoned the chase of the blockade-runner and went after the cruiser, following astern and gaining fast, though never coming within shooting range. The funnels of both ships were pouring out streams of black smoke, but it was the sails, the smartness of the Sumter, and the daring seamanship of her commander that won the race for her. Semmes, who was acting as his own sailing master, hauled his ship close to the wind, thereby shortening the distance of the pursuit. As he had hoped (with much misgiving, he confesses), the Brooklyn, in following the maneuver, got dead into the wind and had to take in her sails. The Sumter under sail and steam made a clean getaway. Semmes was now ready to carry out the orders of Secretary Mallory "to do the greatest injury in the shortest time."

His plan was to pick up such prizes as he could in the Caribbean while steering for the northeast corner of Brazil, off Cape San Roque, where he hoped to catch Union vessels in that much frequented lane. The Sumter's cruising radius was limited by the circumstance that she could carry coal for only eight days' steaming. Semmes economized by using sail as much as possible. He replenished his bunkers in various ports. As it turned out, the Sumter made eight of her seventeen captures before she reached the Atlantic and within the first week of her cruising life of six months.

The first prize was the 700-ton bark Golden Rocket of Maine, bound for the south shore of Cuba in ballast, looking for a cargo of sugar. She was overhauled between the Cuban coast and that of the Isle of Pines on the afternoon of July 3, 1861. A shot across her bows caused her to heave to. A boarding officer escorted the master and his papers to the Sumter, boats brought off the crew and some supplies, and the Golden Rocket was ready for destruction. This was deferred until 10:00 P.M. Semmes adopted a practice which was followed by other commanders when it was safe to do so, of burning ships at night in the hope that the fire would lure other enemy merchantmen to the rescue and into the cruiser's bag. This legitimate stratagem threw the Northern press into paroxysms of invective.

The method of firing a prize was first to chop up the cabin and forecastle bunks, which were usually of white pine lumber, with mattresses stuffed with straw. A pile of chips and straw was laid in the cabin, another in the forecastle. To these were added the butter and lard found in the ship's stores. The boarding crew was then placed in the boats, except the two incendiaries. These fired the inflammable heaps and took their places in the boats, which returned to the cruiser.

Semmes' own description of the burning of the Golden Rocket has been quoted by both of his biographers. It is worth repeating as an example of many similar episodes and as a specimen of the vivid English which its author had at command:

"The wind by this time had become very light and the night was pitch-dark. . . . The boat, which had been sent on this errand of destruction, had pulled out of sight, and her oars ceasing to resound, we knew that she had reached the doomed ship, but so impenetrable was the darkness, that no trace of either boat or ship could be seen, although the Sumter was distant only a few hundred yards. Not a sound could be heard on board the Sumter, although her deck was crowded with men. . . . Suddenly, one of the crew exclaimed, 'There is the flame! She is on fire!' The decks of this Maine-built ship were of pine, calked with old-fashioned oakum, and paid with pitch, the wood-work of the cabin was like so much tinder, having been seasoned by many voyages to the tropics, and the forecastle was stowed with paints and oils. The consequence was, that the flame was not long in kindling, but leaped, full-grown, into the air, in a very few minutes after its first faint glimmer had been seen. The boarding officer, to do his work more effectually, had applied the torch simultaneously in three places, the cabin, the mainhold, and the forecastle; and now the devouring flames rushed up these three apertures with a fury which nothing could resist. The burning ship, with the Sumter's boat in the act of shoving off from her side; the Sumter herself, with her grim, black sides, lying in repose like some great sea-monster, gloating upon the spectacle, and the sleeping sea, for there was scarce a ripple upon the water, were all brilliantly lighted. The indraught into the burning ship's holds, and cabins, added every moment new fury to the flames, and now they could be heard roaring like the fires of a hundred furnaces, in full blast. The prize ship had been laid to, with her main-topsail to the mast, and all her light sails, though clewed up, were flying loose about the yards. The forked tongues of the devouring element, leaping into the rigging, newly tarred, ran rapidly up the shrouds, first into the tops, then to the topmast-heads, thence to the top-gallant, and royal mast-heads, and in a moment more to the trucks; and whilst this rapid ascent of the main current of fire was going on, other currents had run out upon the yards, and ignited all the sails. A top-gallant sail, all on fire, would now fly off from the yard, and sailing leisurely in the direction of the light breeze that was fanning, rather than blowing, break into bright and sparkling patches of flame, and settle, or rather silt into the sea. The yard would then follow, and not being wholly submerged by its descent into the sea, would retain a portion of its flame, and continue to burn, as a floating brand, for some minutes. At one time, the intricate net-work of the cordage of the burning ship was traced, as with a pencil of fire, upon the black sky beyond, the many threads of flame twisting and writhing, like so many serpents that had received their death wounds. The mizzen-mast now went by the board, then the fore-mast, and in a few minutes afterward, the great main-mast tottered, reeled, and fell over the ship's side into the sea, making a noise like that of the sturdy oak of the forests when it falls by the stroke of the axeman."

The next day, the Fourth of July, the Sumter caught the brig Cuba, 236 tons, of Lewiston, Maine, Captain Strout, bound from a Cuban port for London with a cargo of sugar; and another small Maine brig, the Machias, similarly laden.

The usual shot across the bows brought the vessels to. Their manifests bore the British consular certificates establishing the neutral ownership of the cargo. Semmes put a prize crew consisting of a midshipman and four men on each brig and started to tow them into Cienfuegos to await the lifting of the blockade of some Southern port into which they could be sent for adjudication in prize by a Confederate court. He had a theory that captures could be parked in a neutral harbor to be left until called for, like parcels in a check room. He saw no force in the argument that this would make the neutral government accessory to the capture.

The case of the Cuba offered no opportunity to test the theory. The tow line parted, leaving the prize crew to make port under sail. It was only sixty miles away. Nearly fifty years later Captain Strout spun his yarn for the benefit of the *Magazine of History:*

"We were unarmed and were allowed to keep on deck. I got a chance to talk to Jim Babbage and Jim Carroll, my first and second mates, and we determined to recapture the vessel. On July 8 I found the prizemaster [Midshipman Hudgins] asleep on the round-house. Immediately we got possession of all the arms. The prize crew got onto the racket and ran for their weapons. Finding them gone two drew their sheath knives and one got an axe and rushed at where we were. The mainsail was down and lay between us. One of them tried to jump over it and I hit him over the head with a cleaver that I had in my hand. He fell, scrambled back, and did not attempt to return. My mates and the cook were now armed with revolvers and one of my seamen had a cutlass. 'If you stir,' I shouted to the prize crew, 'I will blow your heads off.' They didn't stir. When I ordered them to surrender they yielded and went forward followed by myself and my crew." [1]

In his account of this affair Semmes says that Strout bribed two members of the prize crew. Strout does not mention that. His story continues:

[1] Extra No. 2 (1908), p. 137.

"I had on board only four pairs of irons. I put one on the prizemaster and the others on three of the most dangerous of the others. The rest we tied with ropes. That day I fell in with the brig Costa Rica which took off two of the prize crew, and I headed the Cuba for New York. Nothing of importance happened until the 14th day of July, when the prizemaster, whose irons had been removed at his urgent request, managed to get a pistol and perched himself in the maintop. Then he took out a cigar and lighted it and called down that he had something to say to me. 'Do you intend to carry me to New York?' he asked. I told him that I did. He blew out some smoke, laughed, and said 'Well, you'll never do it alive.' 'All right,' said I, 'then I'll carry you dead.' At that he yelled, 'It's your time to dodge,' and fired at me. The bullet struck the deck at my feet and I did dodge. Johnny Reb told the truth that time. He fired again and I did some more lively hopping. Then I ran below and got my pistol. As my head reappeared in the companionway he turned loose one more time and the splinters flew into my hair.

"I got on deck at last and proceeded to even things up. He was swinging around in the maintop and I was dancing around on the deck. I suppose it was the funniest looking duel that ever was. He used up all his cartridges without hitting me, and I shot at him three times without coming anywhere near him. Then I lodged a ball in the mast just above his head and the next shot I got him in the arm. It was the right arm and it was broken above the elbow. He dropped his weapon to the deck. All this time he had been holding his cigar in his left hand. He was the nerviest man I ever saw. He threw the cigar away and came down. I dressed his wound and locked him up. I kept guard over him until we reached New York on July 21. It was Sunday, I remember, and, though we did not then know it, the guns were roaring at Bull Run."

Captain Strout took the Cuba to New York and delivered his captured captors to the Federal authorities there.

Cases of the recapture of prizes happened occasionally in the privateering days of earlier wars. During the French spoliations of American commerce, there was an instance in which a lone Negro, the cook on a captured ship, overcame the entire prize crew and saved the ship for her owners, who thereupon resisted his claim for a salvage reward.

On July 5, 1861, the Sumter sighted two more American vessels. Semmes cast off the Machias, which had continued in tow, telling her prize master to wait, and went in chase of the brigantines Ben Dunning of Maine and Albert Adams of Massachusetts, making out from Cienfuegos with cargoes of Spanish-owned sugar. They were soon captured, manned with prize crews, and ordered to stand in for the lighthouse. By this time it was after dark. Semmes intended to follow his three prizes (or four, as he supposed, for he thought the Cuba would be among them) into the harbor. But as the Sumter approached the entrance the next morning, a tug appeared coming out with three vessels in tow, the barks West Wind, of Rhode Island, and Louisa Kilham, of Massachusetts, and the barkentine Naiad, of New York, all laden with sugar for Spanish account. Waiting until they had been cast loose by the tug, the Sumter gathered in these prizes also. There is doubt whether these ships were taken on the high seas or in Spanish territorial waters. There were now six prizes with neutral cargo to be sent into Cienfuegos, and another, as Semmes believed, also on her way there.

He wrote the Governor of the town asking hospitality for these vessels until they could be sent into a Confederate port. They remained in the harbor until despatches had been exchanged between Havana and Madrid, when they were restored to their owners. This course convinced Semmes that the Spanish government had been corrupted by Northern gold. The fact was that the Spanish government acted in accordance with a recognized principle of international law, which was codified by the Hague Tribunal in 1907. In November, 1939, the government of Norway applied the rule to the American ship City of Flint, a prize taken by a belligerent because of contraband cargo and taken into a Norwegian port without the excuse of bad weather, unseaworthiness, or other compelling cause. The Norwegian authorities restored the vessel to her American crew.

The Sumter landed her prisoners and replenished her bunkers at Cienfuegos. One regrets to report, on the authority of Semmes, that Lieutenant Chapman, who went ashore to buy coal, *"almost* forgot that he was a married man." After coaling, the Sumter stood away for the Spanish Main to escape Union warships which were known to be in Cuban waters.

Her next call was Curaçao, where she stayed a week, got more coal, did some refitting, and the crew had their washing done.

Between Curaçao and LaGuayra the cruiser caught the schooner Abby Bradford, New York to Puerto Cabello with American-owned provisions. Semmes tried to store this vessel in the Venezuelan port of her destination. The United States Consul protested; the port authorities delayed their decision, and Semmes determined to send the prize to New Orleans in the hope that the prize crew could succeed in running the blockade. He would have done better to destroy her, as was his right. The Abby Bradford was caught by one of the blockaders, restored to her owners, and her prize crew imprisoned.

The next capture was the bark Joseph Maxwell, of Philadelphia. She was carrying some neutral cargo between two Venezuelan ports. Semmes asked permission to put her into Puerto Cabello and received, not a permit, but an order to send her in for a Venezuelan court to determine whether or not she had been captured within the three-mile limit. Semmes preferred to put her in charge of a midshipman with a prize crew and send her to Cienfuegos. The schooner's master and his wife were presented with one of their own boats and told to go ashore on the Venezuelan coast. The ungrateful master "stole" his own chronometer and took it with him. The eight men comprising the remainder of the Joseph Maxwell's crew were detained on board the cruiser. Like the other prizes sent to the Cuban port, she was restored to her owners.

The Sumter proceeded to Port-of-Spain, Trinidad, discharged her prisoners of war, and coaled again. Then on to Paramaribo for more coal. She stayed there ten days, during which her bunkers were enlarged to accommodate fuel enough for four additional days' steaming, twelve in all. At length, after displaying the Confederate flag to the French convicts at Cayenne on Louis Napoleon's birthday, she entered Brazilian waters on September 2, 1861. She passed the Amazon delta and the Equator on September 4, and on the 6th grounded on a shoal, doing damage to her hull which caused trouble later. She backed off and presently came to anchor in the port of Maranham.

Here the Sumter became a local political issue. The nations of her previous ports of call had recognized the belligerency of the Confederacy. Brazil had not yet done so. The position of the cruiser in a Brazilian harbor was anomalous. On receipt of Semmes' application for permission to coal, the President of the Department was puzzled and delayed his reply. The United States Consul protested. Semmes rejoined. The permission was granted. The opposition party in the provincial legislature introduced a resolution calling upon the Governor to explain his action. It came within three votes of passing. Popular excitement reflected the sentiments of the pro-slavery and abolition parties within the country. Semmes' account of the proceedings is at variance with the recorded facts in material points. At this time he was in bad health and embarrassed for lack of funds. His paymaster had to borrow $2,000 from a citizen of Texas who was in business in the town.

Semmes would have been encouraged if he could have seen the report of the American Consul to Secretary Seward.

This contained the first intimation of the real danger to be feared from Confederate cruisers:

"Your Excellency cannot imagine the effect which the presence of the Sumter on this coast has had on American trade. It is quite possible that it will be entirely suspended. Already several cargoes ordered a short time previous have been countermanded."

The Sumter was refitted, painted, coaled, and provisioned, and got away to sea by September 15, 1861. Semmes determined to steer northward and lie in wait in the "calm belt" just above 5° North Latitude. Homebound ships from the south had to pass this way. A steamer, however slow, can overhaul a becalmed sailer. Proof that the Consul's apprehensions were well founded was soon forthcoming. On September 25, 1861, the Sumter caught the brigantine Joseph Parke, of Boston, six days out of Pernambuco in ballast. She had not been able to get a cargo. Taking her people on board his own ship, Semmes put a prize crew on the Joseph Parke and tried to make use of her as a scout. After four days, during which no sails were seen, he recalled the prize crew, used the Parke for a little target practice, and then burned her.

As the hunting was so poor in the calm belt, Semmes determined to try the Lesser Antilles again. The Sumter had now come to the close of her first semester. Her total accomplishment in three months had been the destruction of two enemy ships, some little annoyance and delay to nine others. Her indirect achievement had been to start the mounting fear which was to accumulate throughout the war with lasting disaster to American trade. She had also begun to cost the Federal government heavily in anxiety and in naval effort. Six ships, including some of the most efficient in the Navy, had been detached from blockade duty to search for her. Later others were added. Semmes boasted that altogether about a score of Federal vessels were after the slow, unseaworthy Sumter.

For a month after taking the Joseph Parke, the Sumter

found no quarry. She was roving to the east of the Windward Isles, conserving coal by proceeding under sail above the calm belt. Her crew began to show symptoms of scurvy. Then on Sunday, October 27, 1861, she had a piece of good luck which eliminated that danger. She caught the schooner Daniel Trowbridge, of New Haven, last from New York to Demerara with a cargo of provisions including beef, pork, hams, live sheep, geese, chickens, fancy crackers, cheese, and flour. Three days were required to transfer these fortunate windfalls, together with the crew of the schooner. There were enough provisions to last the Sumter five months. For the first time Semmes was enabled to realize something of his hope to live on his prizes. The Daniel Trowbridge was burned October 30, 1861.

During this portion of her cruise the Sumter usually displayed the Stars and Stripes to deceive the neutral ships she passed, so that they would not report her whereabouts to pursuing vessels of the Federal Navy. The U.S.S. Keystone State, Powhatan, and Dakotah were close upon her track at several points.

On November 9, fifty-five days out of Maranham, Semmes ran into the harbor of Fort-de-France, Martinique, and came to anchor. The physical infirmities of the Sumter and her unrelenting nemesis, an inadequate coal supply, the necessity of obtaining fresh water, of giving the men some shore leave, and of getting rid of the prisoners from the Joseph Parke and the Daniel Trowbridge, dictated this call. The crew were given liberty by watches, each man being supplied with a gold sovereign. They made the best of the social and alcoholic resources of the port. The prisoners were turned over to the American Consul. These were the first prisoners who had been detained on a Confederate cruiser for any length of time.

Throughout the war the Northern press published stories of mistreatment of prisoners of war by Semmes. In his memoirs he repeatedly denies them. It will be necessary to revert to this subject when we come to the Alabama. The weight of the evidence acquits Semmes of inhumanity. A ship is not equipped with cells like a floating jail. The only way to restrain prisoners when they are numerous is with irons. The use of single irons, i.e., handcuffs, allows the presence of the prisoners on deck for light and air. Until February 3, 1862, embracing the entire cruise of the Sumter, the Federal government was treating sailors on armed Confederate vessels as pirates. While this would not have excused reciprocal abuse of Federal merchant seamen, it was hardly an inducement to Semmes to extend to his captives the courtesies due cabin passengers.

Semmes polled the prisoners on the Sumter for complaints and received none. Little importance can be attached to that, for the interrogation took place before they were discharged. The report of the consul at Martinique is more significant. Writing to the Secretary of State on November 26, 1861, Consul Campbell merely says that he has received two masters and eleven men, prisoners from the Sumter, and shipped them to the United States. He describes the activities of the Sumter in Martinique. If the prisoners had made any serious complaints to him after their discharge, he would have reported the fact. Semmes had a strong motive for according humane treatment to captives. His government was courting the good will of the European powers and their people. He would have been unlikely to go out of his way to do anything to forfeit their esteem so early in the war.

To complete refitting, Semmes took the Sumter into St. Pierre, then close at hand, since blotted out of existence by the volcanic eruption of 1902. While he was there, one of his pursuers, the fast, heavily armed steam sloop Iroquois, Captain J. S. Palmer, came in. Learning that the colonial government would enforce the rule requiring an interval of twenty-four hours between the departure of hostile ships, Palmer took the Iroquois far enough outside to exonerate him from the charge of "hovering," and waited. He went at the task half-heartedly and began to pave the way for failure.

On November 18 he wrote the Secretary of the Navy, "I feel more and more convinced that the Sumter will yet escape me, in spite of all our vigilance and zeal, even admitting that I can outrun her which is a doubtful question. . . . Even now, moonlight though it be, she may yet creep out under the shadow of the land and no one be able to perceive her. . . . I have done all I can and if she escapes me we must submit to the distress and mortification."

St. Pierre stood on the shore of an open road twelve miles across. The Iroquois took her station off the center of the bay, prepared to steam in either direction. Palmer arranged with the schooner Windward, which was in port, to signal him by means of masthead lights, indicating the time of the Sumter's departure and her direction. After waiting a week, in the night of November 23, 1861, Palmer saw the signal showing that the Sumter was coming out, steering southerly. Semmes saw it, too; he was looking for it. After making sure that the Iroquois was heading south, he doubled on his course in the darkness and made for the northern end of the bay. A sudden rain squall and the shadow of Mount Pelée aided in the concealment. By the time Palmer discovered the ruse and started north, the Sumter was well away, hugging the northern shore so as to keep within French territorial waters. Palmer hunted for her in vain.

It was a nerve-wracking night for all on board the Sumter. She would have no chance in a fight with the Iroquois. The lookout on the cruiser was so jittery that (quoting Semmes), "if he saw one Iroquois that night he must have seen fifty." He was so shaken that he had to be relieved. Before daybreak the ship, "groping like a blind man," ran almost into the breakers. No one on board knew the position.

It was even worse with Palmer. His failure to take an enemy ship much smaller and slower than his own, while patrolling an area only twelve miles wide, and with coöperation from inshore, drew upon him a court of inquiry and a reduction in rank.

Semmes headed across the ocean under sail, with the dragging propeller acting as a brake. His ship was ill adapted for a long voyage. His hope was to catch a large merchant steamer that he could substitute for the Sumter.

Soon after getting into the Atlantic, on November 24, 1861, he overhauled the handsome full rigged ship Montmorency, of Bath, Maine, from Newport in Wales to St. Thomas with coal. The cargo being neutral, she was bonded. Next day he got the pedestrian little schooner Arcade, of Portland, with a load of staves for Guadaloupe, where she expected a cargo of rum and sugar. The crew was taken aboard the Sumter and the Arcade burned after dark.

The next prize was sighted December 3, 1861, well out at sea. A large ship was seen approaching. The Sumter hoisted French colors and waited until the stranger crossed her bows. A gun brought her to. She was a fine new vessel, the Vigilant, of Bath, Maine, for the guano islands. Prisoners were transferred and the prize burned.

Ten of the seamen of the Vigilant were Negroes. In arranging the prisoners' mess Semmes mischievously seated the black Yankees alternately with the white ones. Later, when the ever-leaking Sumter was laboring in a storm and taking in much water, the Negroes were set to man the pumps. It was work to which the men of the cruiser would have been assigned as a matter of course if there had been no prisoners on board, and imposed no undue hardship upon the Negro prisoners.

On the day (November 25, 1861) on which the Sumter headed out into the Atlantic from Martinique, the bark Eben Dodge, 221 tons, sailed from New Bedford on a whaling voyage to the Pacific. The two vessels met on December 8 in a hard northeaster with weather so thick that they did not see each other until very close. The Dodge was the first whaler to become a prize. Later the Alabama was to take twelve and the Shenandoah some twenty-six of these staunch craft. The chapter relating to the Shenandoah gives some account of them.[1] Like all whaling ships at the beginning of a voyage, the Eben Dodge was well supplied with stores, which were transferred to the Sumter in a heavy sea, along with twenty-two men, making forty-three passengers on board. The Dodge was fired at dusk. "The flames burned red and lurid in the murky atmosphere," wrote Semmes, "like some Jack-o-lantern, now appearing and now disappearing as the doomed ship rose to the top or descended into the abyss of the waves."

The prisoners on the Sumter now amounted to a third of her company. They outnumbered the men of either watch. Among them were three experienced navigators, the masters of the Arcade, the Vigilant, and the Eben Dodge. To forestall the danger of losing his ship, Semmes handcuffed half the prisoners for twenty-four hours, then transferred the manacles to the other half for a like period, and so on. According to Semmes they seemed to like it.

From the 8th to the 30th of December the Sumter made her easting through heavy weather and deserted seas. Then suddenly, in the neighborhood of 35° North and between 16° and 20° West, she stopped sixteen ships in one day, all proving to be neutrals coming out of the Mediterranean. The Sumter's leaky condition had become alarming by this time; so Semmes got up steam and ran for Cadiz, arriving January 4, 1862.

Destiny brought Semmes into Cadiz at a critical moment in a diplomatic negotiation of which he had no knowledge and of which he never learned. The British Ministry were soliciting the support of Queen Isabella in their stand on the Trent affair and tentatively suggesting European solidarity against the United States. The American Chargé d'Affaires at Madrid, Horatio G. Perry, was endeavoring to dissuade the Minister of State, Sr. Calderon, from coöperating with Great Britain and from dealing with the Confederate agent, Rost, who was in the Spanish capital. The insecure government

[1] Chap. X, below.

of Spain, which was to blow away in revolution six years later, was trying to consolidate its impaired strength at home by doing a little diplomatic trading abroad. Calderon's price for joining England and France in presenting a united European front against the North was the restoration of Spanish rule in Santo Domingo, a share of power in the projected Mexican empire, and English pressure on France to concede it. For the moment the maintenance of strict neutrality was the core of Spain's trading position. That was the analysis made by the American Chargé d'Affaires. He studied to exploit it.

On December 7 (1861) he threatened to close the legation if the government should receive any Confederate negotiator (meaning Rost). On January 4 (1862) he reported to the State Department that he had secured the assistance of the opposition leaders in both houses of the Cortes, where the political division was close, and had organized a strong newspaper propaganda.

On that day, Semmes innocently sailed the Sumter into Cadiz.

S. E. Eggleston, United States Consul at Cadiz, protested to the military governor of the port against any violation of neutrality and notified Perry in Madrid. Perry at once sent out a sheaf of telegrams to London, Paris, Rome, Barcelona, and Alicant, to round up American naval vessels which were searching European waters for the Sumter and the Nashville, a Confederate cruiser whose career was overlapped at both ends by that of the Sumter.

Owing to the fussiness of the port health officer, the Sumter's captives from the Arcade, the Vigilant, and the Eben Dodge, were not landed until January 9, when Eggleston reported to Perry that he had received forty-two prisoners off the Confederate cruiser. In the name of his wife, who was a Spanish lady of influential connections, Perry wired Eggleston to give a banquet to these prisoners "and send the bill to us." Eggleston included the officers from sixteen American vessels then in Cadiz, making a dinner of sixty-five. The healths of the President of the United States and the Queen of Spain were drunk at Doña Dolores Perry's expense, with much patriotic oratory. Every newspaper in Spain played up the story.

Two days after the dinner party, Perry called on Calderon and protested against permitting the Sumter to make any repairs whatsoever in a Spanish port. Calderon responded in writing that he had ordered "incessant vigilance" to be kept over the Sumter to see that she got no repairs and provisions "more than what is necessary for the moment," and no munitions.

At the same time Eggleston, under Perry's instructions, was not neglecting the crew of the Sumter. Semmes had been obliged to grant shore leave, as his men had been confined to the ship since leaving Martinique nearly two months before. They went on a heroic binge. "It would be a service of which you might well be proud and which the government would not fail to appreciate," wrote Perry to Eggleston on January 14, "if you could find means to persuade the misguided men who form the crew of the corsair that their only chance of safety lies in a prompt and voluntary submission to the government of their country."

These efforts by the American diplomatic and consular officers, seconded by the *cantineros* and *putaneros* of Cadiz, reacted grievously against Semmes' efforts to get coal and repairs at Cadiz and to keep his crew intact. An additional difficulty was that he had no money. He telegraphed to the Confederate mission in London for funds. These were delayed. He was compelled to ask for credit and was humiliated to find it denied him. Eventually he got the use of the government dockyard for two days, where, if Perry was correctly informed, he was able to make only $7.00 worth of repairs. Then the Governor of the port sent him (January 17) a peremptory order to go to sea. Exasperated, he sailed away. Nine of the crew had deserted to Eggleston's consulate; others were brought on board at pistol point. Urgently needed repairs had not been made. The bunkers were low. The ship leaked. The boilers were in very bad condition. There was no money, and some debts incurred in the port were unpaid.

The Sumter started around the corner toward Gibraltar on January 12 (1862).

In the mouth of the strait she overhauled the 322-ton bark Neapolitan, of Kingston, Massachusetts, Messina for Boston with brimstone and fruit. The cargo was consigned to the Boston branch of Baring Brothers. Semmes decided that it was enemy property and burned the prize in plain sight of both sides of the strait. While the master of the bark was his prisoner, Semmes got a statement from him that the capture had been made more than a league from shore. When the officers of the Neapolitan got to Gibraltar the master and mates repudiated the statement made under duress and swore to a marine protest to the effect that the capture was made within a mile and a half of the Spanish fortress at Ceuta on the south shore. Perry in Madrid promptly demanded damages from the Spanish government for failing to prevent the capture. His purpose was to bring about the detention of the Sumter if she should again enter Spanish waters. The next time Perry saw the Minister of State, Calderon said, "No, no, the Sumter will not again come into any Spanish port," and indicated that she would be arrested if she did. Perry followed this up with a demand that Spanish naval vessels be instructed to stop the Sumter on the high seas, but he could not get Calderon to go as far as that.

Immediately after firing the Neapolitan, Semmes stopped the bark Investigator, of Searsport, Maine, from Garrucha in Spain to Newport, in Wales, with iron ore. The cargo was neutral and one of the owners of the vessel was a Southerner; so Semmes took a bond for $11,250 from the master and let the ship go.

It was dark by this time. By the light on Europa Point and the flames from the Neapolitan, the Sumter put into Gibraltar, where she landed her prisoners. The Investigator was her

THE SUMTER 53

eighteenth and last capture. Her career as a cruiser was at an end.

III

For 102 years, from 1832 to 1934, the United States Consul at Gibraltar was Mr. Sprague. Father, son, and grandson held the post successively. Generations of tourists (including the present reporter) acquired the conviction that the consulate was entailed and that the courteous attentions of Mr. Sprague in Gibraltar were guaranteed by the Bill of Rights.

The arrival of the Sumter of course claimed the attention of the incumbent, H. J. Sprague. A telegram from Perry had put him on the lookout and advised him that Semmes was without funds.

It was a fortnight before the tardy remittance reached Semmes from London. During that time the only money he had was $86, taken from the Neapolitan, and $51, from the Investigator. Meanwhile Sprague had been collecting written promises from the local coal dealers not to make sales to the Sumter. They could hardly refuse the Consul, for many United States vessels patronized them and there was only one Confederate customer. When Semmes tried to get the Governor to sell him coal from the government stores, the request was refused upon telegraphic instructions from London. The fueling of a belligerent warship with Navy coal was a step farther than England was ready to go, immediately after the settling of the Trent affair. Dinner parties and entertainments were tendered to the Sumter's officers, but no fuel.

A few days after Semmes' money arrived, Perry's telegrams brought three United States naval vessels, the Tuscarora, the Kearsarge, and the Ino. They took positions at Algeciras, ten miles away, and cruised about in the neighborhood, effectively blockading the Sumter. Once the Kearsarge ran into Gibraltar and anchored a cable's length from the Sumter. The British authorities objected to this and the offense was not repeated. As the weeks went on while the Sumter lay at anchor, her men began to trickle away in spite of the precaution of allowing only one boat's crew ashore at one time. Attempts to get them back by force were blocked by the police at the Consul's instigation. At Perry's suggestion Sprague offered his protection to deserters who would take an oath of allegiance to the United States. He seems to have used no other inducement. By March 19, two months after arrival, nineteen men had deserted without any replacements.

On the arrival of his funds Semmes determined to send his paymaster, Henry Myers, back to Cadiz to have a supply of coal shipped to him, since the Sumter could not get out to go for it. The paymaster's errand brought about some strange doings in Tangier on the opposite side of the strait. They were not important and are here recounted at undue length from no worthier motive than the entertainment of the reader.

Tangier was ruled by Mohamed Bargash as governor for the Sultan of Morocco. Foreign consuls exercised extraterritorial jurisdiction, i.e., each of them regulated his own nationals without reference to the Moorish government. Some hundreds of Europeans were living in the town, including many human odds and ends with no prejudices in favor of peace.

The newly appointed consul general of the United States, James De Long, unlike Sprague, was neither a Harvard man nor a career diplomat, as will appear (one hopes) from his reports. But he was full of energy and zeal.

In Gibraltar Paymaster Myers picked up a Mr. Tunstall, a Southern man who had been consul at Cadiz prior to the change of administration at home. On February 19, Myers and Tunstall got on board a little French steamer, the Ville de Malaga, which plied around the coast. Before proceeding to Cadiz she had a call to make at Tangier, a matter of an hour or two of steaming. During her stop there, Myers and Tunstall went ashore to take a walk and pay a social call.

In some way not disclosed De Long learned of the presence of these tourists. Although he was not quite sure who they were, he applied to the Moorish constabulary, had them arrested, locked them up in the consulate, and despatched a hasty note to Sprague:

"I have seized Tunstall and the lieutenant of the Sumter and I want you to send the Tuscorora for them immediately."

Sprague was a little alarmed. He thought De Long had overstepped the limits of extra-territoriality by making political arrests. In this he was correct. The capture was a hostile act committed on the soil of a neutral power. Sprague consulted Perry in Madrid. Perry was not disposed to be legalistic. He sustained De Long on the ground that Myers was guilty of treason and of destroying American property at sea. As for Tunstall, he deserved arrest for being in bad company.

These exchanges consumed some time. There was further delay before Commander Craven could spare a ship from watching the Sumter. By the time he sent the little sloop Ino for the prisoners, a week after the arrests, De Long had been through a trying experience. As a matter of fair play he allowed his prisoners to send some messages. They first appealed to the French Consul in Tangier on the ground that they were passengers in a French ship. The Consul pointed out that they had been arrested on shore. Word was somehow communicated to Semmes, who addressed a note to the Moorish Governor and got it delivered via the British Consul. This produced the following communication:

"Praise be to One God.

"To our dear and wise friend the Consul General for the American Nation, James De Long, Esq., which premised we continue to make inquiries regarding your welfare and praying God that you are well.

"We have received a letter from the Captain of the steamer Sumter from the Confederate States in which they inform us that the two men that you have seized are of the best of men and they are guiltless except that they are from the separated Confederate States.

"I know that you have sent to ask from our lieutenant Governor to help you in their seizure, the lieutenant Governor has acceded to your demand, and sent you soldiers to make the arrest without ascertaining the case, but now that we received the said letter informing us of these men that they are of the best of men, and without any fault except a politic affair; and as a matter of this character, I beg that these men should be considered in this country the same that have been at Gibraltar and Cadiz.

"If I am to keep still in this affair after the receipt of the said letter, it would appear that I am dealing different from what other people do. Therefore we ask from you to deliver us these men to remain free as they were in other places, as we wish to act in the same manner that other nations have acted.

"We have no doubt that when you receive this letter you will put them free, as our object is to do good and to cultivate friendship with all the nations and Races.

"Written on the 25th of Shahban year 1276, Corresponding February 25, 1862, and beg from you a prompt answer. God Bless you.

"(Signed) The Employed of the Throne Elevated by God,
"Mohamed Bargash
"God may Protect him."

Instead of acceding to this request, De Long acted with much spirit. From the developments that followed, it appears that Semmes, who says he had written "a cord of letters," found means to sow some seeds of propaganda which fell upon fertile ground among the Christians of Tangier. In his despatches to the State Department and messages to naval officers, De Long tells what happened. It is worth noting that the Moors took no part in the shindy. If the infidels chose to break one another's heads, the faithful saw no reason to interfere.

In his first report De Long wrote,

"I had no way to confine them [the prisoners] without putting them in irons and even then I have to keep four soldiers guarding them day and night.... American citizens may talk and plot treason and rebellion at home (if they can) but they shall not do so where I am if I have the power to prevent it."

While waiting for Craven to send a ship, De Long wrote him,

"My guards are all Moors and the prisoners have tried several times to bribe them, first they offered them a valuable gold watch and one hundred dollars in gold, this is very tempting to semi barbarians, they finally offered to secure to them Five thousand dollars to assist them in making their escape. I had to put them in irons, and Myers got a case knife and sawed off the rivits and got the irons off and jumped out of the second story of the Consulate, but fortunately into the Consulate lot, he then got over the wall into the house of a Moor and was again arrested and taken back to his room and the number of guards increased.... It may be that the rebel portion of the Europeans might combine with the Moors to raise a mob and try to have these men released.... Myers is a desperate fellow.... I learned last evening that there is a secret movement on foot, the Capt. of the Sumter is making many false representations to accomplish some deep plot. I want the presence of a Federal Man of War in this bay."

A week later, after the Ino had arrived, De Long has a lively story to tell Secretary Seward:

"I consulted with the commander of the Ino about the manner of conveying the prisoners on board, and we came to the conclusion to prevent any demonstration that might be made on the conveyance of the prisoners to the beach, that it would be advisable to order thirty Marines to come ashore fully armed to accompany the prisoners.... By the time the marines had landed on the beach the gates of the port was closed and an armed mob of betwen three and four hundred Europeans residing here under the protection of Foreign representatives at this place, had assembled at the American Consulate. The Commander of the Ino, his Purser, Surgeon, and Mr. Train, Master's Mate, and myself, went into the Street. I inquired of one of the mob who could speak English, what they wanted, he replied,—that they were determined to have the prisoners in my Custody released, we immediately made a rush at them, and drove them out of the Street, we then returned into the Consulate and closed the doors. The mob then returned and tried to break into the Consulate.

"I immediately sent a note to my Interpreter to inform the Moorish Minister of what was going on, and to demand of him Soldiers to suppress the Mob, fortunately before my Interpreter got my note, he had gone to the Minister and informed him in relation to the Mob, then the Minister sent a Message to the Foreign Representatives to withdraw their Subjects, and he also sent troops to protect the U. S. Consulate and to disperse the Mob, all of which was attended to promptly.

"The Commander of the Ino accompanied by three of his junior officers, my Interpreter and myself then proceeded to the residence of the Minister at about 2 o'clock P.M., and after a few preliminary remarks, I gave the Minister to understand the ultimatum of what I required, and nothing short of which would I accept, which was in the following words:

"1st That the gates of the port should be opened.

"2nd That the Marines be permitted to march uninterrupted to The American Consulate.

"3rd That he furnish a sufficient number of troops to keep down the Mob, and to accompany the prisoners to the beach.

"4th All of which must be complied with within one hour or I would strike the American flag and quit the country.

"The Minister replied, no, no, your request shall be acceded to but I desire you to hold over until tomorrow, when all will be quiet; I replied that I would consent to no delay for the reason that it would only give the Mob an opportunity to make further preparations.

"This closed the interview and we returned to the Consulate & in less than one hour the gates of the port were opened, the marines marched to the Consulate, the Moorish troops were on hand, and the prisoners were then brought out and marched down to the beach in the presence of at least three thousand spectators without the least interruption and they were placed on board the Ino which sailed last night."

De Long adds some details in his next despatch:

"The Mob got up in the neighborhood of the residence of the Consuls in the Market place, where they had a table with a pen, ink and paper, set out in the middle of the street, signing and pledging themselves in a Solemn Manner to force the release of the prisoners in my custody at all hazards.... The mob was mostly composed of English, French, Spanish and Italian subjects. There was not one Moor engaged in the Mob, on the contrary the Moorish soldiers performed their duty faithfully.... I shall carry with me to the latest period of my life the seens [sic] of the 26th ultimo. I have heard of barbarian mobs in barbarian countries but it is the first time in my life that I have ever heard of nearly the entire Christian population in a semibarbarian country raising a mob to interfere with the acts of a Christian Consul.

"But thank God that I have over come all and sustained the honor of the American flag."

The commander of the Ino, who signed his reports "Josiah P. Creesy, Acting Volunteer Lieutenant, Commanding," zealously supported the Consul. Before escorting the prisoners to the ship he assembled his thirty marines in the consulate and addressed them, "informing them of the danger and risk to be incurred in this determination I had come to, to take the prisoners at all hazards, stating to them that we were engaged in a righteous cause and that the Government of the

United States expects every man to do his duty; consequently this being our duty, we will proceed to perform it, knowing as I do that every man in this room will go with me to the death."

Acting Volunteer Lieutenant Creesy complained to the Department of a lack of coöperation from Commander T. A. M. Craven of the Tuscarora, who was dilatory in acting on communications. Creesy's reports are almost incoherent. Sailor-like, he was not handy with the pen. He seems to have had a real grievance against Craven, who was related to the prisoner Tunstall. During the early part of the war Craven was an unlucky man. As will appear in the next chapter, he had lately been foiled by the British authorities at Southampton in an attempt to catch the Confederate cruiser Nashville. Arriving at Gibraltar sore and discomfited, he embarrassed Consul Sprague by writing insulting letters to the Governor of Gibraltar. The fact that General Sir William Codrington deserved reproach for flagrant discrimination against the Tuscarora, refusing to let her boats come ashore for mail, while allowing the privilege to the Sumter, did not make it politic to write to him accusing him of dishonesty. In the course of the dealings with the prisoners of Tangier, Consul De Long, his sword fleshed with arrests, threatened to take the commander of the Tuscarora into custody if he set foot in Tangier. For his minor deficiencies Craven made the ultimate atonement. In the battle of Mobile Bay, at the last living moment of a sinking ship, his "After you, pilot," cost his life and immortalized his memory.

Consul De Long's last despatch, written before any news of the affair reached the United States, reports a lamentable miscarriage of justice:

"In making the arrest I done it with a full knowledge of what I believe to be the law, and with a view of restraining these men from further depredations upon our commerce. I pursued the whole thing step by step, using the utmost caution to avoid leading my Govt into trouble. Although on the

25th of Feby my life was in the greatest possible danger, brought about by Captain Semmes of the Pirate Sumter through the interference of the Governor of Gibraltar, as well as nearly the entire European population of Gibraltar at this place, where money was offered freely to the Mob if they would secure the release of the prisoners.

"I believe I was the only man in the place on the day of the Mob that was not excited, even Prince Muley Abbas, who is residing here at present, and who is said to be a very intelligent mild innocent sort of a man, when he heard of the Mob, made the remark, 'What the devil has the Christians to do with the American Consul's prisoners.'

"During the short time I have been here my whole time and attention has been devoted to the interest of my Govt, and what is my reward! Last evening three letters came to this place addressed to different parties from Brown, my late predecessor, informing them that the Senate had not confirmed my appointment and that the President had appointed a Mr. McMath of Ohio in my place and that he would be here shortly."

Alas!

The Ino transferred her prisoners to the American merchant ship Harvest Home bound for Boston. They were kept in double irons all the way. When Semmes learned of this it aroused his lasting resentment.

The Harvest Home delivered Meyers and Tunstall at Fort Warren in Boston. Their comedy of errors, which they did not find amusing, was not yet played out. When they sought exchange as prisoners of war, the Navy Department held they were "political prisoners" and could not be exchanged because there were no similar captives in the South. In effect, they were held in prison because they were not subject to arrest. Ultimately they were paroled.

While these events were in progress the Sumter lay at Gibraltar, without coal, without facilities for replacing her worn-out boilers, with her crew dwindling, and with no possibility of escaping the cordon of United States vessels. At her best she was inefficient and slow. By the beginning of April Semmes realized that the cruise was over. He writes:

"When I look back now, I am astonished to find what a struggle it cost me to get my own consent to lay up this old ship. As inexplicable as the feeling is, I had really become attached to her, and felt as if I would be parting forever with a valued friend. She had run me safely through two vigilant blockades, had weathered many storms, and rolled me to sleep in many calms. Her cabin was my bed-room and my study, both in one, her quarter-deck was my promenade, and her masts, spars, and sails, my playthings. I had handled her in all kinds of weather, watching her every motion in difficult situations. . . . She had fine qualities as a sea-boat, being as buoyant, active, and dry as a duck, in the heaviest gales, and these are the qualities which a seaman most admires."

While Semmes was trying to reconcile himself to giving up the Sumter, Perry got a telegram from Charles Francis Adams, who had just learned of the capitulation of Fort Donelson, the first notable Federal victory of the war. The sense of relief still comes to life out of the fading ink of Perry's comment, "Our cause is saved in Europe. Thank God."

On getting the consent of the Confederate commissioner in London, Semmes (April 11, 1862) paid off what was left of his crew, about fifty men, detached his officers, and left the Sumter in charge of Midshipman Andrews, who was murdered by a member of the skeleton crew. A month or two later the ship was condemned by a board of survey convened on orders from headquarters in London, and was sold at auction for $19,500 to Melchior F. Klingender, a stooge for Fraser, Trenholm & Company, Confederate fiscal agents, who changed her name to the Gibraltar and used her as a blockade-runner. After the war the United States government, finding the Gibraltar at Liverpool, filed a suit for possession, which Klingender let go by default. The English court turned her over to the Consul at Liverpool, who sold her at auction June 26, 1866, for £1,140. She ended her life by foundering in the North Sea, where her bones lie not far from those of her more famous successor, the Alabama.

As a commerce destroyer the Sumter was not a success, being too small, slow, and infirm for effective cruising. Of her eighteen prizes only six had been burned; the others survived her. Her value to the Confederacy lay in the fear with which she inspired Union commerce and the lessons of experience she gave her commanding officer, upon which he drew in his next and far more important command.

Semmes went to England for a month; then to Nassau in a passenger ship. There he found orders assigning him to the Alabama.

CHAPTER III

THE NASHVILLE

*Thus if they would not our friends bee,
We lightly stop hem in the see.*
—Hakluyt, *Principal Voyages*

BETWEEN THE BEGINNING and the end of the Sumter's cruise lies that of the Nashville. Her cruising life was short, less than four months. She took only two prizes. Yet her dramatic effect was greater than that of the Sumter because it was related to the Trent affair. When Perry sent out his telegrams from Madrid for naval vessels to come after the Sumter, the ships he was seeking and which came in response to his call were in European waters in pursuit of the Nashville.

She was a 1,200-ton wooden sidewheel steamer with two masts and a hermaphrodite rig and was employed as a passenger liner between New York and Charleston, where she was seized at the outbreak of the war as one of the three vessels that could be used for cruising purposes. Her draft was lightened and her speed improved so that it was asserted she could make $16\frac{1}{2}$ knots an hour. Two guns of English manufacture were mounted on her.

On the night of October 26, 1861, under the command of Captain R. B. Pegram, C.S.N., ex-U.S.N., with a crew of about forty, she ran the blockade out of Charleston, steamed to Bermuda, where she arrived on October 30, took on a supply of coal, and sailed for the North Atlantic on Tuesday, November 5.

Senators Mason and Slidell had originally planned to sail in the Nashville. A last-minute change of plan sent them to Cuba and thence on board the British mail steamer Trent, bound for the Virgin Islands. On November 6, Captain

Charles Wilkes, U.S.N., in the San Jacinto, acting without orders, stopped the Trent in the Bahama Channel, took off the Confederate commissioners and their secretaries in the midst of a small riot on the Trent's deck, and headed for Boston, reaching there on November 19.

On that day the Nashville, being then in Lat. 49° 6′ N., Long. 9° 52′ W., off the Irish coast, overhauled the American ship Harvey Birch, of New York, 1,482 tons, Havre to New York in ballast. This was a splendid prize. Her master, Captain Nelson, swore she was worth $65,000. Pegram took off her company of thirty-one persons and burned the Harvey Birch. He manacled the men, except the officers and passengers.

As the first capture in the North Atlantic ferry lane, the taking of the Harvey Birch was sensational news. It proved to have been unfortunate, for her principal owner was a warm Southern sympathizer.

The *London Times* of November 22, 1861, contained a report from Southampton: "Great excitement has been created here by the arrival in our waters this morning of a steamer of war bearing the flag of the Confederate States of America." The crew of the Harvey Birch were turned over to the American Consul, who put them up at the Sailors' Home and repatriated them the following week by shipping them to New York on the steamer Hansa of the North German Lloyd Line. Nelson hastened to London to tell his story to Charles Francis Adams. The Nashville went into dock for repairs. An attempt was made to set her on fire in the night. The culprit was not discovered. Immediately afterwards several men deserted. Captain Pegram attributed the incendiary attempt to one of them.

News of the Trent affair reached England on November 28 by way of a West Indian mail steamer. The bitter feeling it aroused fanned the flame of anti-Union sentiment which was already burning bright. The press was filled with excoriations of the Federal government and boasts of what England could, and probably would, do to the United States. The newspapers reported verbatim the truculent instructions to Lord Lyons. He was ordered to leave Washington unless he got satisfaction within seven days.

On receipt of Wilkes' report, Secretary Welles had sent that officer a message of congratulation and then spent the next six weeks wishing he had not done so. Taking its cue from the Secretary, the House of Representatives unanimously passed a resolution commending Wilkes. The diplomatic corps protested in a body against this resolution, a proceeding almost without precedent in American history.

This affair practically monopolized the columns of the English papers until attention was diverted by the illness of the Prince Consort, which was announced on December 14. On his deathbed he devoted his attention to moderating the tone of the British diplomatic notes. Upon his death on December 16, the Nashville was one of the first foreign ships to lower her colors in token of respect.

After the funeral of the Prince Consort the newspapers recurred to the Trent and began to give details of the preparations for war. Eight thousand troops were mobilized and embarked for Canada. The government was sounding France and Spain on the question of recognizing the independence of the Confederacy.

All this was pleasant reading for Captain Pegram and his officers while the Nashville lay in dock having her top deck renewed.

On January 8, 1862, the U. S. steam sloop Tuscarora, Commander T. A. M. Craven, arrived at Southampton, where the Nashville, her repairs completed, lay in dock coaled and ready for sea. The next day the news came that the United States had yielded and had released Mason and Slidell to Lord Lyons.

The rejoicing of the British cabinet and public showed how serious had been their apprehensions lest they be called upon to make good their bluff. We shall notice that when the next threat of international war came, nine months later,[1] it emanated from the United States, and Palmerston yielded in September, 1862, as Lincoln had done in December, 1861.

In passing it should be said that it is possible to make out a theoretical defense of Wilkes' action, as Seward explained at great length in his "apology" to Lord Lyons. Wilkes' mistake was in not capturing the Trent herself, British mails and all, and sending her into a United States court for adjudication in prize. He would thus have transferred the controversy to the appropriate forum, where it could have been determined judicially, and Great Britain, in theory at least, would have had no ground of objection to the procedure as it was her own practice. The court would have been cited to certain British decisions sustaining the capture of neutral ships transporting belligerents between neutral ports and to the position of Great Britain in the War of 1812, from which she had not receded, and which, indeed, she still maintains. Indeed, in the Trent case itself, the Crown law officers advised that the vessel was subject to capture. Wilkes thought of this later and excused himself on the ground that he did not wish to inconvenience the passengers and the patrons of the international mails and that he doubted the ability of the San Jacinto to effect the capture. The first is hardly a good reason for not taking a valuable prize, and the second is negatived by the fact that he actually did stop the Trent and let her go again.

All this was afterthought. In overhauling the Trent, Wilkes did not proceed upon theoretical grounds. It was a political act and was dealt with politically. Wilkes placed his government in the preposterous position of having to apologize, not for insulting a friendly power, but for not insulting it enough.

However, it is unlikely that the capture of the ship instead of merely the commissioners would have made any practical difference. Legal arguments in this and other instances were mere ritual which could have been varied to suit a change

[1] Chap. IV, below.

in the form of the episode. The pro-Confederate bloc in the British government had a gift of a ready-made "incident" tossed into its lap, the more acceptable because it was unprovoked. It was exploited for all it was worth. At the cost of some humiliation, Lincoln avoided the snare unwittingly laid by a naval officer, the Secretary of the Navy, and the entire membership of the House of Representatives. The monuments in the case are the appalling mess an impulsive officer can get his government into by arriving at the wrong conclusion when confronted with the necessity of making a quick decision, and the alarming stupidity, shortsightedness, and irresponsibility of politicians in dealing with a delicate but relatively simple international problem. The democratic process can be self-correcting in domestic matters. It may work disaster in foreign affairs.

The only persons in Europe who were not relieved by the avoidance of war were the Confederates there, the members of the first mission, Yancey in London and Mann in Brussels, the officers of the Sumter at Gibraltar and the Nashville at Southampton. Wilkes had played directly into their hand; yet the trick was lost. Yancey was despondent. Semmes recorded his dismay. The British alliance had slipped away,

> "Gone the chance! and at the point
> of such prime success."

The Tuscarora was keeping a close watch on the Nashville. Twice the superintendent of the dock had to chase away nocturnal prowlers sent there by Commander Craven. On January 11 the port authorities cautioned the commanders of both ships to observe the twenty-four-hour interval of departure. The frigate Dauntless was detailed to enforce the rule. To avoid being held up, Craven got the Tuscarora ready for action and took her outside, moving restlessly about the Solent.

At this time the British neutrality rules were being formulated—they were actually issued January 31, effective

The Sumter Firing on the Brigantine Joseph Parke, of Boston.
From Harper's Weekly, *February 1, 1862.*

The Nashville and the Tuscarora at Southampton, England.

February 6—and the port authorities at Southampton were proceeding to carry them out by anticipation. On January 27, the superintendent of the port, Captain Patey, notified Pegram that the Nashville must depart on the 29th, provided the Tuscarora had left twenty-four hours previously. Pegram protested to the Duke of Somerset,

"Your grace cannot fail to perceive from these orders that my movements are made subordinate to those of the Tuscarora and that the commander of that vessel is absolutely empowered to force me into a collision with him on his own terms. If it is indeed true that I am bidden to abandon the asylum whose hospitable shelter I have not abused, and I am thus with my weak ship and slender crew to be placed at the mercy of a powerful man of war with which it would be madness to attempt to cope, I have no alternative but to obey this peremptory order, but I here enter my solemn protest against it in the name of common humanity and that of the government which I have the honor to represent."

This had the effect of changing the arrangements so that the Nashville went out first. On February 4, Pegram sent Patey word that he was about to depart. Patey at once got a steam tender and went down to Cowes, where he notified Craven that the Tuscarora must give the cruiser a twenty-four-hour start. To ensure compliance he moved the frigate Shannon alongside the Federal vessel, with steam up and guns shotted.

The commander and the ship's company of the Tuscarora stood upon her deck and watched the enemy vessel run past them, while a taunting message from Pegram was delivered to Craven, inviting him to give chase if he thought he would catch the Nashville.

The Tuscarora took her departure at the end of the twenty-four hours, not in pursuit of the Nashville, which might have gone anywhere, but bound for Gibraltar, where Craven knew the Sumter was awaiting his attention.

The Nashville recrossed the Atlantic, coaling at Bermuda.

On February 26 she captured and burned the schooner Robert Gilfillan, Philadelphia to Santo Domingo.

On approaching the coast Pegram headed for Beaufort, North Carolina. Only one blockader was on duty, the U.S.S. State of Georgia. At daybreak on February 28 she sighted the Nashville about three miles inshore of her, flying the American flag. The State of Georgia, which was 2 or 3 knots slower than the Nashville, gave chase, firing her Parrott gun. Pegram sent a derisive shot in the direction of the Federal ship and easily ran into Morehead City. The episode caused an outburst of public indignation in the North. Petitions were signed throughout the country calling for the dismissal of the Secretary of the Navy for inefficiency in having only one blockader covering a port which required at least five. Secretary Welles wrote to the senior officer at Hampton Roads, "The Department is unable to learn what measures you can take to keep the Nashville in Beaufort, but they should be characterized by energy."

Her arrival in a Confederate port ended the Nashville's career as a cruiser. An echo of it reverberated for a time. A pamphleteer published a legal brief, arguing that the presence of the two guns of British manufacture, with which the Nashville was armed when she took the Harvey Birch, cast upon Britain a liability to recompense the owner of the prize. The guns had been installed at Charleston. Their previous history was not traced. The argument was conducted *in vacuo* and of course produced no result. It is of interest merely as marking the beginning of the wordy debate which continued from 1862 until the decision of the Geneva Tribunal in 1871 over the rights and duties of neutrals with respect to the armament of belligerent ships.

On arrival at Morehead City, Pegram learned that the government had sold the ship to Fraser, Trenholm & Company, of whom we are to hear more in the next chapter. They proposed to use her as a blockade-runner. Before they could take possession she was obliged to flee from General Burnside's

THE NASHVILLE

advancing land and naval force. She ran the blockade outward, tried in vain to get into Charleston, and was delivered to her new owners in Georgetown, South Carolina. They changed her name to Thomas L. Wragg and used her successfully in the Nassau run throughout the spring and early summer of 1862. In midsummer she ran into Warsaw Sound at the mouth of the Great Ogeechee River in Georgia. Here she was blockaded by three Federal gunboats. In spite of many efforts to get out with a load of cotton, she remained bottled up for eight months. At length the cotton was unloaded and her owners decided to send her out as a privateer, christening her with her third name, the Rattlesnake. By this time the blockading flotilla had been reënforced by the monitor Montauk, Commander John L. Worden.

The Rattlesnake, ex-Thomas L. Wragg, ex-Nashville, lay up the river, protected by a strong earthwork called Fort McAllister, and by stakes and torpedoes planted in the stream below the fort. Because of her speed the Confederate vessel was regarded as a dangerous enemy and Worden determined to destroy her. His progress up the river was halted by the obstructions rather than by the accurate but harmless bombardment exchanged between the Montauk and the fort. He waited another month, bringing the time to February 27, 1863. On that evening, Worden discovered by reconnaissance that the Confederate ship was in motion and presently that she had grounded. He concluded that she would float at high tide next morning. Accordingly, at dawn the Montauk moved up to the barrier, followed by the three gunboats. Halting squarely under the fire of the fort, to which he paid no attention, Worden had the superstructure of the enemy vessel in view across a swampy point. He began to send shells over with remarkable precision. A thick fog now settled down. Through the murk Worden could see the loom of a fire and as he continued to lay down shells through the fog he heard a gun explode and then the detonation of an entire magazine. When the mist rose only some fragments of hull remained.

CHAPTER IV

WAYS AND MEANS

...nervos belli, pecuniam infinitam.—Cicero, *Philipp.* v. 2

I

THE SUMTER AND THE NASHVILLE were of American origin. To obtain other cruisers as well as combat ships it was necessary to look abroad.

From first to last the Confederate government had a large number of representatives in England and France. After the temporary mission of Yancy, Rost, and Mann, James M. Mason became the permanent diplomatic commissioner in London, John Slidell in Paris. A host of other emissaries, spies, *agents provocateurs,* propagandists, came and went, sometimes overlapping and conflicting. The ranking naval officer was Commodore Samuel Barron, who established headquarters in Paris. Lieutenant (afterwards Commander) James H. North, an officer whose genuine ability was handicapped by an irritating fussiness, was delegated to obtain ironclads. Lieutenant George T. Sinclair, of a naval family that gave several officers to the Confederate service, was sent to England to get a cruiser to be commissioned under his command.

The principal agent in procuring cruisers was Commander James Dunwoody Bulloch of Georgia, a maternal uncle of Theodore Roosevelt. Bulloch was a former United States naval officer who had served in every class of ship on the Navy list and had been furloughed to command subsidized merchantmen. Thus he was experienced in both the naval and commercial departments of his problem. For resourcefulness, intelligence, audacity, and devotion to duty he is entitled to high rating. His family background was that of culture and some wealth. Bulloch's qualities are worth underlining because his commission as commander aroused jealousy and dislike among older officers whom he outranked and because disinterested service among those who were sent abroad seems to have been exceptional. C. A. L. Lamar of Georgia, who was in London in the autumn of 1863 to promote blockade running, sent home to his father a letter which is now in the National Archives. "It is impossible [he wrote] to make you conceive, by anything I can write (though you have as I know a liberal opinion of them on that subject) the amount of swindling going on all the time & conducted by Gov'nt agents. Capt. Bulloch is the only one whose name is untarnished. Some of them have made large fortunes"— and the writer goes on to mention names.

Secretary Mallory sent Bulloch to England in May, 1861, to obtain six cruisers. He remained throughout the war (save for incidental absences) subordinating his earnest wish for sea duty in favor of other officers, in order to obtain vessels for them to command.

Before anything could be done in the way of getting ships, it was necessary to have assurance of money. There was no trouble in procuring the passage of appropriation bills. Under the Confederate constitution such measures were proposed by the executive and ratified by the congress. That body, which was made up largely of former members of the Federal congress, made no objection to passing money bills on request. The difficulty was to lay down gold on European counters in payment for the needed military supplies and ships.

Historians who have examined the Confederate fiscal operations are agreed that if a rigid governmental control and expropriation of cotton as a foundation for credit had been set up in the beginning when the blockade was merely theoretical, the credit base thus created might have averted the economic disintegration of the South, held the army together, aligned behind the government the large disaffected minority, and strengthened the leverage for foreign recognition.

That is hindsight. The fact is, it was not attempted until too late. The adoption of such a drastic sumptuary course would have been politically dangerous in the divided and groping counsels of the Confederacy early in the war. Coercive measures might have hastened the threat of "secession from Secessia" which became the nightmare of the Richmond government in the closing days of the war.

We are not here concerned with the internal financing of the Confederacy. Its obligations in the form of bonds and treasury notes did not fall much below par until the autumn of 1861. The depreciation of the paper currency was not acute until the beginning of 1863, when the fantastic inflation began.

The primary purpose of the external financing was the purchase of munitions and supplies for the Army and the procuring of ships, their equipment and running costs. In these transactions the firm of Fraser, Trenholm & Company played an important part. This was a commercial banking house in Liverpool, affiliated with John Fraser & Company of Charleston. The manager in Liverpool was Charles K. Prioleau, of South Carolina. The house was the depositary of Confederate funds in Europe and conducted a profitable business in financing blockade-running operations. It made large advances to the Confederate government. After the war the United States brought suits against the two firms in English and American courts for balances of Confederate funds in their hands, and recovered judgment by consent for $150,000, part of which was realized.

Prior to the battle of Gettysburg and the simultaneous opening of the Mississippi, the possibility of the utter annihilation of Confederate obligations was hardly present in the minds of European financiers. After the first battle of Bull Run the prospect of the success of the Confederacy was greatly enhanced. At the worst it was considered that the Southern states would accomplish a negotiated peace which would salvage their foreign commitments. Accordingly, the hazards of war were used by foreign creditors and investors rather as a pretext for driving profitable bargains than as a reason for withholding credit.

Under these conditions Commander Bulloch and Lieutenant North were able to start ordering naval construction, and other Confederate agents had no difficulty in purchasing munitions and supplies for the Army. The first payments were made by drafts which were honored by Fraser, Trenholm & Company with gold shipped to them through the blockade. This gold was obtained by confiscating enemy-owned funds found in the custom houses and elsewhere and from the first and most successful internal loan floated by the new government ($15,000,000) in the summer of 1861. The total amount of gold possessed by the Confederacy throughout the war, including the proceeds of the foreign loan presently to be described, did not exceed $27,000,000, whereas the war during the first fiscal year, before serious inflation began, cost the Confederate treasury six times that sum. The South fought the war on staple produce and on paper in many forms. While the foreign drafts quickly drained the South of gold, they helped to establish credit with London banks, which thereafter were willing to finance orders on long-term payments on terms of discount highly advantageous to themselves. One bank kept a set of books for the benefit of the Confederate representatives and another for its own. In 1862 Secretary Mallory supplied Bulloch with $1,000,000, an amount which fell short of meeting his authorized requirements. By July, 1862, he had outstanding and unprovided for, £390,000, in accounts payable for naval work. The surviving records of the Confederate treasury, now in the National Archives, show that Secretary Mallory was continually importuning the Secretary of the Treasury to place large sums in sterling to the credit of the naval representatives in England and suggesting expedients for doing so, and that Secretary Memminger was often unable to respond to their requests. It was imperative to find new ways of getting sterling exchange.

Beginning with the summer of 1862, negotiations for floating an external loan were started with an English banking house, whose proposals were ultimately rejected, and with Emile Erlanger of Paris, banker to the Second Empire, whose son married Slidell's daughter. After long delay, which dried up the springs of credit in England and subjected Mason and Bulloch to importunate duns, there emerged the so-called Erlanger Loan, which was advertised by the banking houses and offered to the European public in Liverpool, London, Paris, Frankfort, and Amsterdam, March 18, 1863. The face of the offering was £3,000,000 and the selling price was 90. On the first day, subscriptions to the amount of £16,000,000 were received, chiefly in London.

The bonds bore interest at 7 per cent and were secured by deposits of cotton which was priced for the purpose of the security at 6 pence a pound, or about one-fourth of the then European market rate. One-fortieth of the issue was to be redeemed every six months. The subscribers paid 15 per cent of their subscriptions down and promised to pay the balance in monthly instalments of 10 per cent. The bonds went from 90 to 95½, and the loan appeared to be a great success. Charles Francis Adams called on Lord Russell and told him it was proof of a conspiracy in England "to produce a state of exasperation in America and thus bring on a war with Great Britain with a view to aid the Confederate cause and secure a monopoly of the trade of the Southern states."

Mr. Adams' concern was groundless. The price at which the bonds had been offered, 90 per cent of their face, was too high. Within three weeks they were down to 86. Erlanger attributed the drop to a bear movement on the part of agents of the United States who had purchased part of the issue. Market experts thought Erlanger had priced the issue too high

SEVEN PER CENT. COTTON LOAN

OF THE

CONFEDERATE STATES OF AMERICA.

FOR

£3,000,000 STERLING, AT 90 PER CENT.

The Bonds to bear Interest *at the rate of* **7** *per cent. per annum in Sterling, from* 1st March, 1863, *payable Half-yearly in London, Paris, Amsterdam, or Frankfort.*
The Bonds *exchangeable for* Cotton *on application, at the option of the Holder, or redeemable at par in Sterling in Twenty Years, by Half-yearly drawings, commencing* 1st March, 1864.

Agents for the Contractors in Liverpool: **Messrs. FRASER TRENHOLM & Co.**, 10, Rumford Place.

This Loan has been contracted with Messrs. Emile Erlanger & Co., Bankers of Paris, by the Government of the Confederate States of America, and is specially secured by an undertaking of the Government to deliver Cotton to the holders of the Bonds, on application after sixty days' notice, on the footing aftermentioned.

The nature of the arrangement is fully set forth in Article IV. of the Contract made with Messrs. E. Erlanger & Co., which is as follows :—

"Each Bond shall, at the option of the holder, be convertible at its nominal amount into Cotton at the rate of Sixpence Sterling for each pound of Cotton, say 4,000 lbs. of Cotton for each Bond of £100, or Francs 2,500, and this at any time not later than six months after the ratification of a treaty of peace between the present belligerents. Notice of the intention of converting Bonds into cotton has to be given to the representatives of the Government in Paris or London, and sixty days after such notice the Cotton will be delivered :—if in peace, at the ports of Charleston, Savannah, Mobile, or New Orleans; if in war, at points in the interior of the country, within ten miles of a railroad, or stream navigable to the Ocean. *The delivery will be made free of all charges and duties, excepting the existing export duty of one-eighth of one cent per pound.* The quality of the Cotton to be the standard of New Orleans middling. If any Cotton is of superior or inferior quality, the difference in value shall be settled by two Brokers, one to be appointed by the Government, the other by the Bondholder; whenever these two Brokers cannot agree on the value, an umpire is to be chosen, whose decision shall be final."

It is at the same time provided, that holders who do not convert their Bonds into Cotton, shall be entitled to retain the Bonds, and receive interest at the rate of 7 per cent. per annum in Sterling, payable half-yearly, in London, Paris, Amsterdam, or Frankfort, at the option of the holder, until repayment of the principal at par.

An Annual Sinking Fund of 5 per cent. is provided for, whereby 2½ per cent. of the Bonds unredeemed by Cotton shall be drawn by lot half-yearly: the first drawing to take effect on the 1st March, 1864, and to be continued on the 1st September following, and on the 1st March and 1st September in every succeeding year, so as finally to extinguish the Loan in twenty years from the date of the first drawing.

Prospectus of the Erlanger Loan, Page One.
From the National Archives.

The Bonds to be issued at 90 per cent., which is to be paid as follows:—

5 per cent.		on Application.
10	,,	on Allotment.
10	,,	1st May.
10	,,	1st June.
10	,,	1st July.
15	,,	1st August.
15	,,	1st September, less dividend 3½ per cent.
15	,,	1st October.
£90		

Subscribers will have the option of paying the instalments in advance, on allotment, or on any of the above dates, under a discount of seven per cent. per annum on such pre-payments; but in default of due payment of the respective instalments, all previous payments will be liable to forfeiture.

[By payment, under discount, the price of the Cotton is reduced to about 5¼ d. per lb.]

After Allotment, Scrip Certificates will be issued to bearer. These certificates, after payment of the last instalment, will be exchanged for Bonds to "Bearer" in sums of £100—£200—£500—£1000 each, with Coupons attached, payable 1st March, 1st September, as stated above.

Arrangements have been made for the execution of the Bonds in Paris.

From the proceeds of the subscription, the Contractors and their Agents are authorised to retain sufficient funds to pay the first two Coupons.

The drawings for the operation of the Sinking Fund will be duly advertised previous to the half-yearly redemption.

An authenticated copy of the Act of Ratification of the Contract may be inspected either at the offices of Messrs. FRESHFIELDS & NEWMAN, the Solicitors to the Contractors, or of Messrs. CROWDER, MAYNARD & Co., Solicitors to the Agents of the Contractors in London.

Application for allotment to be addressed to

Messrs. FRASER, TRENHOLM, & Co., 10, Rumford Place,

from whom, and from the Brokers,

Messrs. T. TINLEY & SONS, Brown's Buildings.

Messrs. TOD & ASHTON, Liver Chambers.

Forms of Application may be obtained.

In the event of no allotment being made, the deposit will be immediately returned.

A Public Subscription is simultaneously opened in London, Paris, Amsterdam, and Frankfort.

FRASER, TRENHOLM, & CO.,
Agents to the Contractors in Liverpool.

10, RUMFORD PLACE, LIVERPOOL,
19th *March*, 1863.

Prospectus of the Erlanger Loan, Page Two.
From the National Archives.

because he was too greedy. His firm was to receive all the proceeds above 77, plus a 5 per cent commission. Whatever the reason, as time for payment of the second instalment of the subscriptions approached, there was every prospect that the downward movement would cause the subscribers to take the loss and abandon the issue. The only salvation was for the Confederate agents to bull the market by large purchases of their own bonds. Nearly £1,500,000 in gold was spent for this purpose and the price was driven back above 90, but half the issue was then in the hands of the Confederate government. These were reissued subsequently at 60 and 66. At their lowest, these bonds commanded a higher price than any U. S. bonds in Europe during the war. Professor Schwab has computed that the net amount realized in expendible form from this $15,000,000 loan was $6,250,000. To get the cotton which lay back of the bonds, the Confederate government impaired its credit at home.

The attraction of the Erlanger bonds was that the holder had the option of demanding payment in 6*d* cotton at any time on two months' notice. On demand (if made before the end of the war) the Confederate government agreed to deliver the cotton at a point in the South within ten miles of a railroad. The bondholder had to get it to market. If the demand was postponed until after the war, the cotton was to be delivered at Charleston, Mobile, and New Orleans. A group of the bondholders formed a corporation called the Albion Trading Company to get the cotton out. Nothing came of that enterprise.

The subscribers to these bonds were speculating in cotton and in the prospect of its delivery. Upon these hazards European investors were prepared to bet $75,000,000. It must be said for the sportsmanship of English capitalists that they were ready to back their fancy with their cash.

On the question of ultimate delivery, the investors had the support of so responsible a journal as the *London Economist* which said the foreign lien upon the cotton clothed it with a neutral character that would enable the creditors to realize upon it after the war, irrespective of which side should win. Upon the destruction of the Confederacy the United States seized all the assets of the defunct government that could be found and did not honor liens which had been created to arm the enemy. In 1871 the British government presented a claim on one of these bonds. The United States resented the mere mention of it and Mr. Gladstone made a note that such claims were not to be urged.[1]

Of the proceeds of the Erlanger loan $5,200,000 was allocated to the Navy. Under the direction of C. J. McCrea, "agent for the loan" in Paris, funds were furnished for the operating expenses of the cruisers Florida, Rappahannock, and Georgia, and obligations to French shipbuilders were discharged.

Another method of raising money was adopted very late in the war. The Confederate government itself went into the blockade-running business with its own ships and instituted a strict regulation of the other blockade-runners. It assumed absolute control of exports and imports and began shipping cotton to Fraser, Trenholm & Company. This system was not set in operation until the summer of 1864, too late to rescue the declining Confederacy.

In one way and another, the shipbuilders who did work for the Confederacy were paid, as were the suppliers and munition makers who fleeced the South *more suo*. Those who were left holding the bag were the subscribers to the bonds and the bankers who took them in payment or as collateral. The holders of Confederate securities gambled at long odds for high stakes and in the end were merely the losing team in a highly speculative game.

The commanding officers of the Confederate cruisers were usually (though not invariably) furnished with enough money to purchase fuel and supplies and to pay in gold the high wages they offered to their crews.

[1] Granville to Schenck, March 20, 1872. *For. Rel.* 1872, II, ii, 436, 440.

II

The legal obstacles in the way of acquiring naval vessels in England were not those interposed by the principles of international law. That lofty region of jurisprudence gave the Crown lawyers and those retained by Commander Bulloch no uneasiness. The concern of the lawyers was with a municipal statute, the Foreign Enlistment Act.

In the first quarter of the nineteenth century the revolts of the Spanish Colonies in South America, accompanied by all sorts of adventuring and filibustering on the part of soldiers and sailors of fortune, made it necessary for the United States and Great Britain to establish some definitions to govern their own neutrality and the activities of their citizens. The two nations adopted very similar neutrality laws; the Act of Congress was passed in 1818; that of Parliament in 1819. They were in force in their original form thoughout the Civil War. Both were criminal statutes. An elementary rule of English and American courts is that a penal law is to be construed literally; that is to say, you cannot be punished for coming close to the line of offense, so long as you do not actually overstep it.

The task of the Confederate agents in getting ships was to skirt the edge of the Foreign Enlistment Act as nearly as possible without going over. In this they had the assistance of astute counsel who advised that they could "sail a fleet of ships through the Foreign Enlistment Act." Their position was sustained by one of the most scholarly of English judges, Sir Frederick Pollock, in the case of the Alexandra.[1]

The Foreign Enlistment Act made it a misdemeanor for anyone without special license to equip, furnish, fit out, or arm any vessel for a belligerent, or to endeavor to do so, or knowingly to assist in so doing, under penalty of fine and imprisonment and forfeiture of the ship.

Counsel gave it as their opinion that "The mere building

[1] See p. 81, below.

of a ship within Her Majesty's dominions by any person (subject or no subject) is no offense, whatever may be the intent of the parties, because the offense is not the building but the equipping."

This opinion clearly charted the course that Bulloch followed with all the cruisers he contracted for. In his own words, "In no case was any builder or vendor informed what was the purpose of the purchaser. No ship was ever supplied with any portion of her equipment within Her Majesty's dominions nor was the builder or vendor of any ship employed to assist in the equipment without her Majesty's dominions."

The plan adopted was to order a ship for an individual, to be built as a merchantman, without a vestige of armament or military equipment on board. She would depart from England, under a British master and crew, for some remote rendezvous, where she would meet another merchant vessel laden with arms and equipment and carrying passengers, who turned out to be Confederate naval officers. A quick transfer would be made at sea; title to the cruiser would be passed to the Confederate government by the delivery of a document signed by the individual owner and brought along by the English captain or one of the "passengers." The cargo vessel, now lightened of her load, would depart; and the cruiser, in respect of *materiel*, was ready for work.

This method provided a ship without a crew. The Foreign Enlistment Act made it a misdemeanor for a British subject to enlist in a foreign naval service without special permission, and for anyone within British jurisdiction to induce him to do so. The Confederate commanders, after taking over the cruisers outside British jurisdiction, endeavored to persuade the merchant crews to enlist in the Confederate service by offers of high wages. They met with varying success, as will appear. Those who enlisted were not where the law could catch them. The seamen who did not enlist were transferred to the ship that brought out the armament, and taken home. These plans were followed in the cases of the Florida, the

Alabama, the Georgia, the Tallahassee, and partially in that of the Shenandoah.

The method of procuring vessels was promptly challenged by Charles Francis Adams, with the result that it was sanctioned by the English courts. Fraser, Trenholm & Company built a small wooden steamer, which they named the Alexandra in compliment to the popular fiancée of the Prince of Wales. Their intention, which was not concealed, was to convert her into a gunboat outside British waters, run her through the blockade, and present her to the Confederacy in some Southern port. Upon the insistence of Adams, the Attorney General had the Alexandra arrested in April, 1863, before completion, and tried in the Court of Exchequer for the forfeiture of the ship for violation of the Foreign Enlistment Act. Chief Baron Pollock, applying the rule of strict construction of a penal statute, charged the jury strongly in favor of the vessel. A verdict was rendered for her restitution to her owners and £4,000 in costs were assessed against the Crown. An application for new trial was argued before the full court in November, 1863. Pollock was sustained in a report 210 pages in length,[1] containing much ponderous discussion of international as well as municipal law. Ineffectual appeals followed and the ship was finally released. Later she was again arrested in Nassau. She never became a cruiser.

The decision in the Alexandra case confirmed rather than guided the course of the British Ministry with respect to cruisers, for before it was rendered, the Florida, the Alabama, and the Georgia had gone to sea.

During the pendency of the Alexandra case, Adams continued his expostulations. Whatever the effect of the Foreign Enlistment Act and its technical interpretation, he felt he was on firm ground when he based his position on the comity between friendly nations. He and Consul Dudley at Liverpool had spies in every shipyard, and as keel after keel was laid down he kept a stream of remonstrances flowing into

[1] *Attorney General* v. *Sillems*, 2 Hurlstone & Coltman 431.

the Foreign Office, with supporting proofs. He submitted altogether thirty-four protests against British violations of neutrality. Indeed, no one who was not willfully blind could escape knowing the purposes for which the cruisers were being built. Adams' difficulty was with the quality of his evidence. The only witnesses whose names he was at liberty to disclose were Liverpool water-front characters and renegade Confederates. He got such affidavits as he could afford to use and submitted them to the Crown law officers, who responded with the diplomatic equivalent of "Rubbish!" Nevertheless they conducted a private investigation of their own and were sufficiently impressed to take a belated and ineffectual action to stop the Alabama. In the end Adams was vindicated by the award of the Geneva Tribunal in 1871. It was a barren triumph, for a money indemnity could not restore the crippled merchant marine to the ocean, or redress the lost prestige of the United States, or relieve the nation thenceforward from the necessity of adjusting its foreign policy to the hegemony of England.

Adams' protests were more effective against another type of vessel which the Confederacy tried to get in England—ironclad fighting ships. The mesh of intrigue, espionage, and duplicity in which these vessels became entangled can receive only brief mention here for its bearing on the cruisers.

Fighting equipment for rams could not be added at sea. It was structural. The only thing to do was to go ahead with the construction, secretly if possible, brazenly if necessary, relying upon the sympathetic credulity of British officials.

To relate the rams to the cruisers the following time-table may be useful. By August 31, 1861, contracts had been let for the construction of the cruisers Florida and Alabama. In March, 1862, the Florida sailed. In the spring Bulloch ordered the construction of the cruiser Georgiana. On May 20, Lieutenant North contracted with James and George Thompson of Glasgow to build a powerful ram. In July Bulloch placed an order with Laird Brothers of Liverpool for two smaller rams. On July 29, in spite of the government's faint-hearted effort to stop her, the Alabama got away. In the same month (July, 1862) Lieutenant Sinclair ordered a cruiser, the Pampero, to be built on the Clyde. Adams continued his protests. On September 1, Lord Russell wrote Adams that the evidence for detaining the ironclads was insufficient. In reply Adams sent his famous letter of September 5, 1862: "It would be superfluous in me to point out to your Lordship that this is war."

There was nothing new in the threat except its immediacy. Even before the inauguration, Seward was advising Lincoln to foment a foreign war as a means of reuniting the country. He clung to this incredible purpose after the beginning of the war. It is reflected in the truculence of the language in which he framed his communications to foreign powers. The more violent of these were toned down by Lincoln and Adams before they reached the chancelleries.

There is this to be said for Seward's bluster: it worked. While the argument is only *post hoc, propter hoc* and many considerations contributed to the outcome, the face of the record shows that Seward stormed and England yielded.

The Ministry had, in fact, already determined to order the rams held up. Their status had been the subject of deliberation and diplomatic exchanges in Washington and London throughout the preceding six months, and the inspired *London Times* had begun to prepare public opinion to support the ministers in detaining them. Aside from the natural reluctance to precipitate a war, England was not in a position to undertake one. The two Canadas were defenseless. Russia, thirsting to avenge the Crimean humiliation and with Poland in ferment, was openly befriending the North in order to obtain ice-free American ports of refuge (New York and San Francisco) for her navy. British commerce lay open to reprisals. The United States was rapidly acquiring a formidable Navy, including specially designed commerce raiders. A bill authorizing the issuance of letters of marque had been introduced in Congress with administration support. Britain, having refused to outlaw American privateers, was confronted with the prospect of private American raids upon British commerce.

The strangely assorted triumvirate then in command of English affairs, the jaunty Palmerston, Gladstone the opportunist politician, and the Machiavellian John Russell, determined upon a policy of appeasement. On September 8, 1862, they notified Laird Brothers to stop work.

This point marks a second change in the British attitude, which had already been modified by the outcome of the Trent affair. Legal considerations never played an important part in it. Until it became clear that the United States was ready and willing to fight, little attention was paid to the arguments of Mr. Adams. After the Ministry became convinced that Lincoln and Seward meant war, and after the long succession of Confederate victories was interrupted at Fort Donelson, Shiloh Church, and New Orleans, the plausible dialectics of Mason and Bulloch were addressed to deaf ears. The Confederacy could no longer hope for active British support but only for "benevolent" neutrality.

The Georgiana escaped from Liverpool January 22, 1863. Attempting to run into Charleston for her armament, she was stopped by the blockade, beached by her commander, and destroyed by shells from the blockaders.

Although work on the rams was suspended, they remained at their builders' yards. The field of Confederate effort now shifts to France. Some mention of this has been made in Chapter I. On October 8, 1862, Napoleon III himself initiated the suggestion to Slidell that the Confederate government might build ships in France. On January 7, 1863, L. Arman, a shipbuilder of Bordeaux, who was a member of the Corps Legislatif, offered to build ironclads. On April 13 contracts were made with Arman for two corvettes, which could be used as cruisers, and with J. Voruz, ironfounder of Nantes, also a member of the Corps Legislatif, for two more, all "subject to the Emperor's approval." On June 6, the Minister of Marine authorized Arman to arm the ships. Arman gave out that they were being built for a packet line between San Francisco and Japan and China, and were being armed as a protection against piratical Chinese junks and to make them salable to the Japanese or the Chinese government. On June 16, Bulloch contracted with Arman for two more rams. By June 30 title to the unfinished rams at Laird's yard in Liverpool was transferred to A. Bravay et Cie of Paris, purporting to act as agents for the Khedive of Egypt, with a gentleman's understanding that the transfer was fictitious.

And then, on September 10, 1863, when the news from Vicksburg and Gettysburg was still fresh, John Bigelow, United States Consul General at Paris, bribed a clerk in the employ of Voruz. For 15,000 francs this man produced original documents from the shipbuilder's files, disclosing and proving the foregoing transactions. Minister Dayton at once called at the Foreign Ministry and laid the documents on the table.

Louis Napoleon exploded with the horrified amazement proper to a dictator when confronted with the disclosure of dealings to which he had been privy from the beginning. He made scapegoats of the shipbuilders and ordered them to stop work or prove that the ships were not intended for the Confederacy.

Meanwhile, Bulloch had been trying to deliver to A. Bravay et Cie the unfinished rams lying at Laird's yard in Liverpool, so that they might be completed in France. In pursuance of the policy of appeasing the North, the British Navy had picketed Laird's plant with enough armed vessels to intern a battle fleet, and even lashed a gunboat alongside one of the rams. Bulloch finally succeeded in getting from the English authorities permission for the delivery of the rams to Bravay on condition that Napoleon should ask for it. By this time, ships tainted with Confederate interest had become, in the argot of the underworld, "hot." The Emperor did not wish to handle any more such ships and refused to make the request.

This brings us to February, 1864. We have two unfinished rams under guard at Liverpool; one at Thompson's on the Clyde; a cruiser on the Clyde (in custody); two covettes at Bordeaux; two at Nantes; two rams at Bordeaux; and the Rappahannock [1] interned at Calais; eleven ships, all very "hot." Three Anglo-Confederate cruisers (the Alabama, the Florida, and the Georgia) were at sea, at the peak of their depredations.

As no request was forthcoming from the Emperor for the delivery of the rams which were occupying space at Laird's and monopolizing the time of the naval guard, the Attorney General started an Exchequer suit against Bravay et Cie, putative owners, for the forfeiture of the ships, a proceeding similar to that against the Alexandra. This suit was settled without trial. In the settlement the rams were completed as units of the Royal Navy, Laird Brothers got their builder's profit, Bravay and the Khedive of Egypt faded out, and the greater part of £30,000 found its way from the British Exchequer into the Confederate treasury as the price of the building contracts. This money was applied to the purchase of the Sea King, which became the cruiser Shenandoah. The two rams thereafter served Queen Victoria as H.M.S. Scorpion and H.M.S. Wyvern.

The great ironclad nearing completion at Thompson's yard on the Clyde was certain to be prevented from departing to join the Confederate Navy. Although Denmark was a belligerent power, no one in England was interested in hampering her naval efforts. Accordingly, no objection was interposed when the ram was sold to the Danes. The purchase price came in at a timely moment to help meet the interest payment on the Erlanger Loan which fell due in September, 1864, thus preventing a default in those bonds before the end of the war.

[1] See Chap. VIII, below.

Sinclair's cruiser, the Pampero, at first called the Canton, had been arrested in a suit brought by the English government in the Scotch Exchequer Court, a case precisely like that of the Alexandra. By agreement of the parties, she was condemned and turned over to her builders to be operated as a merchantman, on condition that she would not be sold for two years without the consent of the Crown.

The disposal of the six vessels in France (four wooden corvettes and two ironclads) was protracted over a period of ten months after Dayton's discovery of the Franco-Confederate plans. There were abortive attempts to make fictitious sales. During these dilatory proceedings, Louis Napoleon became persuaded that if he would manifest a conciliatory disposition toward the North (which appeared to be winning the war) the United States might recognize Maximilian's government in Mexico. Appeasement became an element in French as well as British policy. Accordingly, when Seward had become so exacerbated over the delay in disposing of the ships as to cause Dayton to make an unequivocal threat of war (June 8, 1864), the Emperor saw M. Arman. What followed was reported by Bulloch on June 10:

"M. Arman obtained his promised interview with the Emperor, who rated him severely, threatened imprisonment, ordered him to sell the ships at once *bona fide,* and said that if this was not done he would have them seized and taken to Rochefort. Captain Tessier also brought me word that the two corvettes at Nantes were ordered to be sold, and the builders of those ships sent me by him a copy of the letter from the Minister of Marine conveying the order to them. The order is of the most peremptory kind, not only directing the sale, but requiring the builders to furnish proof to the Minister of Foreign Affairs that the sale is a real one."

And Bulloch ends on the plaintive note of outraged simplicity which sounds now and then through the writings of American diplomats of this period, "I certainly thought this kind of crooked diplomacy had died out since the last century."

Arman sold the two Bordeaux corvettes and one ram to Prussia, which was a belligerent nation but a winning one, and arranged (or said he did) for a sale of the two Nantes corvettes to Peru. Commander Rodgers, U.S.N., visited the vessels at Bordeaux in disguise. The beauty of their models and the perfection of their equipment fascinated him. He said they were like yachts; the finest ships he ever saw.

Arman sold the other ram, called the Sphinx, to Denmark under the name of the Stoerkodder and she was sent to Copenhagen. By the time she arrived, Denmark had lost Schleswig and Holstein and did not want the ship. Her name was changed to Stonewall and she was sent to Spanish waters under the command of a Confederate naval officer, Captain T. J. Page. She was blockaded in the port of Corunna by the Niagara under Commodore T. T. Craven (brother of the heroic T. A. M. Craven mentioned in Chapter II) and by the sloop of war Sacramento. The Stonewall moved out of the harbor and tried to provoke the Federal vessels to an attack. Craven declined to be drawn into a fight and the Stonewall, thumbing her nose at the two Federal vessels, which had fifteen guns to her three, sailed for Cuba. Craven was court-martialed for failing to engage the Stonewall, and sentenced to two years' suspension. The Secretary of the Navy disapproved the sentence as too light and convened another court, which reached the same conclusion as the first one. Thereupon the Secretary again disapproved the sentence as too light, and added a dream-like quality to the whole proceeding by restoring Craven to duty.

By the time the Stonewall reached Havana the war was ended, and the Spanish authorities turned her over to the United States. The government sold her to Japan for $400,000, and lent Commander George Brown to take her to Yokohama, where he held her for two years in the harbor until he was able to identify one of the contending factions in

Japan as the Japanese government. Under the name of Azuma (sometimes called Kotetsu, "the first ironclad") she was still in service in 1888, when Japanese sailors were using her ram as a diving board. She was doing duty as a hulk in 1908.

As the result of all his transactions, Arman was left at the end of the war holding a substantial balance of money belonging to the Confederate government, the precise amount of which was in dispute. The United States brought suit against the shipbuilder in a French court to recover the fund. The French courts, confronted with the vexatious problem of the right of the United States to maintain a suit for Confederate property, debated it and at length evaded it by dismissing the case on the ground that the American evidence was tainted with corruption. Some of the proofs consisted of papers obtained by Bigelow when he bribed the employe of Voruz. So the United States recovered nothing and the dividends of Arman's French creditors—for he was insolvent —were correspondingly increased.

The Confederate attempt to obtain naval vessels abroad resulted, in sum, in obtaining five effective cruisers, built in England, each of which will be spoken of in turn. There were other ships, merchantmen built or bought for private owners to be operated as blockade-runners. Some were acquired for the same purpose by the Confederate government. These have no connection with the naval effort. Their story belongs to that of the blockade.

III

The Washington administration, too, had its problem of ways and means. It did not lack resources; the Navy was steadily increased throughout the war. The question was one of method. What ships could be spared to pursue the cruisers? What plan of operation should they adopt?

The pursuit ship was confronted with the same questions as the cruisers, many times magnified. The areas of operation were obvious—the North Atlantic packet lanes, the paths to the West Indies, the zone between Brazil and Africa, the route around the Cape of Good Hope. That is a great deal of water. The cruisers had the advantage. The quarry they sought were numerous and widespread; whereas the objectives of the pursuers were only two or three ships in those vast reaches of ocean. The needle in the haystack is a peculiarly apposite metaphor.

The primary requisite for a cruiser is speed; for the vessel that seeks her, greater speed. In the Civil War camouflage was used in a primitive way, with whitewash and gray paint. The Confederate commanders employed a readier stratagem —simple disguise. They dressed their ships to resemble British naval vessels and often flew British naval ensigns. We shall see how this helped the Florida to run into Mobile; the Alabama to come to close quarters with the Hatteras. The pursuing ship could not be sure whether she was chasing a Confederate in disguise or wasting time in following a British warship. An attempt to tell the story of the cruisers from the viewpoint of their pursuers would produce merely a long dull tale of frustration, relieved by two or three successes, such as the blocking of the moribund Sumter, the belated destruction of the Alabama, and the capture of the Florida.

To lure vessels from the blockade was one of the purposes of the cruisers. After the first detail of ships to pursue the Sumter and the Nashville, the Union command did not take the bait. The strengthening of the blockade was an element of the Federal grand strategy of the war, which was to bisect the South vertically, slice it laterally, and squeeze the life out of the pieces. At the beginning of the war the Union Navy consisted of about sixty ships in commission. At the close of the war there were seven hundred. Of this number only fifty-six were detailed to search for Confederate cruisers. When the latter approached the coast, the Navy Department hastily sent out many miscellaneous craft of all sorts *except blockaders* to defend the harbors. The depletion of the blockade for this purpose was declined. It would have been folly to detach slow ships which were useful on their stations, to rove the seas in search of three or four fast ones. The diary of Gideon Welles contains many entries narrating his resistance to demands from alarmed coastal cities for a detail of powerful ships to defend their harbors.

The most efficient of the Union pursuit ships was the Vanderbilt. In the late 1850's, "Commodore" Cornelius Vanderbilt constructed a 3,300-ton steamer called by his name [1] and intended as a candidate for a government subsidy in the Atlantic ferry. She was a powerful wooden sidewheeler, faster than any vessel in the Navy. Her coal consumption, 80 tons per day, was prodigious at that time and was only possible because of her very large bunkers. As an Atlantic packet she was hopelessly expensive to operate without a subvention. Vanderbilt obtained a mail contract which enabled him to run the ship at a profit until 1861, when it was suspended. He then tried briefly to use her as a Union privateer, without success, and presented her to the government. She was armed with two 100-pound rifles and twelve 9-inch guns.

In September, 1862, when the depredations of the Confederate cruisers began to be severely felt, Captain Charles Wilkes was placed in command of a flying squadron. This officer had become an insufferable nuisance to the Navy. He was sixty-three years old; in service, eight years junior to Farragut, eleven years senior to Porter. He had commanded the great naval exploring expedition to the Antarctic and Pacific in the forties with credit to the Navy and distinction

---

[1] Not the same ship as the Confederate blockade-runner Vanderbilt. It is necessary to beware of confusing vessels because of identity of names. Each of the navies had a Vanderbilt, a Shenandoah, a Florida and an Alabama. At one time the U.S.S. Alabama was pursuing the C.S.C. Alabama. The Georgia was a Confederate, the State of Georgia a Union ship. The Confederacy had two Atlantas, two Tennessees, two Virginias. The names of ships were frequently changed, adding to the difficulties of the investigator. The C.S.C. Tallahassee had four names; the Georgia two; the Alabama two; the Rappahannock three, etc.

to himself. After the Trent episode, for which he had been commended by the Secretary of the Navy and the House of Representatives, he became a popular hero, whose prestige was not diminished by the subsequent disavowal of his action. In short, he was in an almost unassailable position to make trouble with impunity. Sunning himself in political favor, he seems to have considered himself superior to the rules of naval discipline. To capture the Confederate cruisers, Wilkes was assigned a squadron of seven vessels, two of which, the steam sloops Wachusett and Dakotah, were fast and powerful enough to cope with any of the Confederate ships. In the nine months during which he continued in this duty he had altogether some sixteen vessels in his command for the purpose of apprehending two enemy ships in the same waters, i.e., the West Indies trade routes.

Instead of carrying out his instructions, Wilkes devoted his attention to catching blockade-runners and annoying innocent English vessels, adding to the embarrassment he had previously caused in overhauling the Trent and aiding the enemy by fomenting British resentment toward the North and friendliness to the South.

Wilkes had a habit of detaining and attaching to his own command naval vessels he encountered that had been sent on special duty. For this he was denounced by Farragut, who threatened to retaliate by taking over any of Wilkes' ships that came his way.

The Vanderbilt was sent out by the Navy Department under Commander C. S. Baldwin with specific instructions to pursue the Alabama. Baldwin's orders laid down the course he was to follow and demonstrated that some one in the Department had anticipated the Alabama's plans with remarkable precision. The orders, if obeyed, would almost certainly have brought the two ships into conflict a year before the final termination of the Alabama's destructive career.

The Vanderbilt was unlucky from the start. One of her first exploits was the capture off St. Thomas on February 25,

1863, of the large British steamer Peterhoff, London to Matamoros with neutral cargo. Baldwin, who suspected her of being a blockade-runner, sent his prize into the Federal Court in New York for adjudication. English indignation over the stopping of the Trent was inflamed by the capture of the Peterhoff. After four years of litigation the Supreme Court, in a leading decision, found that she was innocent and restored her to her owners.

Three days after taking the Peterhoff, while still cruising off the Virgin Islands, the Vanderbilt met the Wachusett. Wilkes, who outranked Baldwin, at once transferred his flag to the larger vessel. He was delighted with his acquisition and enthusiastically reported the fact to the Department. He held her from February 28, 1863, until June 13, when he was peremptorily relieved of his command. By that time the Alabama was some three thousand miles away, having taken eighteen prizes in the interval.

Commander Baldwin then followed out his interrupted orders. Everywhere he went, the Alabama had departed a month ahead of him, until the two ships were off the Cape of Good Hope, where the cruiser was enabled to evade the Vanderbilt through warnings by British residents at the Cape. Later the Vanderbilt embarked upon an ineffectual pursuit of the C.S.C. Florida off Halifax. In the end, the accomplishment of this magnificent fighting ship was precisely nothing.

We shall come upon the Wachusett again. Other pursuit ships, the Kearsarge, built especially for this work, the Niagara, the Dakotah, and the lonely Wyoming, which was assigned to patrol the entire East Indies, the China Sea, and the western Pacific, will appear in the narrative of the particular cruiser with which each had to deal. Still others kept fruitless watch in the Atlantic. Sometimes they were sighted and evaded by the cruisers without being identified by name. In the final score, the Kearsarge has to her credit the blocking of the Sumter and the destruction of the Alabama; the Wachusett, the capture of the Florida; and the Niagara, that of the Georgia after she had ceased to be a Confederate vessel.

The United States had reserves to draw upon for making sallies in search of enemy cruisers on occasions of sudden alarm. The stout little fleet of revenue cutters was placed at the disposal of the Navy. The Navy Department was authorized to requisition the services of any merchant vessel. The craft thus made available were unarmed and were not designed for naval use, but could be employed in emergency to search for raiders. It will appear that at various times when the C.S.C. Florida, the Tacony, the Alabama, the Tallahassee, and the Chickamauga were discovered to be severally operating near the coast, a large number of ships of all sorts, from tugs to all types and sizes of merchantmen, were hastily drafted, armed, and despatched with their merchant personnel to patrol near-by waters. While these would not have been a match for one of the larger cruisers, they were valuable as scouts. Although none of them ever sighted an enemy, the rumor of their proximity fended off the cruisers, caused them to deflect their courses, and thus saved craft that otherwise would have been captured.

CHAPTER V

THE FLORIDA AND HER OFFSPRING

Kites but a little space behind the doves.
—Æschylos, *Prometheus Bound*

I

FOLLOWING THE PLAN of having ships built in England without armament and adding their equipment elsewhere, Bulloch, early in 1861, contracted with the engine-building firm of Fawcett, Preston & Company of Liverpool for the construction of a vessel for his personnel account. The hull, masts, and rigging were sublet to Wm. C. Miller & Sons, who had plans for an English gunboat as the base. The hull was to be of wood, a requirement which increased the cost and retarded the construction of the vessel, since English shipbuilding had by this time turned to iron, at least for framing, because of the shortage of heavy timber and the abundance of ore in England. The use of wood for the Florida and the Alabama was doubtless indicated by the fact that they were destined to be rovers and likely to require repairs in ports where iron was not available. The large scantling for the sternpost, stem, and keelson proved to be costly and hard to get in Liverpool. The ship was a steamer of 700 tons, bark-rigged, with two smokestacks and three masts. She had four gun ports. Bulloch let it be known that she was destined for sale to an Italian firm in Palermo. Charles Francis Adams vainly protested to the Foreign Office that she was intended for the Confederate Navy. She was registered as a British merchant vessel under the name of the Oreto, to be changed to the Manassas as soon as she should be commissioned, and sailed down the Mersey in ballast on March 22, 1862, under the command of John Low, an Englishman who was warranted provisional master, with a British crew of fifty-two men, ostensibly bound for Palermo and Jamaica, but actually consigned to Adderly & Company, the correspondent of Fraser, Trenholm & Company, in Nassau.

At the same time the steamer Bahama was at Hartlepool in Durham, on the opposite side of England. The Bahama was loaded with cannon, rifles, shot, and shells.

When the Oreto reached Nassau on April 28, 1862, after a passage of twenty-seven days made under sail to save coal, Messrs. Adderly & Company turned her over to Lieutenant John N. Maffitt, C.S.N. Her crew promptly left the ship because they did not want to join the Confederate Navy. Maffitt shipped twenty-two new men in Nassau with results that proved disastrous, as will presently appear. His orders were to "cruise at discretion, the Department being unwilling to circumscribe your movements in this regard by specific instructions." "The Secretary," wrote Maffitt, "complacently ordered me to fit out and cruise as though I controlled a navy yard and had engines, men, etc. at my command."

In a day or two the Bahama from Hartlepool came into Nassau. The transfer of arms and munitions began but was interrupted. The violation of neutrality was too flagrant to be countenanced. The Oreto was arrested, released, arrested again. A *pro forma* trial was held in an admiralty court. An English naval officer at Nassau examined her and reported that she could be equipped for battle within twenty-four hours. Bulloch had written that "the hammock nettings, ports and general appearance of the ship sufficiently indicate the general purpose of her construction." For the defense, a merchant of Nassau, hardly a disinterested witness considering the money that was flowing into the Colony, testified that he had been on board the ship and she seemed to him to be a commercial vessel. Much to the disgust of the American Consul, she was released by Mr. Justice Lees on the ground that no violation of neutrality had been shown. This mock trial, in which the prosecutor was as eager to lose as the defense was to win, was staged to make a face-saving record for the colonial authorities. These proceedings consumed the time until August 6. On that day Maffitt sent the Navy Department a voucher (now in the National Archives) for $248 for "boat hire, bribes to police, and runners." The next day the ship was released, and the day after that the Oreto's English captain took her to an uninhabited island some sixty miles from Nassau. Lieutenant Maffitt and eight Confederate naval officers were on board as passengers. There were only thirteen men left in the crew. Two days later a schooner, the Prince Albert, left Nassau with eight guns, shot, shells, and provisions, but without rammers, sponges, sights, locks, and other necessaries which had been left behind by oversight. When the Prince Albert appeared at the rendezvous, the Oreto took her in tow. In his journal Maffitt describes the transshipment of the cargo:

"Now commenced one of the most physically exhausting jobs ever undertaken by naval officers. All hands undressed to the buff and with the few men we had commenced taking in 6 and 7¼ inch guns, powder, circles, shell and shot, &c. An August sun in the tropics is no small matter to work in. . . . On the morning of the 17th (August, 1862) got under way, hoisted and cheered the Confederate flag, and christened the Oreto by her new official cognomen of Florida (the name Manassas having been abandoned), parted with the Prince Albert and stood to the southward and westward." But the crew brought on board with them a deadly enemy, *Stegomyia fasciata*, the yellow fever mosquito. The sickness, which was prevalent in Nassau, made its first appearance on board on August 15, while the work of transferring armament was under way. Several men were taken ill and the ward room steward died. Maffitt, who had to act as his own surgeon, describes the condition of that horror of sailormen, a fever ship. As of date August 17, "the yellow fever by this time had gained complete ascendency and in our absolute helpless condition were forced to enter a Cuban port (Cárdenas). Moreover we found that neither beds, quoins, sights or rammers had been sent to us.... On the 20th dispatched Lieutenant Stribling and Mr. Vesterling to Havana to obtain, through agents, more men and a doctor. The fever had complete possession of the vessel, but as yet none had proved fatal for I watched every case with the most particular care. 'Twas a sorrowful sight to see our quarterdeck turned into a complete hospital. All the men who were able to work we kept fitting side tackles, breachings, &c."

"August 22nd. My duties as physician have prostrated me considerably; do not feel well. At 2 P.M. was taken with a slight chill which I fancied originated from getting wet in a thunder squall. Took a foot bath and felt better for a time. At 4, while giving medicine to the sick, was seized with a heavy chill, pain in the back and loins, dimness of vision, and a disposition to vomit. The painful conviction was forced upon me that I was boarded by this horrible tropical epidemic. I sent for Mr. Floyd and Mr. Lyman and gave full directions in regard to the duty of the vessel.... Knowing that fever always affects my brain, I did all that I thought necessary with promptness, even directing the medicines and the care of the sick during the night."

For a week Maffitt was desperately ill. Then,

"The first unpleasant news conveyed to me on becoming quite sensible was that my dear stepson, Laurens, was seriously ill with fever. Poor boy, he had set up with me and manifested a most tender solicitude for my recovery. I was distressed that my debilitated condition prevented attention to his case. Dr. Barrett of Georgia, a warm hearted Irishman, volunteered for the vessel giving up an excellent situation in the Government hospital in Havana in order to demonstrate his devotion to the South in this time of need.

"August 30. At 6:30 P.M. poor Laurens was taken with black vomit; at 7 the noble boy went gently to sleep, beloved and regretted by all who knew him. This blow came like the raven wings of fate, blackening my very soul and nearly producing a relapse. Poor Mr. Seely (John), our third assistant engineer, and three men departed this life about the same hour. Mr. Floyd is down with the fever; also Midshipman Sinclair."

Under the circumstances there was nothing to do but head for a Confederate port in the hope of running the blockade, attending to the sick, getting the necessary outfit, and recruiting a crew. Maffitt started for Mobile. Men continued to sicken until, on sighting the blockading line, only the officers and four foremast hands were available to work a ship with a normal complement of one hundred. Maffitt himself had to be supported when it was necessary for him to stand. Lacking a pilot the Florida was compelled to run in by daylight.

On approaching Mobile on the afternoon of September 3, 1862, Maffitt had a stroke of luck he could not have anticipated. Of seven Union warships assigned to the blockade of the port, five were away on one errand or another. Of the two remaining on duty, one, the Oneida, was undergoing engine repairs which reduced her speed, leaving the Winona as the only blockader ready for her work. A Union armed schooner came up just before the Florida arrived. As the cruiser resembled the English gunboats which frequently inspected the blockade, Maffitt undertook to run through disguised under British colors. The ruse deceived Commander George H. Preble of the Oneida until the Florida was less than a hundred yards away. Foreign naval observers were required to ask permission before passing the blockade. When the incoming ship did not do this and failed to answer a hail, Preble realized that he had been duped and began to shoot. So did the Winona and the schooner, which were further off. When the firing began the Florida and the Oneida were running alongside, the Confederate vessel making 14 knots to the blockader's 7. Maffitt could not man his guns. He merely ran for it. Four shots took effect, doing considerable damage on board the Florida. She was scarred by 1,400 shrapnel balls. The Oneida had to yaw to bring her guns to bear. By the time this maneuver was completed the Florida was safe over the bar, anchored under the defense of Mobile. One man was beheaded and three wounded.

Commander Preble was dismissed from the naval service for "inexcusable neglect in permitting the armed steamer Oreto, in broad daylight to run the blockade." After being out of the service for nine months he was reappointed and restored to his rank by President Lincoln.

Fever continued to plague the Florida while she lay at Mobile. Here are some extracts from Maffitt's diary:

"September 9. Stribling very ill; will not permit anyone to administer his medicine but me and I am hardly able to stand. Midshipman Sinclair rather worse; case assuming a doubtful phase...

"September 10. Nothing but sickness.

"September 11. The same. I have now no hope for poor Stribling....

"September 29. Received a complimentary communication from the Navy Department but no hint of promotion....

"October 12. At last after great exertion I have some mechanics at work. They all dread the vessel and desired to await a fever killing frost ere coming on board. Slow, slow, slow. This fitting out in an open bay where so much is to be done is bad business."

Maffitt stayed in Mobile four months. He repaired his ship, got a new crew of about a hundred men, and prepared to resume operations. He was furnished with $50,000 for expenses. This was replenished from time to time. The experience of the Sumter had demonstrated that without ports to which they could be sent for adjudication, a raider could not live on her prizes.

The night of January 15-16, 1863, was dark, with a strong north wind. At two o'clock in the morning the Florida, camouflaged with a coat of whitewash and burning coke to avoid telltale smoke, came out into the main channel across the bar. Seven blockaders were riding in line two miles out. One of them, the fast steamer R. R. Cuyler, had been detailed to Mobile expressly to catch the Florida. The squadron and the cruiser had sighted each other while the latter was waiting behind the point before dark on the previous evening.

Against these odds Maffitt made his dash. The Florida ran between the Cuyler and the flagship Susquehanna. After about half an hour the Cuyler started in pursuit. It was stated later that there was a rule of the ship requiring the watch officer to rouse the commander and await his arrival on deck before slipping the cable. The commander admitted that he was in bed but insisted that he arrived on deck in five minutes. The flagship signaled the Oneida to join the pursuit. She saw the signal but did not see the Florida and did not budge. When the Cuyler finally got under way, she chased the cruiser the rest of the night and all the next day. By the morning of January 17, the Florida was burning the brig Estella on the north coast of Cuba, while the Cuyler was looking for her off the corner of Yucatan. The Oneida followed the chase a day late. She went to the Cuban coast but failed to locate the Florida, which, in the meantime, called at Havana.

An inquiry followed which was of little avail to the owners and insurers of the sixty prizes subsequently taken by the Florida and her tenders.

The Florida was on her way back to Nassau. Before reaching that port she caught and burned the brig Corris Ann, Philadelphia to Cárdenas; and the Windward, Matanzas to Boston. She arrived in Nassau ten days after leaving Mobile; received a rousing reception; stayed thirty-six hours and took a supply of coal for three months, both the stay and the supply being in excess of that permissible under the instructions of the home government. Maffitt also used Bermuda and Barbados as bases and never had any difficulty in getting coal in violation of the British instructions which, it had become apparent by this time, were regarded by colonial authorities as elastic when profits might accrue.

II

When she left Nassau at the end of January, 1863, the Florida had been in commission for five months, four of which had been spent in Mobile. Her luck had been bad from the beginning. Her total accomplishment was the taking of three small prizes. Her value as a raider remained to be demonstrated. In the next six months she bagged seventeen prizes and mothered a brood of four new rovers which caught twenty-seven more.

This period, the winter and spring of 1863, was that of the peak of effectiveness of the commerce destroyers. Their work synchronized with a general Confederate advance on land. The war was at flood; the Southern cause prosperous. In the fighting of the first two years the balance of success lay with the Confederacy. The year 1862 ended on the Rappahannock "in gloom and disaster to the federal cause." In the spring of 1863 Chancellorsville heartened the South. Lee, recovering from the reverse at Antietam, pressed northward again. The Mississippi was still dammed by Confederate guns. The blockade, while tightening, was still full of holes. It was wishfully believed in Richmond that the people of the North were not supporting the war. Similar disaffection in the South was less articulate. If the Confederacy had already been compelled to resort to conscription, the United States, with greatly superior man power and a multitude of arriving immigrants, was able to postpone it only until March of 1863. Although currency inflation and shortage of supplies had begun to affect domestic life in the South, hope inspired the people to endure privation. It would be summer and then autumn before Gettysburg, Vicksburg, Lookout Mountain, and Missionary Ridge turned the tide.

Three of the cruisers, the Alabama, the Florida, and the Georgia, were zigzagging over the same wide belt of sea.

Nassau, New Providence, in the Bahamas, "the Principal Rendezvous of the Anglo-Confederate Blockade-Runners." *From* Harper's Weekly, *September 3, 1864.*

"The Pirate 'Tacony' Burning Merchant Vessels and Fishing Craft." *From* Harper's Weekly, *July 11, 1863.*

"Destruction of the Clipper Ship 'Jacob Bell' by the British Pirate 'Florida.'" *From* Harper's Weekly, *March 21, 1863.*

Operating independently, their commanders pursued two main objectives: to alarm the Northern ports by threatening to raid them, thus diverting blockading ships for their protection; and to capture or frighten away American commerce traversing the broad and populous belt between Cape San Roque and Cape Palmas. The Florida's effort in 1863 was made chiefly in and just above the North Torrid Zone, through which passed all the ships bound to and from the Orient by way of either cape. The Florida's offspring struck terror along the New England Coast.

On leaving Nassau the cruiser was chased for three hundred miles by the U.S.S. Sonoma, finally escaping because of a breakdown of the machinery of the Federal vessel.

The first prize was the most valuable taken during the war by any of the raiders, the 1,382-ton ship Jacob Bell, Foo Chow to New York with a full load of tea, cassia, camphor, firecrackers, and matting. No finer ship was registered at New York. Forty-seven persons were taken off, including the captain's wife, who was approaching confinement. Maffitt surrendered his cabin to her. A few days later the party were put aboard a Danish brig for St. Thomas. The Jacob Bell was burned February 12, 1863, in Lat. 24° N., Long. 65° W., north of Puerto Rico. Of this ship Midshipman Terry Sinclair wrote,

"She rounded to,—and as she lay thus with black hull, gilt streak, scraped and varnished masts, and snow white sails, there was a general expression of admiration coupled with regret that such a thing of beauty must be destroyed."

On February 24 the Florida called at Barbados for coal and a gaudy exchange of hospitalities.

On March 6, in Lat. 15° 13′ N., Long. 54° 38′ W., the ship Star of Peace, Calcutta to Boston with a valuable cargo of oriental merchandise, including a quantity of saltpeter for the E. I. duPont de Nemours Company, was taken. Her officers were paroled; the men, as usual, put in single irons. After she had been set alight, she was used for target practice. Late in the evening, when the Florida was thirty miles away, the sea was still brightly illuminated by the burning saltpeter.

The next prize was the schooner Aldebaran, New York to Maranham with flour, provisions, and clocks. Vessel and cargo were uninsured against the war risk. She was burned notwithstanding the protest of her captain that he was a Southern sympathizer. A few days later eleven of the prisoners from the Star of Peace and the Aldebaran were put on board an English brig bound for Scotland.

On March 28, in Lat. 31° N., Long. 33° 35′ W., the Florida took the 590-ton bark Lapwing, Boston to Batavia with provisions, lumber, furniture, and a large cargo of coal. The crew and store of provisions were transferred to the captor. Maffitt placed four officers and fifteen men on board the prize, with two 12-pound howitzers, intending to use her as a collier. The two vessels parted, met a fortnight later for a transfer of coal to the cruiser, and separated, appointing another rendezvous.

On April 20 the Lapwing took a fine prize of her own, the 1,278-ton ship Kate Dyer, seventy-two days out of Callao for Antwerp with guano. This ship, twice the size of her captor, was taken by a ruse. Included in the cargo of the Lapwing was a family carriage, which some Bostonian was shipping to Java. One would like to know the story behind that consignment. A sawed-off spar of the Lapwing was mounted on two wheels of the carriage. The formidable looking weapon was partly hidden to improve the deception. A shot from the little raider and a glimpse of the half concealed "gun" brought the prize to. Because of her neutral cargo the Kate Dyer was bonded and allowed to proceed.

Again the Lapwing met the mother ship and fed her more coal off the Brazilian penal island of Fernando de Noronha north of Pernambuco. The two ships parted, appointing another meeting. Owing to bad weather this tryst was not kept. The Lapwing was leaking, unseaworthy, and sluggish. Fearing that he might fall into the hands of the U.S.S. Vanderbilt, now patrolling these waters, Acting Master Floyd determined to destroy his ship. On May 30 (1863) he ran to within seven miles of Barbados, manned a boat with his fellow officers and the crew, and fired the vessel fore and aft. The company of the late C.S.C. Lapwing rowed ashore, where they were greeted by a large crowd of cheering blacks, who lifted Floyd above their heads and carried him to the custom house. On the same day the Vanderbilt came into the harbor. The Confederate officers took passage in an English bark for Queenstown and later rejoined the Florida at Brest.

III

After parting company with the Lapwing the first time, the Florida captured the bark M. J. Colcord, New York to Cape Town with provisions, transferred the crew to a Danish brig and burned the bark. Continuing in the populous tropical belt, with numerous sails in sight, Maffitt caught and destroyed a valuable prize on April 17, the ship Commonwealth, New York to San Francisco with general merchandise. A French ship received ten of the Commonwealth's people. Then came the bark Henrietta, Baltimore to Rio de Janeiro with general cargo, and the ship Oneida,[1] a splendid catch laden with tea and silks from China to New Bedford.

On April 28 the Florida was at Fernando de Noronha, where she landed prisoners from her last three prizes; The C.S.C. Alabama had left there only a week before. The hospitality which the Governor had extended to the Alabama did not meet the approval of his superiors, and a new man was sent to replace him while Maffitt was there. The zealous new incumbent ordered the Florida to depart. She did so at once, meeting the Lapwing at sea for the second and last time.

While still off the Brazilian coast, May 6, 1863, the Florida caught the large brig Clarence, Rio de Janeiro to Baltimore

[1] Not the blockader of that name.

with coffee. Lieutenant Charles W. Read, of the Florida, submitted to his commanding officer a daring proposal—nothing less than to man the Clarence with twenty seamen and one small howitzer gun, retaining on board the brig's papers, which showed her American registry, her manifest, etc., and continue on her original voyage. Once inside Hampton Roads and past Fortress Monroe in the guise of an accredited American merchantman, he hoped to surprise an armed steamer or even a Federal gunboat by boarding in the night, transfer his crew to the new prize, set fire to the shipping in the harbor of Baltimore and, after losing or destroying his ship, try to make his way with his men to the Confederate lines.

Maffitt replied, "I agree to your request and will not hamper you with instructions. Act for the best and God speed you."

We must therefore leave the Florida in the warm purple water and follow the career of the Clarence and her immediate successors.

Slowly making his northing, Read had no adventures for a month. Then, on June 6, off Cape Hatteras, he stopped the bark Whistling Wind, Philadelphia to New Orleans with coal for the Federal government, covered by war risk insurance. Naturally the Whistling Wind was burned. The next day Read overhauled the schooner Albert H. Partridge, New York to Matamoras, and took an unusual sort of bond. She was loaded with arms and clothing destined for citizens of Texas. Read sent her on her way after requiring of her master a written obligation to complete the voyage and deliver the cargo as consigned. He may have thought that a Yankee who had gone out to aid the enemies of his country for gain should be bound as strictly as possible. He did not know that trading with the enemy through the military lines was proceeding with the connivance of both governments.

On June 9 the Clarence took the brig Mary Alvina, Boston to New Orleans with supplies for the Union Army. Burned.

From the newspapers and prisoners he got from these

prizes, Read learned that his plan for entering the Chesapeake was impracticable. The Clarence would not have been permitted to pass Fortress Monroe even if she had been sailing under her former master and prosecuting her original voyage in good faith. No vessels were allowed to pass the fort except those loaded with supplies for the Army and these proceeded under escort. Read therefore decided to stay outside the capes and try with his one gun to catch an army transport.

On June 12, directly off Cape Henry, he had a busy and fruitful morning, taking three prizes before eight o'clock. The first was the bark Tacony, Port Royal to Philadelphia in ballast. Read lured her toward the Clarence by flying the American flag union down. When the Tacony approached on her errand of mercy, a boatload of men from the Clarence boarded her and subdued her crew with pistols. As the Tacony was a better vessel than the Clarence, Read determined to transfer his "armament" and flag to her. First, however, the schooner A. M. Schindler, also from Port Royal to Philadelphia in ballast, claimed attention. While securing this prize and moving the gun from the Clarence to the Tacony, another schooner came along, the 387-ton Kate Stewart, Key West to Philadelphia in ballast, with a number of women passengers. As the howitzer was on the way from the Clarence to the Tacony, the only weapon available for the capture of the Kate Stewart was a wooden gun on board the Clarence. The schooner succumbed to that. Thus, before breakfast, Read had four ships to dispose of. He also had fifty passengers. He made a bonded cartel of the Kate Stewart to take them ashore; completed the transfer to the Tacony; and burned the Schindler and his former flagship, the Clarence, while the aroma of her cargo of coffee drifted over the sea. The Kate Stewart with the prisoners reached the South Jersey shore the next day and put ashore the ex-captain of the Tacony, who caught a train for Philadelphia and got telegraphic word to the Navy Department of the previous day's work of the Clarence and the fact that the Tacony was now cruising in her stead.

The Secretary of the Navy telegraphed to the commandants at Philadelphia, New York, and Boston, directing them to commandeer and arm ships and send them in chase. Pursuant to these orders more than thirty armed vessels took the sea within the next two days. One of them was the same schooner, the Kate Stewart, which had brought the prisoners and the news to Philadelphia. Among so many improvised pursuit ships naturally some were unfit for the duty. The U.S.S. Commodore Jones "bounced like an india rubber ball from one sea to another, throwing water 50 to 60 yards ahead and on each side of her." The naval school ship Marion, manned by boys, had to return to New York (after being struck by lightning three times) because everyone on board was seasick. The U.S.S. Seminole leaked so badly that the constant operation of three steam pumps did not diminish the water in her hold.

A firm in Boston was authorized, on its own request, to send out ships with arms furnished by the government.[1] In calm, gravely measured words Governor Andrew of Massachusetts reminded President Lincoln, Secretary Welles, and Senator Sumner of the service of the Commonwealth to the Union and asked the assignment of an ironclad to guard Boston Harbor. The Navy Department had none to spare and telegraphed the commandant at Boston, "Charter more steamers and send them after the Tacony; all that can be sent in 48 hours."

The Boston Chamber of Commerce and various large groups of merchants and underwriters memorialized the President for protection for the fishery. Vice-President Hamlin and the Maine Senators journeyed to Washington while Congress was in recess, to urge protective measures. The Common Council of New Haven, the Mayor of Portland, and

[1] Technically not privateers since they were not authorized to take prizes for their own account.

the inhabitants of Provincetown begged for gunboats. The Navy Department was doing everything possible short of depleting the blockade. Two armed sailing vessels were sent on a three months' cruise to protect the fishermen in the Gulf of St. Lawrence.

The New York Chamber of Commerce petitioned the Secretary of the Navy for organized convoys for all vessels sailing for the British Isles, for all vessels bound for Brazil, and for all vessels bound eastward around the Cape of Good Hope and westward around Cape Horn, the escort to remain in company as far as the Tropic of Capricorn. The adoption of a large-scale convoy system would have depleted the blockade. Besides, it would not have worked where it was most needed, i.e., in southern waters. A fleet of sailers in various stages of loading, destined for remote ports, under the command of masters to whom the idea of a schedule was wholly foreign, could not readily have been assembled for departure at a particular time and place and could not have been relied upon to meet the escort at sea. During the voyage such a fleet would have been limited to the speed of its slowest member and hampered by the divergent ideas as to course and seamanship of the most independent and highly individual set of men in the world, American merchant sailing captains, one of whom was said to have said, "God Almighty rules on land, but I am master on this ship." They would not have remained in company and would not have accepted naval orders. On the initiative of the government rather than the owner, naval escorts were provided from the Mosquito Coast northerly through the West Indian danger zone for the steamers of Cornelius Vanderbilt and those carrying the California mail to and from the Caribbean side of the Isthmus, four ships being assigned to this duty. This relatively simple convoy brought complaints from the captains that the naval vessels slowed them up and interfered with them.

None of the pursuit ships came up with the Tacony. They heard rumors of her from the sails they spoke. She was variously reported as being an ex-British gunboat and an ex-Baltimore fruiter. The fact that no accurate description of the little cruiser was available made it necessary to speak every vessel in sight. One of the pursuers spoke fifty sail.

Meanwhile the cause of this activity was continuing the cruise begun by the Clarence. The cruise of the Tacony continued unmolested for twelve days and netted nineteen "prizes." The inverted commas are intended to suggest a doubt as to the status of some of these captures.

The first five were unexceptionable. Following the three captures by the Clarence on the morning of June 12, Read, now on board the Tacony, rounded out his day off the Virginia capes by taking the brig Arabella, Aspinwall to New York. He bonded her because of neutral cargo. The Tacony's course was laid for New England. By the 15th she was well out to sea opposite the mouth of the Delaware, where she burned the brig Umpire, Cárdenas to Boston with sugar and molasses.

On the 20th and 21st the little cruiser was off Nantucket in the North Atlantic ferry track. Here with her one gun she captured the ship Isaac Webb. It was like drawing out Leviathan with a hook. The Isaac Webb was inbound to New York from Liverpool with 750 passengers. Having no means of disposing of this host, Read bonded the prize. The next day he gathered in another great vessel, the clipper ship Byzantium, London to New York with coal. The same day the bark Goodspeed was taken. The Byzantium and the Goodspeed were burned.

The Tacony now turned her attention to the New England fishing fleet. The Cape Ann schooners were out for their summer fares of cod, mackerel, and halibut. They formed the foundation of a great industry. With good reason it was a point of etiquette among the New England gentry never to give a formal dinner without serving codfish. The sculptured cod in the Boston State House symbolizes a basic element in the economy of Massachusetts. From 1816 until 1858, fishing was aided by a Federal bounty. The withdrawal of this assistance in the latter year had not caused a shrinkage of the fleet by 1863. Indeed the industry flourished until 1865. In that year the Cape Ann men brought in more than three million dollars' worth of fish; the Cape Cod men another two million. This was in excess of any previous catch.

The crews of these vessels were the best type of Yankee sailors. Many of the ships were family enterprises, every man on board being related to every other. Cape Ann boys went to sea at the age of ten, which was regarded as mature, for they had learned the name of every line and sail as soon as they could articulate words. You did not come of age until you were ten because in early youth you were liable to seasickness and might cry, which is unmanly in a seaman.

Fishing was conducted on a profit-sharing basis. The vessel was the property of perhaps three part-owners, one of whom was her master. The fish were caught on hand lines and, by 1863, with trawls, which are heavy lines anchored near the bottom, having smaller lines attached at intervals carrying baited hooks. The trawls were handled from boats, a hazardous occupation in rough weather. Seines were not in use in 1863.

The schooners went out supplied with salt so that the catch could be partially cured before returning. When Congress repealed the Federal bounty in 1858, it substituted an exemption of salt from tariff duty as a gesture—it was no more—of compensation.

The work was hard and dangerous; the hours were all the hours there were except those necessary for sleep; the rewards were not bountiful for the individual. But the life was independent, and so satisfactory that no one engaged in it succumbed to the lure of western migration. The only occupations that drew men from fishing were the merchant and naval services of which the schooners were the nursery and school.

Upon the schooners that were out in June of 1863, the Tacony descended with gun shotted and torch ready. In three days she took eight of them, ranging from 69 to 94 tons. Every one of these prizes hailed from Gloucester. None was insured against this type of loss. Six of them were burned; one bonded as a cartel; seventy-five prisoners taken from the others; the eighth was the Archer, to be spoken of further on.

The capture of small fishing vessels near shore violates an elementary rule of international law. The United States Supreme Court puts it thus:

"At the present day by the general consent of the civilized nations of the world, and independently of any express treaty or other public act, it is an established rule of international law, founded on considerations of humanity to a poor and industrious order of men, and of the mutual convenience of belligerent states, that coast fishing vessels with their implements and supplies, cargoes and crews, unarmed and honestly pursuing their peaceful calling of catching and bringing in fresh fish, are exempt from capture as prize of war."

The legitimacy of the Tacony's work depends upon whether the fishing boats she caught were a little too large and a little too far out at sea to be obnoxious to the rule. Their capture did not help the Southern cause or hurt the Northern. It did not appreciably cripple the fishing fleet, for the captures formed less than 2 per cent of the tonnage engaged in the industry that year. Storm sometimes took a heavier toll than that. The total effect was the impoverishment of a number of fishermen. The destruction was not an act of war but a simple atrocity. Such episodes form a part of the realities of any war. They may excite the indignation of the naïve. Our quotation from the Supreme Court is not from a Civil War case. It is from that of the Paquete Habana, one of thirty or more small Spanish fishing smacks taken by the United States Navy off the coast of Cuba during the war with Spain in 1898.

The chief injuries to the fisheries during the Civil War were inflicted by the government of the United States: The expanding Federal Navy was short of sailors and paid a liberal bounty for enlistment. It was a common experience for

Gloucester Harbor and Part of the Fishing Fleet during the Civil War Period. *From a photograph exhibited at the Centennial Exhibition in Philadelphia in 1876. Courtesy of the Gloucester Chamber of Commerce.*

THE REVENUE CUTTER "CALEB CUSHING" BLOWN UP BY REED AND THE OTHER PIRATES WHO HAD SEIZED HER.

From Harper's Weekly, *July 11, 1863.*

THE FLORIDA

the Gloucestermen returning from Newfoundland or from George's Bank to be deserted immediately on reaching home by every member of the crew. A considerable proportion of the crew of the U.S.S. Kearsarge when she sank the C.S.C. Alabama consisted of Gloucester fishermen. The schooners thus deserted had to be dismantled and laid up. Another blow to the fisheries was the emancipation of the Negro. Fish being cheap, the planters purchased immense quantities to feed the slaves. Freedom destroyed this market. These effects were temporary, however. The present condition of the fishery is not attributable to the Civil War and is outside the bounds of our present study.

By way of coda to the fugue of the fishermen, the Tacony captured, on June 24, the ship Shatemuc, Liverpool to Boston with immigrants, and bonded her. The newspapers taken from the prize told Read that more than twenty gunboats were searching for the Tacony. He determined to cheat them by destroying her. On the day the Shatemuc was taken he captured the last of his fishermen, the little 90-ton schooner Archer; he transferred his "armament" and crew to her and set fire to the Tacony. "No Yankee gunboat," he noted in his journal, "would even dream of suspecting us. I therefore think we will dodge our pursuers for a short time."

The cruise of the Archer lasted two days. It culminated in a feat of brilliant audacity which terminated the military careers of the vessel and her commander and crew.

The steam revenue cutter Caleb Cushing was lying in the harbor of Portland, Maine, where she was outfitting to take the sea in search of the Tacony. Her commander, Captain Clark, had gone ashore to be treated for illness. On Friday, June 26, he died and was succeeded by Lieutenant Merryman. Second in command was Lieutenant Davenport, who came from Georgia. On Friday night half the crew and all the officers except Davenport were on shore.

On Saturday morning the Caleb Cushing was missing from her moorings. The first conjecture was that Davenport had run away with her; the second, that she had been captured by pirates. The Collector of Customs commandeered two passenger steamers and a tug from the shipping in port. He got some guns and a detail of infantry from Fort Preble and a posse of citizens. Everyone in Portland who had any sort of sailing craft followed the steamers out of the harbor. Presently a fisherman reported that he had seen the cutter early in the morning being towed to sea by two boats. At the same time the man in charge of the marine observatory sent down word that he could see the Caleb Cushing in the offing but could not tell whether she was manned by pirates or traitors under Davenport. No one ashore knew until four o'clock in the afternoon that she was being navigated by Read and twenty-three of the crew of the Archer, who had stealthily boarded her from the schooner's boats at two o'clock in the morning, cut her out, shackled her men, and got her to sea under the noses of the Federal garrison.

Early in the afternoon the throng on the water front heard the sound of guns and learned from the observatory that a naval engagement was in progress between the pursuing steamers and the cutter. Soon they saw a column of dense white smoke and heard an explosion. Word came from the observatory that three boats had left the cutter and she had blown up.

The triumphant passenger navy returned to port bringing the boatloads of men who left the Cushing before Read fired her, the irons now being upon the men of the Archer.

One of the passenger steamers went out and got the Archer, upon which Read had left three Confederates and a fisherman. The Federal authorities took charge of all the prisoners and sent them to Fort Warren, refusing to yield them to the local police. "Our citizens," said the *Portland Transcript,* "could scarcely reconcile themselves to the idea of not hanging somebody." They had to be content with distributing as souvenirs all of the extra clothing of the Confederates taken from the Archer. The prison authorities permitted Read to send to Richmond for money to buy a change of clothes for his men. The Portlanders were, indeed, much agitated. Before daybreak the following Monday morning all the bells started ringing an alarm. Citizens rushed into the streets with their firearms. The rumor was that a Confederate gunboat had come in to rescue the prisoners. It turned out to be merely the well-known harbor tug, the Tiger, going about her work with some of the armed guard still on board.

IV

We left the Florida, parent of this brood of bantam cruisers, in the South Atlantic, on May 6, 1863. Her engines were not giving satisfactory performance. Coal was needed. Maffitt put into Pernambuco. The recent courtesies to the Alabama in Brazilian ports had brought the United States consuls into angry collision with the local officials, who came to the conclusion that policy required a stricter adherence to neutrality. Accordingly Maffitt was ordered out within twenty-four hours. On his expostulation that his ship could not be made seaworthy in that time, he was allowed three more days against the consul's bitter protest.

The Florida's head was then turned north. Maffitt expected to pick up the Lapwing for more coal and make the "dash against New England commerce" which Secretary Mallory was fond of suggesting. Cruising over fifty degrees of latitude, from 10° South to 40° North, between May 12 and July 12 (1863), the raider took eight prizes. The first four were fine catches. The great ship Crown Point, New York to San Francisco with assorted cargo, was burned on May 13. On June 6 the same fate overtook the 1,000-ton ship Southern Cross, west coast of Mexico to New York with logwood. On June 14 the ship Redgauntlet, Boston to Hong Kong with coal and musical instruments, was overhauled. Maffitt spent twelve days in transferring the coal to the Florida before burning the Redgauntlet.

On June 16 the large ship B. F. Hoxie, from the west coast

of Mexico, was captured. Her master said he was bound for England with neutral cargo. Maffitt did not believe him. Her papers appeared to him to be bogus, and members of the crew were vague about their destination. The Hoxie was the nearest approach to a treasure ship taken by any Confederate cruiser. In addition to a cargo of logwood, he was carrying $105,000 in silver bars. Maffitt took off the people and the silver and burned the ship. The silver was good prize, properly distributable among the officers and crew of the captor. That was not done. No Confederate prize court was available to condemn and apportion it. Presumably it was used to pay the cruiser's expenses.

The Florida was now within fifty miles of New York and crowded with prisoners. To relieve the congestion the next two prizes were bonded—the whaling schooner V. H. Hill, of Providence, and the packet ship Sunrise, New York to Liverpool with passengers.

On July 8, in the latitude of New York and the longitude of Boston, the Florida had a brush with a Union warship, the U.S.S. Ericsson, a small four-funneled sidewheeler. With three small guns and twenty men the Ericsson was no match for an antagonist armed with eight guns and carrying a crew of about a hundred. The ships sighted one another around noon. The Confederate at once went for the Ericsson, got within range, and fired three shots, which fell a little short. Lieutenant Commander Miller rightly stood away at full speed. His escape was aided by a dense fog, which descended suddenly and lifted half an hour later showing the Florida four miles astern. Maffitt took up the pursuit, but the Ericsson made the better speed and as she was increasing her distance Maffitt gave up the chase about five o'clock.

The New York papers taken from the Sunrise told Maffitt that the coast was alive with Union war vessels looking for the Tacony. Although he does not make note of it, they must also have informed him of what happened the week before at Gettysburg and Vicksburg. He felt that he would be risking his ship by remaining in that part of the ocean. Pausing the same night to burn the brig W. B. Nash and the whaling schooner Rienzi, whose crew took to the boats and rowed away on observing the capture of the Nash, he laid a course for Bermuda.

Arriving at St. Georges on July 16, the Florida exchanged, gun for gun, a 21-gun salute with the shore battery. While extending this honor the Governor also took the precaution to send Maffitt a copy of the British neutrality regulations. This seems to have been "for the record." The regulations required belligerents to depart in twenty-four hours. At the end of eleven days the Florida left of her own volition.

The ship had now been at sea nearly five months. She required a general overhauling and new officers to replace the four sent off on auxiliary cruisers, one who had been drowned, and two who were sick. Maffitt decided to go to Brest.

On the way he bonded an immigrant packet ship bound for New York and in the English Channel burned the ship Anglo Saxon. On August 23 he entered the harbor of Brest.

V

The neutrality of the port of Brest proved to be accommodating. To Ambassador Dayton's protest that the Florida was capable of proceeding under sail and therefore repairs to her engines were not necessary, the Emperor replied, "Because a duck can swim is no reason for clipping her wings"; thus illustrating, perhaps, a decline in the flavor and bouquet of French wit between the First Empire and the Second.

On his arrival at Brest, Maffitt gave his officers leave to visit Paris. A rumor spread through the crew that only officers were to be allowed ashore. Two-thirds of the men promptly mutinied. The occasion and the place were ill-chosen for such a demonstration. Ambassador Dayton in Paris protested against the shipping of men to replace the mutineers. While the diplomatic exchanges were in progress, the Confederate agents in London rounded up sixty men, including a number of Italians, formerly members of Garibaldi's red shirts, now looking for further adventures. These were sent to Brest, and enlisted. A new commanding officer was also assigned to the ship to relieve Lieutenant Maffitt, who was seriously debilitated by his attack of yellow fever, Lieutenant Charles Manigault Morris, of South Carolina, who commanded the Florida throughout the remainder of her career.

In February, 1864, Morris left Brest with the Florida at two o'clock of a thick rainy morning. He laid a course across the Atlantic by way of Madeira and Teneriffe, stood west until the fortieth meridian was reached, and then turned southward and eastward toward the familiar cruising ground below the Tropic of Cancer between the points of Africa and Brazil. Many vessels were spoken, but no American until March 29, when the large ship Avon, of Boston, from Howland Island in the North Pacific with guano for Cork, was burned. Her likeliest seamen were induced or compelled to enlist on the cruiser. The others were sent to England on passing ships.

Just above the Equator the Florida veered easterly without results, reversed her course and came into Martinique on April 26, 1864. Coaling here, she went to Bermuda, where the usual hospitalities were extended. A British man-of-war went out to invite her in and dipped the Union Jack to her, while the English officers doffed their hats to the Confederate ensign. Coal and supplies were replenished. For a time the vessel cruised off Bermuda, calling there once or twice for supplies. On May 16 she caught the schooner George Latimer, Boston to Pernambuco. The prize yielded a welcome supply of bread, flour, and lard. Burned. Prisoners transferred to an English ship.

Another unprofitable month went by until June 17, when the hermaphrodite brig W. C. Clark, Boston to Matanzas with lumber, was taken and burned. There was no more luck until July 1, when the 403-ton bark Harriet Stevens, Portland to

THE FLORIDA

Cienfuegos with lumber, was burned fifty miles off Bermuda. The prisoners were put on a Danish bark bound for Cork. The Harriet Stevens yielded 312 pounds of gum opium, which was sent to the Confederate hospitals by a blockade-runner. In the nearly four months which had now elapsed since leaving Brest, the Florida had taken but four prizes. She was very expensive to operate and it was important to find a way to render her more effective. Dropping in again at Bermuda, Morris received a letter from Secretary Mallory containing his favorite suggestion, another "dash at New England commerce." This course undoubtedly offered the best prospects. It also involved a close approach to the American coast at great danger to the cruiser. Fortified by the Secretary's suggestion, Morris was at liberty to take the risk. Leaving Bermuda at the end of June, he caught and burned, on July 8, the 331-ton whaler Golconda, homeward bound from the Pacific. This vessel, a bark which had been altered from an old ship, was laden with 1,240 barrels of sperm and 600 barrels of whale oil, a part of which was being shipped home from the whaler Gipsey, later to be destroyed by the C.S.C. Shenandoah.

The next day as the Florida approached the neighborhood of the Virginia Capes, the schooner Margaret Y. Davis, north bound from Port Royal in ballast, was burned, her crew being put on an English schooner. The same afternoon the steam tug America was sighted towing the bark Greenland, laden with coal for the Federal squadron in the Gulf of Mexico. The tug cast off and ran for the Delaware Capes, while Morris burned the tow.

The Florida was now off Hampton Roads, where prizes were numerous. On July 10, the most profitable day of her hunting, she burned the barks General Berry, New York to Fortress Monroe with hay for the Army, and Zelinda, Matanzas to Philadelphia in ballast. The destruction of the Golconda, Greenland, General Berry, and Zelinda burdened the cruiser with sixty-eight prisoners. Morris accordingly made a bonded cartel of his next capture, the schooner Howard of New York, the third prize taken on July 10.

The same afternoon, as her fourth victim for that day, the Florida made a sensational catch. At 2:00 P.M., 66 miles S.E. by S. off Cape Henlopen, she started to chase the brig-rigged steam liner Electric Spark, New York to New Orleans with a valuable cargo of merchandise, forty-two passengers, a crew of thirty-nine, the United States mails, and $12,000 in postage stamps. By a stroke of luck, shortly before rounding up the steamer, Morris overhauled the English schooner Lane with a deck load of fruit. He bought the fruit for $720, threw it overboard in order to make room for the prisoners from the Electric Spark, and sent them on board.

The tug America, which had been towing the prize Greenland when the latter was captured, made the fifty miles back to Fortress Monroe and reported to Admiral Lee of the blockading squadron shortly after noon. Before five o'clock Lee had four vessels at sea in pursuit of the Florida, and the Secretary of the Navy was sending telegrams to every naval station from Philadelphia to Portland to send out ships which were back in port after the search for the Tacony three weeks earlier.

The Lane with the prisoners from the Electric Spark reached New York on July 12. The news they brought redoubled the efforts to catch the Florida.

The disposition Morris made of the Electric Spark was shrewd. After parting with the Lane, and as long as daylight lasted, he kept company with the prize. At midnight he scuttled her. By so doing he created a mystery. In Washington it was supposed that so valuable a ship would be preserved for the Confederate Navy. No one believed she had been destroyed. Much time and energy were wasted in looking for her. Her captors created consternation in all the Northern ports. Every available ship was turned out to hunt the cruiser and her prize. Merchant skippers began seeing ghost ships. Off Grand Manan one of them sighted three steamers all resembling the Florida except that they were sidewheelers. As far away as Cherbourg it was reported that the Florida and the Electric Spark had been seen together off the Grand Banks, and the Kearsarge started in that direction to look for them. The Consul at San Miguel, Azores, saw a ship in flames and thought it was a victim of the Florida. It turned out to be a whaler trying out blubber. When the Electric Spark had been lying on the bottom of the sea for nearly two months she was positively identified riding in an inlet 150 miles east of St. Johns, Newfoundland. A rumor spread that she or her captor was about to attack the steamers of the Fall River Line, and Union vessels were ordered to patrol Long Island Sound. The powerful U.S.S. Vanderbilt was sent to hover off Halifax. Other pursuit craft were sent through the Gut of Canso in the Gulf of St. Lawrence. A ship was dispatched to the little French islands of St. Pierre and Miquelon off Newfoundland. The U.S.S. Shenandoah cruised from Cape Henry to Cape Henlopen, recrossing her own track twenty-four times in a fortnight. A captured blockade-runner being reconditioned at the Boston Navy Yard was hurried to sea before completion, under the waggish name of Tristram Shandy. The U.S.S. Wyoming came wearily up the Delaware River, trudging home after five years of cruising off the coast of China. She was suffering from almost every infirmity that can afflict a ship. She was not allowed even a night's rest. The commandant of the Philadelphia Navy Yard said she could stand another week and sent her out on the day of her arrival. She got as far as Nantucket when her engines fell apart like the One Hoss Shay and she limped back to Philadelphia. The rapidly expanding Navy of the United States was able to send in chase of the Florida a third as many ships as had made up the entire United States fleet in commission four years previously.

While these activities were in progress the Florida was steaming smartly for Madeira. More intelligent and less panic-stricken efforts were made to pursue her. The U.S.S. Iroquois was ordered to the Cape of Good Hope via Rio de Janeiro, an approximate anticipation of Morris' plan for his cruise. The Ticonderoga was also sent south.

VI

Departing from Madeira the Florida returned to the old hunting ground between Africa and Brazil. On September 26, 1864, she captured and destroyed her last prize, the bark Mondamin, Rio de Janeiro to Baltimore in ballast.

By this time the sport in the Atlantic had become so poor that the attention of the Confederate Navy was turned upon the Pacific whaling fleet. Although no orders to Morris to proceed to the Pacific are among the surviving records, it was understood that he was to go there. He headed the Florida for Bahia for a final refitting and to give the men a run on shore after two months at sea in anticipation of a much longer voyage. The ship arrived in Bahia on the night of October 4 at nine o'clock.

Daylight disclosed a Union warship in the harbor, the steam sloop Wachusett, Commander Napoleon Collins. The Dona Januaria, a Brazilian corvette, had taken a position between the two belligerents.

The commanding officers of the Union and Confederate vessels paid respects to the local authorities, who exacted promises from Morris and from the American Consul in behalf of Collins that the neutrality of the port should be respected, and it was—for two days.

Consider the position of Napoleon Collins. He was lying in the harbor of a technically friendly nation, in effect, a guest in a friend's house. Almost alongside—save for the intervening Brazilian corvette—lay an enemy warship which was directly and indirectly responsible for the capture of sixty defenseless merchant and fishing vessels of his country and was in port preparing to continue that work. At the same time the American Consul and the enemy commander had given express promises to the Brazilian government that there should be no hostilities in the harbor. Collins said he did not know of the Consul's promise.

Collins' first step was to send Morris, via the Consul, a challenge to come outside and fight. The bearer of the message, a Brazilian Southern sympathizer named Videky, who did not know its contents, felt that he had been imposed upon. He wrote to Morris, "Be sure that whenever I shall meet that faithless scoundrel who calls himself a consul of the United States of America and goes by the name of Wilson, I shall take my revenge and treat him as he deserves it." Senhor Videky went looking for Wilson, but the Consul had taken refuge on the Wachusett.

Morris sensibly sent word that he had come to Bahia for a particular purpose and when that was accomplished he would leave and would abide by what might follow. In a match battle the Wachusett would have the advantage of somewhat superior force.

Collins felt that if he stood upon punctilio and the raider should escape, he would be guilty of unpardonable laxity. He decided to flout the amenities and go after the Florida. The Consul, Thomas F. Wilson, was on board the Wachusett. He approved the proceedings and volunteered for duty. Crossing the bow of the Brazilian ship, on the night of October 7, 1864, the Wachusett rammed the Florida a little abaft midships, knocking down the mizzen mast and the main topmast and enveloping the deck in a tangle of lines and canvas.

The danger in this operation was that the impact might unseat the Wachusett's boilers, dislocate the steam pipes, stop the engines, and scald the engine-room crew. These contingencies were met by accepting the offer of one of the assistant engineers, George W. Melville, who volunteered to remain below alone and reverse the engines immediately after the shock. As it happened, the Wachusett struck the Florida obliquely and sustained no damage below deck. Melville's gallant conduct on this occasion has been obscured by the greater distinction he won subsequently as chief engineer of the ill-fated Jeannette and the savior of the survivors of her company on the luckless De Long arctic expedition. He closed his long career as engineer-in-chief of the Navy.

After striking the Florida, Collins fired two shots at her, which did not take effect. Fast exchanges of pistol shots across decks wounded three of the Union men. Morris and half of his crew, relying on the rule of neutrality and the mutual promises, had gone ashore. Lieutenants Porter and Stone, the senior officers of the Florida, could do nothing except surrender the ship and the sixty-nine men who were on board.

The commander of the Brazilian corvette, Gervasio Macebo, behaved with admirable prudence. He would have been warranted in engaging the Wachusett. If he had sunk her, the United States would have had no just grievance, but his vessel might have come to grief. In any event an international controversy would have arisen. He sent an officer to the Wachusett, who addressed the officer of the deck in Portuguese and was answered in English. The Brazilian said he threatened to fire on the Wachusett and that she promised to desist from the capture, which was then complete. The Wachusett said no such promise was made. The Brazilian fired a shot in the general direction of the Union vessel to "ratify the arrangement." Thus the representative of Brazil had squared his government with that of the Confederacy if the insurrection were successful, without offending the United States in the event of the triumph of the Union.

In apologizing to Brazil, Secretary Seward wrote that the action of Commander Collins was "an unauthorized, unlawful, and indefensible exercise of the naval force of the United States within a foreign country in defiance of its duly established and duly recognized government." Very true, and likewise true that in logic two wrongs do not make a right. Nevertheless, in ordinary human relations it is said to be the equivalent of tat and turn-about is fair play. You have only to turn over to page 146 to discover that the previous year a Brazilian Governor of whom a Confederate officer wrote, "International law don't bother him," had permitted the cruiser Alabama to bring a prize into port, loot her there, and use the harbor as a base from which to run out, take two more prizes, and return the same day to present the local surfmen with the boats of the captives. Brazilian neutrality was liable to such lapses, for feeling ran strongly against the United States. The coffee plantations were worked by Negro slaves, an abolition movement had begun, and the possibility of servile rebellion incited by news from the North was disturbing the repose of the planters. Secretary Seward also informed Brazil that the prisoners taken from the Florida were "enemies of the human race."

Lieutenant Morris and the men of the Florida who were left ashore in Bahia made their way to England. About two-thirds of the crew remaining on the Florida were transferred to the Wachusett, the others continuing on the cruiser. As members of the enemy's fighting force, they were somewhat more rigorously dealt with than the merchant seamen taken off the prizes. With the exception of the officers, many of them were kept in double irons for nearly two months. The surgeon of the Florida attended the sick of the Wachusett, including a case of smallpox. In recognition of this courtesy, Lieutenant Morris' personal effects were restored to him.

The Wachusett, with the Florida in tow, made first for St. Thomas, where they met the victorious U.S.S. Kearsarge.[1] In St. Thomas eighteen of the prisoners who were burdening the Wachusett were permitted to escape, thus offending another foreign government, that of Denmark (owner of the island), which promptly protested.

The Wachusett with her tow now steamed for Hampton Roads. The Florida's officers were sent up to Washington, where they remained for a few days in the Old Capitol Prison. The men were shipped to Point Lookout, Maryland,

[1] See Chap. VII, below.

at the mouth of the Potomac. Then everyone was returned to Fortress Monroe and put again on the Wachusett, which left the Florida there and proceeded to Fort Warren in Boston Harbor. At Fort Warren the prisoners were kept on short rations. While marching to the cook house for dinner some of the officers tried to concert a plan for capturing the fort. When this was discovered all the prisoners were kept in close confinement without exercise and their meals were brought to them. About the end of January, 1865, these "enemies of the human race," fifty in all, were paid $20 apiece from the Federal treasury and paroled in Boston on condition that they leave the country within ten days. As the $20, or what they had left of it, was not enough to pay their passage to England, the master of the liner Canada carried them to Liverpool on credit and collected the balance due on arrival.

Collins was court-martialed for violating the territorial jurisdiction of a neutral government. He pleaded guilty and was sentenced to dismissal. The Secretary of the Navy disapproved the sentence. The whole affair has the appearance of prearrangement.

In every modern war naval officers have found themselves confronted with the necessity of deciding for themselves whether to commit Collins' offense and accept the personal and international consequences, or to keep the legal record clear and lose a chance to cripple the enemy. Commenting on this, the naval historian, Captain D. W. Knox, remarks:

"The decision in such cases is always most difficult for a naval officer; fully cognizant of the illegality of his course and of the outward embarrassment to his government from the necessary formal disavowal of it, yet faced with a clear need of action in behalf of his country's best interests and believing that the public and the officials at home will be pleased, at least secretly." [1]

The same observation might be applied to the conduct of Wilkes in the Trent affair, the difference being that Eng-

[1] *History of the United States Navy*, p. 288.

land was a powerful nation and Brazil a weak one. Wilkes guessed wrong when he should have known better; Collins risked spending the rest of his life in the limbo of discredited men, and fortunately guessed right. Enemy gunfire offers easier terms than such alternatives. The fundamental difficulty is that of reconciling legal rules with war.

In making amends to Brazil the United States should have restored the Florida to the harbor of Bahia. This was made impossible by the circumstance that she was sunk in a collision with the Army transport Alliance in Hampton Roads. The collision was said to have been accidental. There were two courts of inquiry with inconclusive results. The matter soon ceased to have any importance, for the war was drawing to a close and presently there was no government left to reclaim the vessel.

The Wachusett remained in commission until 1887. In 1884 her commanding officer, Captain A. T. Mahan, left her deck to write *The Influence of Sea Power in History* and two dozen other books which revolutionized the public attitude toward the navy in every country and introduced the word "navalism" into the vocabulary of international politics.

CHAPTER VI

THE ALABAMA
AND THE TUSCALOOSA

When the Alabama's *keel was laid,*
  Roll, Alabama, *roll!*
They laid her keel at Birkenhead,
  Oh roll, Alabama, *roll.*
    —Joanna C. Colcord,
      Songs of American Sailormen

I

THE ALABAMA CREATED a literature. It is so extensive that the explorer is left free to follow his own course from seamark to seamark, touching at such points as are of interest to him. No more effective than the Florida, this cruiser was more dramatic and occupies a far larger place in history. This is because the circumstances of her birth brought on a sharp diplomatic collision between the United States and England for the second time within a year, and because her cruise of 75,000 miles, equivalent to three circuits of the globe, was performed continuously without serious mishap or interruption under one commander, the same officers, and largely the same crew, and ended in one of the most perfect battles ever witnessed. After the war her name became attached to a group of international claims, of which about one-third were attributable to her work. In Europe today the word "Alabama" suggests the ship or the claims to many persons who are unaware of the state exceeding England in area and Scotland in population, whose capital was the first seat of the Confederate government.

When Commander Bulloch went to England in June, 1861, to get ships, he had no expectation of staying there. His ambition was centered on sea duty. Secretary Mallory gave him to understand that he should have command of the first vessel commissioned. That was the Florida. When she was nearing completion Bulloch was called home on an errand. On his recommendation Maffitt was placed in command of that ship. Bulloch fully expected to be assigned to the second one.

On August 1, 1861, he signed a contract with Laird Brothers of Liverpool to build for his personal account the 290th vessel which had been turned out by that long-established yard. In accordance with custom the builders set up a signboard at the head of the building slip bearing the serial number 290. Later the New York newspapers absurdly reported that the sign indicated that 290 British capitalists had subscribed to the cost of the vessel. During construction British officials had the run of Laird's yard. So had the agents of Consul Dudley and Minister Adams. The name of the purchaser was concealed and the fact that the ship was destined for warlike use was not expressly communicated even to her builders. She was not to be armed. Indeed, when she finally departed from Liverpool she could have been captured by anyone at hand with an old horse pistol. But she was specially designed for conversion into an armed cruiser by a few hours' work on the open sea. She "had unusual resources within herself such as no other man-of-war of her day could boast. She carried the means of making all ordinary repairs to her machinery, spars and armament while at sea or in ports where mechanical facilities could not be commanded."[1] Laird boasted that she was "the finest cruiser of her class in the world." No seaman who looked at her could doubt that she was intended for naval use. In short, no one was deceived except the shipbuilders themselves and Lord John Russell.

Yet it was long before Charles Francis Adams could get anything in the way of credible evidence to lay before that purblind old gentleman.

[1] Arthur Sinclair, *Two Years on the Alabama*, p. 3.

In the meanwhile Bulloch had been to Richmond and back, the Florida had gone to sea, and Bulloch had experienced the bitterest disappointment that can befall a line officer. When the new vessel was ready for sea and he had completed his arrangements to take her out, had appointed a rendezvous with the Florida and had concerted with Maffitt a plan for a joint cruise, he was informed that Semmes had been assigned to command the new cruiser. What influences were at work in Richmond we do not know, beyond the fact that Lieutenant North, in England, was trying to get the appointment, having tried previously to get command of the Florida. Semmes himself was in Nassau, where he had gone after relinquishing the Sumter.

But on March 8, 1862, when Bulloch returned to Liverpool from his visit to Richmond, he had no suspicion that anyone else would command the new ship. Finding that she was not as far advanced as he had hoped, he expedited the work. On May 15 the vessel was launched and received the name Enrica, which she bore until she ceased to be a British merchantman. Her engines were installed, and on June 15 the Enrica made her trial trip. There remained a number of items of unfinished work which the builders proceeded to complete. Meanwhile Bulloch engaged the services of an English master, Captain Butcher, to take the ship out. While on his recent voyage home, Bulloch had spotted a suitable place for effecting a transfer of armament, off the island of Terceira in the Azores.

The Enrica was a 900-ton wooden vessel, 230 feet long, beam 32 feet, draft when loaded 15 feet, barkentine-rigged, with a large spread of canvas. She had 300 hp engines with lifting propeller and a condenser. Her speed under steam was about 10 knots; under steam and sail her maximum performance was 13¼ knots. Her exceptionally lofty rigging was a means of identification by enemy ships.

It was not until June 23, 1862, nearly eleven months after the vessel had been ordered, that Mr. Adams had any evidence of her character worth submitting to the Foreign Office. The complaint he then made resulted in an investigation by the customs officer at Liverpool and a perfunctory whitewash.

Still supposing that he was to command the vessel when she should be commissioned, Bulloch made his personal preparations for departure. He appointed a staff from among the available Confederate officers, took the Enrica into Birkenhead dock, coaled her, and shipped her supplies. Except that the employment of a crew was postponed until the last moment to avoid advertising her impending departure, all was ready for sea. Bulloch also chartered the bark Agrippina to carry out the ammunition and the battery consisting of six 32-pounders to be placed in broadside, a pivoted 100-pounder rifle, and a pivoted 8-inch smooth bore.

Then, on a day early in July, Bulloch received orders to turn the command over to Semmes, who was said to be on his way to England from Nassau on the steamer Bahama.

On July 21, 23, and 25, Adams filed additional evidence with the Foreign Office. It consisted of affidavits that left no possible doubt of the character and purpose of the ship. Still, there remained the question whether she was so far "equipped" as to constitute a violation of the Foreign Enlistment Act. Adams also had the U.S.S. Tuscarora, then at Southhampton, ordered to patrol St. George's Channel.

On Saturday, July 26, Bulloch "received information from a private but most reliable source that it would not be safe to leave the ship in Liverpool another 48 hours." The inference is irresistible that the cue came straight from Downing Street.[1]

Smarting under his grievance, Bulloch had to engage a crew for the Enrica and get her off; load and dispatch the Agrippina; keep in touch with his agents, who were sending in telegrams reporting the movements of the Tuscarora; and

---

[1] The actual source of the tip seems to have been a clerk in the Foreign Office named Victor Buckley.

watch for the arrival of the Bahama bringing Captain Semmes.

Early Monday morning, July 28, the Enrica came out of the dock, ostensibly to make another "trial trip." To add to the illusion, she was dressed with flags, and a party of ladies and gentlemen were invited. The tug Hercules went along as tender. After luncheon Bulloch told his guests that he had decided to have the ship remain out all night. He accompanied them ashore in the tug, telling the pilot to take the cruiser about fifty miles down the Anglesey shore to Point Lynas.

The Enrica still had no sufficient crew. It was to get more hands that Bulloch returned to Liverpool on the tug. He had already started a shipping master rounding up men.

At seven o'clock the next morning, Tuesday, July 29, the tug was ready to set out again, this time with various fittings that had been left behind in the hurried departure of the previous day; about forty seamen to be shipped for the voyage; an equal number of women; and Bulloch, who had not been to bed. About 4:00 P.M. the tug came alongside the Enrica in Moelfra Bay.

Here ensued a maddening delay. The reader will have to submit to it, as Commander Bulloch did, with his best grace.

Seamen who were "outward bound," i.e., unemployed, were the recipients of attentions from a group of waterside entrepreneurs known as crimps. The crimp supplied board, lodging, and liquor on credit. In coöperation with the professional women of the dockside, he also provided social life. Thus the sailor, outward bound and broke, was furnished with hearth, home, refreshment, and night life, all in anticipation of his next pay. The prices were commensurate with the risk and the simplicity of the victim, say several multiples of the market rates to cash customers. Upon shipment it was the practice to advance the man a month's wages to defray his obligations to the crimp and his collaborators. This system provided the ships with a reservoir of labor and the seamen with social security. It also created a business opportunity for a class of conscienceless scoundrels to exploit simple-minded men and women. It could work only where there was a fairly steady demand for marine labor.

The women who went down the Welsh coast on the tug were the doxies of the seamen, going along to collect the advance wages.

Bulloch should have understood this, for he had been in the shipping business in New York where the same system prevailed. Nevertheless, he tried to put the women off the tug before starting. They would not go. He tried to prevent them from boarding the Enrica. They swarmed up the ladders and over the side, exciting the admiration of the officers by their seaworthiness. Once aboard, they said they were hungry. There had been nothing to eat on the tug, which had been out from breakfast to tea time. Bulloch ordered supper for them; then grog.

He asked the men to sign articles for a voyage to Havana or any intermediate point, guaranteeing their return to England. They agreed, the advances were turned over to the girls, and the latter returned to the tug.

This system has been reformed by making it unlawful to pay a seaman any part of his wages in advance or to honor any assignment of them when earned. Jack is now discharged at the end of a voyage with a pocket full of pay, instead of only partly full. The crimp's occupation is gone. The girls have developed a new technique. When Jack has spent his pay and is outward bound, he is now to be found frequenting art galleries. The seamen's charities will give him something to eat and, if not too crowded, a bed. Indubitably it is better. Whether Jack and his doxy get as much fun out of the modern system is an improper inquiry, not to be included in the questionnaires of those who go about doing good, though they ask about everything else.

If the reader has found this interruption tedious, let him consider its effect upon Commander Bulloch. As he stepped aboard the tug that morning a telegram was handed to him telling him the Tuscarora was coming. He knew the gentry in Downing Street were contriving to arrest his ship. The unarmed Enrica was held up in Moelfra Bay for eight hours, with danger approaching from two directions, while the half-world of Liverpool collected its dues.

It was midnight of a rough and rainy night when the last of the girls got over the side. Dirty as the weather was, Bulloch and Butcher could not risk staying in St. George's Channel until daybreak. The menace of the oncoming Tuscarora precluded the usual southerly route. They laid a course around the north of Ireland. By eight o'clock in the morning the Enrica was off the Calf of Man. At six that evening Bulloch and the pilot hailed a fishing boat off Giant's Causeway and went ashore, leaving Captain Butcher to take the ship to the meeting place in the Azores. The fisherman landed his passengers at a little inn on the Antrim shore. Bulloch writes:

"During the evening it rained incessantly and the wind skirled and snifted about the gables of the hotel in fitful squalls. Bond (the pilot) and I sat comfortably enough in the snug dining room after dinner and sipped our toddy of the best Coleraine malt; but my heart was with the little ship buffeting her way around the rugged north coast of Ireland. I felt sure that Butcher would keep his weather eye open and, once clear of Innishtrahull, there would be plenty of sea room, but I could not shake off an occasional sense of uneasiness."

Bulloch undressed for the first time in four nights and went to bed in the little Antrim inn. Next morning he got a boat and pulled around inside the Skerries for Port Rush; thence by train and ferry back to Liverpool.

In point of fact the Cabinet did decide on that day, Tuesday, July 29, to detain the Enrica, and so instructed the collector of customs at Liverpool. The decision of the ministers was clouded by a dramatic episode which, without affecting the outcome, added a touch of tragedy to their action. Mr. Adams' dossier was completed on Friday, July 25. On Saturday it was sent to the Queen's Advocate, Sir John Harding, for his opinion. No one knew except Lady Harding that several days previously her husband had suffered a nervous breakdown and was totally and hopelessly mad. The distraught woman was concealing the fact and holding all papers. As Bulloch received his warning the same day the file was sent to Harding, i.e., Saturday, July 26, and as the ship got out of Liverpool early on the Monday morning, it is hardly possible that this affliction contributed to her escape. By Tuesday the Cabinet had the papers back and acted without benefit of the advice of the Crown counsel.

The Ministry regarded the departure of the cruiser with mixed feelings. Lord Russell communicated his official chagrin to Adams. In private conversation, John Bright, who was not given to making rash statements, taxed Russell to his face with being privy to the tip to Bulloch. Without explicitly denying the charge, the Foreign Minister complained that Bright was traducing him. The extent, if any, to which ministers connived at the escape of the Alabama under their noses, will never be known.

II

Through August, 1862, Swift's Comet, making its rounds, hung a luminous brush across twenty-five degrees of sky above Mont Pico. Its last previous appearance, in 1739, had portended the War of Jenkins' Ear, with much destruction of commercial shipping in the waters now about to be infested by Confederate cruisers. In the Azores the sea was calm, the nights clear, the stars unusually bright. Three ships, the Enrica, the bark Agrippina, and the British steamer Bahama were lying a marine league off East Angra Bay, Porto Praya, Terceira, an unfrequented spot. The Agrippina arrived first with the battery and 250 tons of coal. The Enrica followed. Then, on August 20, the Bahama, having carried

Captain Semmes from Nassau to Liverpool, brought him with his officers, his indispensable law library, and Commander Bulloch to the rendezvous. Four days of furious work sufficed to arm and coal the cruiser. On August 24 she was put in commission, a ceremony consisting of lowering the British Merchant, raising the Confederate colors and captain's ensign, and reading Captain Semmes' commission to command the C.S.C. Alabama. The names of naval vessels do not usually appear upon their hulls. The only lettering upon the exterior of the Alabama, spread across her stern in gilded carving, spelled the words, *Aide toi et Dieu t'aidera.*

Thus, on August 24, the new Confederate cruiser was in commission, staffed with twenty-four officers and not one enlisted man. It was a critical moment. Semmes mustered the crews of the Enrica and the Bahama on board the former, now the Alabama, and delivered a short patriotic address which left the English sailors cold. Then he began to speak of money. They would receive about double the usual wages, paid in gold, and "lots of prize money," which would be appropriated by the Confederate congress for the ships that must be destroyed. Cries of "hear, hear" greeted this part of the speech and Semmes thought it prudent to close his remarks abruptly. The men knew they were masters of the position. They drove hard bargains. Stokers got £7 per month; ordinary seamen £4 10s. With no living expenses, these were unheard-of wages. Semmes' loose talk about prizes brought him into trouble later. The undisciplined minds to which it was addressed took it for a license to do individual freebooting aboard the captures to which they were sent as boarding parties, and to bring off private loot, particularly liquor. It was long before severe discipline broke up this practice.

Eighty-three men enlisted in the Confederate Navy. The others returned to England on the Bahama, as did Bulloch. Semmes was satisfied. He was about twenty men short of a full crew, but he had enough to handle the ship. Others could be recruited from prizes or in ports of call. About half of the original crew remained with the Alabama throughout her life. The rest deserted in various ports and were replaced.

That night the little flotilla parted company. Bulloch reported to the Navy Department that the Comet was burning with a brilliant blaze.

III

The life of the Alabama was twenty-two months, starting August 24, 1862, and ending June 19, 1864. Eighty-five per cent of her prizes were taken in the first half of that period. Her effective cruise was, therefore, of about eleven months' duration.

The order issued to Semmes to take command of the vessel is not to be found in the surviving records of the Confederate Navy and is not included in his journal or memoirs. It is safe to assume that it was no more definite than the orders to the commanders of other cruisers and left the direction of his operations largely to his discretion, so that the accomplishments of the Alabama may be said to be his work.

He began by combing the neighborhood of the Azores for whaling ships which frequently called there. In the course of a month he caught nine of them. The first one had just killed a whale and had it alongside. Several of these vessels, homeward bound from long voyages, had valuable cargoes of oil. Others were starting out. They were burned, as was a little schooner carrying passengers from Fayal to Flores. Semmes landed the passengers in his cutter and sent the whaling crews (except those of the last two captures) ashore in their own boats. As the weather was fine and the greatest distance from the coast was not more than twenty miles, this disposition of prisoners caused no hardship, though the Northern press characterized it as inhuman.

After cleaning up the whalers the Alabama headed west into the track of commerce between Northern and European ports. Cruising here and off the Banks of Newfoundland for a month, she had very good luck nothwithstanding a severe storm which did much damage on board.

The prizes taken in these waters, ten in number, were large vessels with valuable cargoes. It was October and American wheat was moving eastward. Six of the prizes were carrying grain and flour. As there was already a wheat shortage in Europe, the loss of these cargoes, in itself perhaps not sufficient to have a perceptible effect on the market, was nevertheless a factor in the fluctuation of British and French sentiment. English observers noted that wheat was no less important than cotton and that measures antagonistic to the United States were of doubtful policy.

The first two of this group of prizes were taken on October 3. The Emily Farnham, New York to Liverpool, was released on bond because of neutral cargo. While she was under examination and Semmes was conducting his "prize court," the great grain ship Brilliant, New York to London, was captured. She was nearly as large as the Alabama. Her company and the people from the last two whalers were placed on the Emily Farnham. The Brilliant was burned. Master's Mate Fullam, an Englishman, noted in his diary:

"It seemed a fearful thing to burn such a cargo as the Brilliant had, when I thought how the operatives in the cotton districts would have danced with joy had they shared it among themselves. I never saw a vessel burn with such brilliancy, the flames completely enveloping the hull and rigging in a few minutes, making a sight as grand as it was appalling."

Of the same ship Semmes writes, "I was much moved by the entreaties of the master of the Brilliant (Captain Hagar) to spare his ship. He was a hard-working seaman who owned a one-third interest in her. He had built her and was attached to her and she represented all his worldly goods. But I was forced to steel my heart." Captain Hagar may well have lamented the loss of his ship for the war risk insurance carried upon her was wholly inadequate.

The bark Wave Crest, another grain carrier, eight days

out from New York to Cardiff, and the hermaphrodite brig Dunkirk, grain from New York to Lisbon and Cadiz, were burned October 7. The Dunkirk was taken by moonlight after a long, exciting chase in a strong breeze, pursuer and pursued racing before the rising wind with studding sails alow and aloft. No steam was used. Semmes sat up all night astride the hammock nettings, watching the performance of his ship in high good humor.

The next captures were neutrals—a flock of curlews, blown far out to sea, wing-weary and starving, settled in one of the lifeboats. To avoid arousing the superstition of the crew against harming birds, they were fed and watered, and flew off toward the west.

The Tonawanda, Philadelphia to Liverpool, was taken October 9 and retained in company until the 14th, as she had seventy passengers including thirty women. On the 11th the ship Manchester, New York to Liverpool, was burned. On the 14th Semmes reluctantly bonded and released the Tonawanda as a cartel because he had no other way of disposing of her people and those of the three preceding prizes. One of the people from the Dunkirk and one from the the Tonawanda remained on the Alabama. The first was a man who had deserted from the Sumter at Cadiz and now found himself sentenced to serve on another cruiser for the duration of her voyage without pay or prize money. He did not complete the sentence because he was court-martialed again for drunkenness and set ashore on a barren island in the Caribbean. The other was Dave, a seventeen-year-old black boy from the Northern slave state of Delaware. Dave was assigned as personal servant to the surgeon of the Alabama. He steadfastly refused to accept the liberty offered him by various United States consuls, until on June 19, 1864, he gave up his life.

Four more prizes, taken between October 15 and 28 (1862) do not call for notice except that one of them yielded six live pigs which were a welcome addition to the Alabama's ever-diminishing stock of fresh food. Their people were held on the captor awaiting disposition. A total of eleven men from prizes had by this time enlisted on the cruiser.

On October 29 a small lumber brig, the Baron de Castine, was taken about three hundred miles east of Atlantic City. She was an old vessel. Semmes put all his prisoners aboard her, took the usual bond, and told her master to advise the New York Chamber of Commerce that the Alabama would be off that port by the time the message reached them. The brig went to Boston, but the inhabitants of New York had already learned of the proximity of the cruiser from Captain Hagar of the Brilliant, who had been transferred from the Emily Farnham (which continued her voyage) to an inbound ship which had reached port by October 15.

The Chamber of Commerce held a special meeting to hear Hagar's graphic story and passed resolutions, which were sent to Washington. Insurance underwriters also sent in an appeal for pursuit ships. The Boston Marine Society and the Chamber of Commerce petitioned for the protection of their port. Naval vessels were sent out from Hampton Roads, Philadelphia, New York, New Haven, and Boston. Word was sent to Wilkes commanding the West Indies squadron. This search was initiated and conducted with much less hysteria than those for the Tacony and the Florida the following summer, which have been described. The depredations of the commerce destroyers had not yet had a severe effect upon American commerce. It was the subsequent career of the Alabama herself, and the failure of the efforts to catch her, which enraged and terrified the ports in 1863.

The returning prisoners brought tales of brutal treatment. These boil down to the fact that part of the time the Alabama was crowded; that prisoners were placed in irons, as was unavoidable; and that the officers as well as the men of Semmes' first eighteen prizes had been manacled during the short time they were kept on board the cruiser. Semmes said he adopted the latter practice in retaliation for the treatment of the paymaster of the Sumter when he was shipped back from Gibraltar. A sounder reason, doubtless the true one, was that the Alabama herself would have been in danger of capture as a prize if he had permitted skilled navigators among the prisoners to have access to his lawless and unpredictable new crew of aliens before he had become confident of his control over them.

When he sent the message by the brig Baron de Castine, Semmes fully intended to raid New York. This project was balked by a shortage of coal. Master's Mate Fullam noted in his diary, "We were startled and annoyed to find that only four days' coals were on board. To astonish the enemy in New York harbor, to destroy their vessels in their own water, had been the darling wish of all on board."

Semmes determined to sail for Martinique. The tender, Agrippina, which had carried the battery to Terceira, had been ordered to act as a collier for the Alabama and was appointed to supply her with coal at several places, of which Martinique was the first. The Agrippina was waiting for the Alabama there.

On the way, the Alabama burned two prizes. One was a whaler which had on board a quantity of cabbages and turnips. These were welcome for, after seventy days at sea, the cruiser's men were showing signs of scurvy. The other was a ship from Calcutta with a general cargo and some passengers, including two women and three little girls. The officers of the Alabama were turned out of their cabins to accommodate them. These prizes added nine recruits to the Alabama's crew. The prisoners were landed at Martinique.

Arriving at that island on November 18, Semmes found the Agrippina. He also found that her purpose there was known, so he sent her along to Blanquilla, off the Venezuelan coast. The next day, when the Alabama was ready to follow, after quelling a brief mutiny caused by Martinique rum, Semmes found that he was blockaded by the U.S.S. San Jacinto, the ship that had stopped the Trent, an "old wagon" but more powerful than the Alabama. Preparing for action or flight, he sent his money ashore. On learning that the local bankers required 5 per cent for holding the deposit, he took it back on board. The play of the Sumter and the Iroquois was reënacted. To avoid twenty-four-hour rule Commander Ronckendorff of the San Jacinto stood outside the roadstead and attempted to police it with boats. A system of signals by rockets was arranged with an American brig in the harbor. The signals were duly set off, while the Alabama, like the Sumter, slipped out under cover of darkness and rain.

After coaling at Blanquilla and giving the crew shore liberty on an island where they could find neither liquor nor entertainment, Semmes determined on a cruise in the Caribbean in the hope of picking up a California steamer to or from the Isthmus. He traversed the Mona Passage by moonlight, and the Windward Passage; burned a small bark and bonded a schooner with neutral cargo; and then, on December 7, he found the California packet.

The Ariel was a third larger than the Alabama. She was a unit of the great system of transport linking the east coast with the west by steamers from New York to Aspinwall (now Colon), by rail across the Isthmus, and by connecting steamers to San Francisco. The Alabama caught her on the southbound trip through the Windward Passage. Semmes was hoping for a northbound liner. That would have been the "treasure ship" of which the cruisers dreamed. All he got from the Ariel was about $1,500 specie (as against a hoped-for million), a quantity of small arms and ammunition, and the United States mails. The Ariel had on board more than seven hundred people: her crew, 140 U. S. Marines bound for west coast service, and 532 passengers, half of them women and children. The passengers were part of the western migration which proceeded steadily throughout the Civil War and paid the Panama Railway some six million dollars a year. Semmes disarmed the marines and put them under parole, to the great chagrin of Captain David Cohen. A festival was held in the saloon of the Ariel with champagne broached from her pantry. The passengers drank the health of Jefferson Davis and the prize crew that of Abraham Lincoln. The ladies cut all the brass buttons from the Confederate uniforms for souvenirs.

There was no way of disposing of the Ariel except by sending her into a neutral port to discharge the prisoners and leaving her there to be restored to her owners like the early prizes of the Sumter. Accordingly Semmes took the customary bond and let the ship go. It was a severe disappointment, underlined by the knowledge that it negatived the possibility of capturing a treasure ship, for the Ariel herself was the next scheduled northbound packet. On that voyage she left her golden cargo on storage in Aspinwall. Thereafter these ships were protected by naval escorts. The great quest for gold ended in nothing more notable than a lively social party and the discomfiture of a captain of marines.

Semmes now embarked upon the execution of an audacious plan. Newspapers found on the Ariel told of the preparation of a Federal military expedition under General Banks which was to land at Galveston, then in Union hands, and invade Texas. Semmes conjectured that the troop ships, having no reason to apprehend a naval attack, would not be convoyed. He proposed to go through the Yucatan Channel into the Gulf of Mexico and capture some of the transports off Galveston. Adverse winds and a machinery breakdown protracted the voyage to a month. Christmas was celebrated by giving the men a run on shore upon an uninhabited key. The coal tender Agrippina turned up there, transshipped the remainder of her cargo, and was sent back to Liverpool for a new supply to be brought to the island of Fernando de Noronha, off the coast of Brazil.

Arriving off Galveston about noon January 11, 1863, Semmes was astonished to discover a Federal gunboat shelling the city. The Confederates had taken the place ten days previously and five Federal warships had been sent to recapture it. The Banks expedition had been diverted to New Orleans.

The Alabama approached gingerly under sail, showing British colors. About three o'clock the flagship Brooklyn signaled to the U.S.S. Hatteras, Captain Blake, to go out and investigate the visitor, which drew off slowly, decoying her pursuer away from the rest of the fleet throughout the remainder of the afternoon. Blake, alert and suspicious, signaled a description of the stranger to the flag ship. Receiving no response, he prepared for action and continued to obey orders. When within hail Semmes announced his vessel as "Her Majesty's ship Vixen." Blake sent off a boat to verify this identification. By this time the stars were out; the two ships were twenty-eight miles off shore and less than four hundred yards apart.

The Hatteras was an iron-hulled, sidewheel, excursion boat from the Delaware River, where she had coped with nothing more warlike than a Ladies' Aid outing or a Sunday School picnic. She was a mere shell. Her battery was about half as heavy as that of the Alabama. Farragut called her "my poor little good-for-nothing Hatteras."

Blake's boat was hardly in the water when the Alabama fired a broadside. The Hatteras returned the fire. There were hot exchanges. Thirteen minutes later, at Blake's request, Semmes sent his boats to rescue the Union crew, except two who had been killed.

The Brooklyn and two other Union ships saw the flashes on the horizon and searched vainly all night for traces of the combatants. In the morning the flagship, returning to Galveston, came upon two upright topmasts protruding just awash from a submerged wreck which could not be identified. Presently a piece of flotsam was recognized as the hurricane deck of the Hatteras.

Semmes took his 130 prisoners to Port Royal, Jamaica, paroled them, and put them ashore. They were destitute. The English residents refused them hospitality. The American Consul shipped them home. The colonists had other company—the crew of the Alabama were given shore leave with access to a sailortown and money to spend for the first time in six months. They were reassembled with some difficulty at the end of five days. Semmes had to dismiss his paymaster here for drinking with the crew. This man afterwards turned up in England as a witness for the United States in some of the litigation over the Confederate ships. He was not of sufficient importance to rate the vituperation Semmes lavished upon him. He was merely a moral slum whose brief ill-fame need not be reviewed. His defection and his testimony neither harmed nor helped anyone.

IV

The destruction of the Hatteras is a punctuation point in the career of the Alabama. On leaving Jamaica, January 25, 1863, she headed for the ocean highway between Pernambuco and Cape Palmas. Here throughout the spring of 1863 the Alabama, the Florida, and the Georgia brought about the great hejira of American commerce, the effect of which upon our national economy is still acute.

By the time she crossed the Equator, March 29, the Alabama had taken thirteen prizes, burning nine and bonding four. Their cargoes included lumber, flour, lard, salt, candles, wines, brandy, sardines, olives, jute, linseed, whale oil, guano, and general merchandise. Their ports of departure, call, and destination were New York, New Bedford, Cienfuegos, Ponce, Guadeloupe, Buenos Aires, Montevideo, Callao, Calcutta, Bordeaux, Cork, and London.

Below the line the first catch was the ship Louisa Hatch, of Rockland, Maine, Cardiff to Singapore with a cargo of coal, which was being shipped to the Far East as a speculation. It was a happy windfall for the cruiser. Semmes took the Louisa Hatch to the rendezvous he had appointed for the Agrippina, the island Fernando de Noronha. This volcanic peak northeast of Cape San Roque was, and still is, a Brazilian penal colony "on the wayside of the commerce of all the world, sighted by more ships and visited by fewer than any other spot in earth." It is "awfully hot when the sun shines" and almost equally so when it does not. The social arrangements are democratic. The Governor was most hospitable, being glad of visitors with money to exchange for antiscorbutic foodstuffs at exorbitant prices. Members of the staff of the Alabama dined at Government House with a forger and a counterfeiter, who did the honors graciously. The Governor outdid himself. Not only did he permit the Alabama to bring a prize into port and loot her there; he also permitted her to run out one afternoon and capture two whalers whose boats had come in, burn one, and bring the other back into the harbor for spoliation. On leaving, Semmes presented the boats from these ships to the surfmen of the island "in return for sundry kindnesses and attentions." The Louisa Hatch and the other whaler were taken beyond the marine league and burned. The crews of these three prizes augmented the population of the colony until taken off by Brazilian ships.

The Governor's courtesies were disapproved by the home government. By the time the Florida reached the island, seven days after the departure of the Alabama, he had been recalled.

The Agrippina should have been at Fernando de Noronha by the time the Alabama reached there. Semmes waited for her impatiently and in vain. At length he concluded that she had found a better market for her services and had abandoned her obligation to him. That was not the case. The Agrippina was merely delayed and, although she never again served a Confederate cruiser, she spent many weeks trying to come up with one in a South American port to make delivery of her cargo of coal. After waiting eleven days the Alabama went to sea on April 21.

She was headed southerly for Bahia. On the way she burned a whaler, a large ship bound for Shanghai with coal, a small clipper for Shanghai, and a handsome outbound California clipper with general cargo. The destruction of these prizes burdened the Alabama with more than a hundred prisoners. Several of them were women. Young Lieutenant Sinclair records a heartfelt comment, "The ladies, bless their sweet hearts, are desirable company at all times and places with but few exceptions. One of the exceptions is the crowded wardroom of a man-of-war."

The Alabama arrived at Bahia on May 11, 1863. Two days later the Georgia came in and word was received that the Florida was less than four hundred miles to the north, at Pernambuco.

At this time the only pursuit ship in the South Atlantic was the U.S.S. Mohican. The Vanderbilt, which should have been there, was detained in the West Indies by Wilkes. The Mohican was close upon the trail. At Pernambuco she was a week behind the Florida. At Bahia she missed the Alabama and the Georgia by three days. The consuls at Pernambuco and Bahia were using every means to ascertain the movements of the Confederate ships and communicate them to the Mohican. On May 27 the Consul at Pernambuco reported that he had been working sixteen hours a day for a month and was physically exhausted. An American commercial firm in Pernambuco sent a messenger to the Cape Verde Islands with a letter for any American man-of-war that might be found there, advising of the activities of the Florida and the Alabama.

As early as May 29, nine marine insurance companies in New York learned that the Florida and the Alabama were operating near the Equator and reported to the Secretary of the Navy, who at once relieved Wilkes of the command of the West Indian squadron for "wholly inexcusable" misconduct in holding the Vanderbilt, and ordered that vessel to join the search. The problem presented could not be solved, as in the case of raids along the North Atlantic coast, by sending out miscellaneous craft for short dashes. Only fast ships with sufficient coal capacity to give them a long cruising radius could be sent to equatorial waters in search of enemy vessels especially designed and built for the work they were doing there.

The Alabama stayed at Bahia ten days, departing on May 21. Until July 6 she cruised in latitudes varying from 12 to 14 degrees south of the Equator and in longitudes from 30 to 35 degrees West; that is to say, off the Brazilian coast between Bahia and Rio de Janeiro. In this vicinity she took eight prizes bound for Calcutta, Rio de Janeiro, Montevideo, Buenos Aires, San Francisco, and Antwerp (from Callao). Five of them were burned and two bonded.

One of these was the 500-ton bark Conrad, Buenos Aires to New York, with a cargo of Argentine wool, taken June 20. Lieutenant Sinclair says, "A more beautiful specimen of American clipper could not be produced, new, well-found, and fast." Semmes armed the Conrad with two brass 12-pounders which had been found on an earlier prize; put Lieutenant Low and fifteen men on board; renamed and commissioned her as the C.S.C. Tuscaloosa.

Semmes determined to try the hunting off the Cape of Good Hope on the track of vessels homeward bound from the East Indies, where the Georgia also was headed. He ordered the Tuscaloosa to cruise on her own and join him at the Cape.

For sixteen lonely days he saw no sail. Then the ships for northern Europe began to appear and many were overhauled. All proved to be neutrals. On July 6 Semmes noted, "I have ... spent a busy Sabbath Day, without having time even to read a chapter in the Bible, and all for nothing—one Dutchman and two Englishmen."

V

On July 29 the Alabama came to anchor in a small landlocked harbor a few miles north of Cape Town. Her life was now half over and it may be said that her effective work had been done. She had taken fifty-four prizes, whereas in the remaining eleven months of her career she took only ten. The next two months, which she spent cruising on and off the Cape of Good Hope, were the most barren period of her cruise, netting only one prize. During this time, however, there were some curious transactions on shore, in which international law was heavily laced with Cape brandy.

From time to time the crew of the Alabama was a source of anxiety to the officers. Hastily recruited from the riffraff of the Liverpool sailortown, they were as inferior human material as a man-of-war had ever assembled. A few veterans of the British navy did not suffice to leaven the lump. They had given trouble at Martinique and at Jamaica. At Cape Town it became serious. On August 1 Semmes noted, "I have a precious set of rascals on board, faithless in the matter of abiding by their contracts, liars, thieves, and drunkards." Shore leave could not be denied men who would have mutinied to get it and who had been at sea more than two months. Each shore party resulted in losses by desertion. The hospitality and shelter of the American consulate were at the disposal of deserters. The seductions of the Consul and the attractions of the port cost the Alabama twenty-eight men. Semmes appealed to the police. With the utmost goodwill toward the Confederate cause, the municipal authorities could not see their way to arresting British subjects who had committed no offense, in order to compel them to serve against their will in a foreign warship. Just before leaving South African waters the Alabama got about a dozen replacements by shipping as "passengers" drunken men obtained from a crimp, and enlisting them beyond the three-mile limit. Semmes paid the crimp for bringing the drunks on board, at the same time reviling the Consul for harboring the other drunks whom they had replaced.

Two episodes, one on August 5 and the other on the 8th, brought on legal complications. The first was the capture of a prize, the bark Sea Bride, of Boston, approaching Cape

Town with miscellaneous merchandise. The Alabama caught her within sight of shore. The entire population of Cape Town, on foot, in all the available cabs, and in every sort of boat, including several racing shells, went out along shore to witness the capture. The consul at once protested that the bark was taken in the territorial waters of the Colony. There was much debate and a war of affidavits. The colonial authorities finally concluded that the Sea Bride was more than three miles offshore. His experience in Cuba with the first prizes of the Sumter had taught Semmes not to bring a capture into port. He sent her up along the west coast of Africa until she came to the country of the Hottentots. Lying off a place called Angra Pequeña, Semmes sold the Sea Bride and cargo to a citizen of Cape Town for $16,940 in cash. The purchaser knew he could not get a good title to an uncondemned prize; indeed Semmes cautioned him. He knew, too, that if he brought his purchase into Cape Town, she was technically liable to be held for her American owner. He counted on being able to dispose of the cargo at a profit on his total investment. For this purpose he took the Sea Bride around the Cape to Madagascar, where apparently she was put under a local flag and disappears from the record. Semmes collected the price in gold. Although it was prize money, it was never distributed among the officers and crew of the captor. It was applied to the operating expenses of the ship.

The other occurrence was the arrival on August 8 of the Tuscaloosa (ex-Conrad), which had been cruising, had captured a prize and bonded it because of neutral cargo, and now came to rejoin the mother ship as ordered.

Again the Consul protested. He said the Tuscaloosa was an uncondemned prize and must be detained for her owner. In this the Admiral of the Port supported him. Rear Admiral Sir Baldwin W. Walker, R.N., was a warm Southern sympathizer, most hospitable to the Confederate officers. But he was also a stickler for obeying the rules. On the arrival of the Tuscaloosa Semmes claimed the same rights for her as for the Alabama, saying the two vessels were alike commissioned cruisers of the Confederate States Navy. The Admiral observed that the Tuscaloosa was peddling a cargo of wool. He considered this inconsistent with the status of a naval vessel. He maintained that the bark was a prize and, having come into a neutral port, must be held for her owner.

The colonial Attorney General overruled the Admiral and she was permitted to go to sea. The case, which was now moot by reason of the Tuscaloosa's departure, was referred to London. In due course a ruling was received reversing the Attorney General and sustaining the Admiral. It turned out that this was merely for consumption by the Consul and Secretary Seward.

In January, 1864, the Tuscaloosa came into Cape Town again. She had been cruising without success between Africa and Brazil, and had called at a Brazilian port. She was now back at the Cape to meet the Alabama in accordance with orders. Having received the ruling from Downing Street, the Governor seized her and notified the American Consul. Lieutenant Low was aggrieved. He had been permitted to depart on the former occasion, and now his ship was taken from him. The matter was again referred to London while the vessel was held. This time the Duke of Newcastle, who had made the previous ruling when he knew the Tuscaloosa had gone to sea and could not be reached, said the circumstances had changed. Having been permitted to come in and go out once, said His Grace, her commander had a right to assume that he might do so again. "Her Majesty's government have, therefore, come to the opinion, founded on the circumstances of this particular case, that the Tuscaloosa ought to be released, with a warning, however, to the captain of the Alabama that ships of war of the belligerents are not to be allowed to bring prizes into British ports and that it rests with Her Majesty's government to decide to what vessels that character belongs." For the Governor's consolation the noble duke added, "I am by no means surprised that the conclusions to which you were led have not in all instances been adopted on fuller consideration by Her Majesty's government." The reader will perhaps agree with Professor Soley that "Comment on these proceedings is hardly necessary."

Before the announcement of the final ruling permitting the Tuscaloosa to depart the second time, Lieutenant Low had left Cape Town; the Alabama had returned thither and left again and there was no Confederate personnel there to take her to sea. She remained at the Cape until restored to her owners at the end of the war.

VI

The Alabama hung about the Cape from July 28 to September 24, 1863. The sea was populous with all flags except the Stars and Stripes. On August 16 the C.S.C. Georgia came into the neighborhood. The two cruisers did not meet.

Meanwhile the U.S.S. Vanderbilt, released by Wilkes immediately before relinquishing command of the West Indies fleet, had resumed the chase which had been interrupted for six months. Commander Baldwin followed the course originally laid down for him by the Department. His orders, issued in January and carried out beginning with June, were:

"When you are perfectly satisfied that the Alabama has left the Gulf or the West Indies and gone to some other locality, you will proceed along the coast of Brazil to Fernando de Noronha and Rio de Janeiro, making inquiries at such places as you think advisable. From Rio continue your course to the Cape of Good Hope, thence back to St. Helena, Cape Verde, the Canaries, Madeira, Lisbon, the Western Islands, and New York. If at any point word is obtained of the Alabama or any other rebel craft, you will pursue her without regard to these instructions."

As we have seen, the Vanderbilt was close behind the Georgia and Alabama in Brazilian waters. Replenishing his rapidly consumed coal supply at Rio de Janeiro, where he met the Mohican, Baldwin cruised for a fortnight off Brazil and then crossed to St. Helena, midway the South Atlantic, where he stopped for coal. Here on August 15 he learned from a northbound vessel that the Alabama and Georgia were off the Cape.

The Vanderbilt arrived there on August 30, the morning after the Georgia left. The Federal ship played a game of hide-and-seek with the Alabama for a week. They were in and out of the same South African ports a day or two apart, without sighting each other. The only injury the Vanderbilt did the Alabama was to carry off two piles of coal upon which Semmes was counting.

Concluding that the Confederate cruiser had turned eastward, Baldwin started in that direction on September 7. The pursuer thus became the pursued, though neither knew it. The Alabama remained off the Cape until the 24th, when the speedy Vanderbilt was 2,600 miles to the northeast at Mauritius. Semmes then started in that direction. Seconded by an eddy of the Agulhas current and by the Brave West Winds, the Alabama, proceeding without steam, logged 221 miles in a day and crossed the Indian Ocean at an average rate of 171. She missed the Vanderbilt by keeping far to the south of Mauritius, traversing a lonely sea where nothing was to be seen for nineteen days except a huge albatross, which was caught on a hook and line and sat a while on deck in injured dignity before taking off on its ten-foot spread of pinions.

The Brave West Winds whipped into a gale which brought the Alabama, a month out from the Cape, fairly into the area of the Dutch East Indies.

The Vanderbilt returned to Cape Town from her unsuccessful search at Mauritius, was refused coal, seized 250 tons that Semmes had stored on an island outside British jurisdiction, stopped a British bark that had on board part of the Tuscaloosa's cargo of wool, and came into serious collision with the colonial authorities for this action; and then, in accordance with her original orders, went back to policing the ocean highway off Brazil.

VII

Semmes had high hope for his East Indian adventure. The presence of a Confederate cruiser in those waters was unsuspected, though long feared, by homeward bound American craft trading from the Orient by way of the Cape of Good Hope. The Strait of Sunda, between Java and Sumatra and Malacca Strait, between the latter island and Singapore, were roadways which offered good prospects.

The hope was disappointed because the volume of shipping was smaller than Semmes anticipated, many ships being held in port through fear, and because a delay of twelve days for painting ship at Pulo Condore, French Cochin China, gave time for the rumor of the Alabama's presence to spread through the Java Sea. Three prizes were burned at Sunda Strait just three months after the last previous capture, that of the Sea Bride. Two of them, destroyed off Java Head, were westbound from Manila with hemp and sugar; the third was the fine clipper ship Contest from Yokohama to New York with tea, silk, and curios. These three prizes were burned between November 5 and 11 (1863).

At this time Semmes was having more than usual trouble with his crew. The chief officer of the Contest, while aboard the cruiser as a prisoner, observed, "Crew much dissatisfied, no prize money, no liberty, and see no prospect of getting any. Discipline very slack; steamer dirty, rigging slovenly. Semmes sometimes punishes but is afraid to push too hard; men excited; officers do not report to captain; crew do things for which they would be shot on board American man-of-war," and more to the same effect. Semmes' journal entries confirm this. He was tired, homesick, discouraged by the news of the war which reached him down to October dates through the Singapore newspapers; he was feeling old, disgusted with his crew and without friends among the officers except his devoted First Lieutenant Kell.

After cruising along the west coast of Borneo and lying

over at Condore he tried Malacca Strait. On December 22 he put into Singapore, where he found nineteen tall American merchantmen laid up in the harbor, out of his reach. He heard of others tied up at Bangkok, Canton, Shanghai, and Manila. At Singapore twelve men deserted; half a dozen were recruited. The U. S. steam sloop Wyoming, sole representative of the Navy on the China station and a fair match for the Alabama, was in the Java Sea. Commander McDougal learned of the presence of the enemy on November 22. The two ships had been within twenty-five miles of one another, unknown to either, though Semmes knew the Wyoming was in the waters and made preparations to engage her. McDougal searched all likely spots without result. At Singapore he was close enough to intercept some letters for Semmes from the Confederate agents in that port. Believing that the Alabama would continue into the China Sea, McDougal took the Wyoming from Singapore to the other great entrepôt of the East, Manila, thus unwittingly taking a direction opposite to that of his adversary.

Leaving Singapore on Christmas Eve, the Alabama was no sooner out of the strait than she took a prize which was unique among the Confederate captures, because it was a duly registered British ship, the bark Martaban of the Straits Settlements, formerly the Texan Star, with a cargo of rice for Hong Kong, shipped by Mr. Abraham Cohen of Maulmain, representing the well known house of Behn, Meyer & Company. The transfer to British registry was only ten days old. The captain admitted to Semmes that it was a device to escape capture. Accordingly Semmes burned the prize. When this was reported to Vice-Admiral Sir James Hope, he issued a sharp order to British naval officers, supported by an opinion of Lord Stowell, to "capture and send to England for adjudication in the admiralty court every vessel by which a British vessel (i.e., with legal British papers) is burned at sea." This would have sent the Royal Navy in chase of the Alabama except for a footnote that the case of the Martaban was to be regarded as doubtful. The Confederate cruisers took notice and no other such episode occurred.

Christmas Day was spent at Malacca, where the Martaban's prisoners were landed. The next day in Malacca Strait two prizes in ballast were burned.

The condition of the Alabama's bottom had been giving Semmes concern for some time. With the hull of his ship and the morale of his crew both in need of overhauling, he had no choice but to return to Europe. As early as December 15 he had determined to do so. While he could not forecast his reception, he knew the prospect of hospitality was better in France than in England, where awkward questions arising out of the Foreign Enlistment Act would have been added to the problem of neutrality. On the last day of the year the Alabama reeëntered the Indian Ocean, bound for France, her Commander anxiously hoping that she would be made as welcome as the Florida had been. Without knowing the existing status of Franco-Confederate relations, he realized that his government had lost the advantage of its earlier military prestige. Thus beset with anxiety, ill health, an ill-conditioned ship, and an unruly crew, on New Year's Day, 1864, Semmes took the Alabama out of the northwest end of Malacca Strait and turned her head once more towards Cape Town. The return course was far to the north of the one followed on the outbound voyage. It took more than three times as long and included the burning of a small prize in the center of the Indian Ocean; two calls to discharge prisoners and get fresh food, and the overhauling and release of a pilgrim ship bound from Singapore to Jiddah with a large company of the faithful on their way to Mecca. According to Semmes, the boarding party converted all of them to the Southern cause by the assurance that Confederates practiced polygamy.

Sailing southerly through the Mozambique Channel, the Alabama ran into the harbor of Cape Town on March 20. After coaling at the Cape and arguing about the Tuscaloosa, which was under detention, Semmes went once more into the Atlantic and cruised for a month in the Torrid Zone. Toward the end of April he burned his last two prizes, the ship Rockingham, Callao to Cork with guano, and the fine clipper Tycoon, New York to San Francisco with general cargo. This splendid capture was the Alabama's sixty-fourth and last prize, her fifty-fourth bonfire at sea. In the course of her wanderings the cruiser had overhauled or spoken 294 vessels of every flag afloat. Forty-five days later she sailed into Cherbourg for the purpose of docking, general overhauling, and giving her officers and crew a long holiday if French neutrality and Federal warships would permit.

CHAPTER VII

CHERBOURG,
JUNE 19, 1864

... all thy men of war, that are in thee, and all thy company which is in the midst of thee, shall fall into the midst of the seas in the day of thy ruin.—Ezekiel, 27:27.

WE HERE COMBINE into one narrative a number of eye-witness accounts of the battle between the Alabama and the Kearsarge, which took place in the mild sunlight of a Sunday morning June 19, 1864, off Cherbourg, on a sea as calm as a dish. The waters were those, as Semmes reminded his English seamen, in which their countrymen had begun the rout of the Armada nearly three centuries before.

The Alabama arrived at Cherbourg at noon on June 11. Semmes would better have put into Havre, where there were privately owned docks. Those at Cherbourg were French naval property. Permission to use them had to be obtained from the Emperor, who was making holiday at Biarritz. No decision could be reached for several days. Because of this the one-day rule was relaxed. Semmes put ashore thirty-eight men from his last two prizes.

The Kearsarge, which was built at Portsmouth, New Hampshire, in 1861, had been on special detail for a year to hunt the Alabama. She was at Flushing when Captain Winslow got a telegram from Ambassador Dayton in Paris. The men on shore were recalled by firing a gun. Winslow addressed his crew:

"Men, I congratulate you in saying that the Alabama has arrived at Cherbourg, and the Kearsarge, having a good name in France and England, is to have her cruising ground off that port."

Then he stood drinks twice around. Semmes, who knew his enemy was on the way, could have escaped with empty bunkers, an easy prey when caught. He did not try it.

On the morning of the 14th Winslow steamed into Cherbourg Harbor and sent a boat ashore to request the port authorities to turn over to him the men whom Semmes had landed there. This was refused upon Semmes' protest that it would augment the crew of the Kearsarge in a French port on the eve of battle. Winslow thereupon took the Kearsarge out beyond the breakwater without having come to anchor. Here he received a message from Semmes, relayed through the United States Consul, saying that if the Kearsarge would remain outside until the Alabama finished taking on coal, they could accommodate one another with a fight. It was a gesture. Winslow had come to the end of a year's search. Nothing could have induced him to depart, and Semmes had no real option. Judah Benjamin, writing to Slidell on September 24, 1864, complained that the Emperor's delay in acting on the request for permission to dock had forced the Alabama to go out and engage the Kearsarge. In any case, an extended stay in Cherbourg would have brought reënforcements to Winslow. The Alabama had to go out or be laid up for the rest of the war either by the French government or by Union warships. Semmes had no wish to avoid the encounter. He had a fair chance to win. We shall see that he came within an ace of winning. He had been stung by taunts in the Northern press accusing him of being a bully who never took on anyone his size or did anything except despoil helpless merchantmen. Semmes might have attempted to slip out in the night. If successful, he would have found himself with a disaffected crew, condemned to further voyaging when almost in sight of home. He was not the man to risk ship and men for a show of bravado, but when this coincided with military necessity he was not sorry. He fought because he had to and because he wished to.

At the same time, he and his officers regarded the prospect with anxiety. On Saturday night he noted in his journal, "The combat will no doubt be contested and obstinate but the two ships are so equally matched that I do not feel at liberty to decline it. God defend the right and have mercy upon the souls of those who fall as many of us must. Barometer low and weather unusually cold and blustering for the middle of June." On Sunday morning he asked young Sinclair how he thought the day would turn out. This was unusual condescension to a minor subaltern. Semmes seldom consulted anyone except Kell. He was looking for encouragement. The astonished boy answered vaguely, for he thought the outcome dubious.

The men were in better heart. Most of them were English sailors inwardbound from a long voyage. Naval discipline, however lax, had shaped them into a fairly orderly crew. Six of them were ex-naval artillerists of the British service. With a fight in prospect they were loyal to the ship and eager to win. They were tired of being called "the scum of England" by the Northern newspapers they got off the prizes. But, deeper, they were not fighting for their own; they were merely working at a job; their bright hopes of prize money had been disappointed because the Alabama had found it impossible to realize on her prizes; more than anything they wanted to get home to their tea.

Semmes communicated with his superior, Commodore Samuel Barron, senior officer of the Confederate Navy in Europe, who was in Paris, and obtained formal permission to use his own discretion, meaning, "If you win you will be decorated; if you lose, take the consequences." On the Saturday night he advised the men to make their wills and sent the ship's money and valuables ashore. Farewell parties were tendered the crew in the cafés of Cherbourg. The men had been cautioned and behaved themselves sedately. Boatswain Mecaskey and his men stayed on board to stopper down rigging and stow top hamper.

Every hotel and lodging house in the town was booked

to capacity by visitors come to see the show. The battle took on the aspect of a scheduled event. A load of sightseers from Paris came out on the first regular excursion train of the season, took up positions on the bluff with their luncheon boxes, and munched their *dejeuner* while observing the contest. Mass being over, the curé shepherded a little flock of nuns out of church and found places for them, followed by the rest of the congregation. Spectators took up positions on the bluff south of the town or in second-story windows along the front. The affair even had a theme song, composed by the Alabama's poet laureate,

> "We're homeward bound; we're homeward bound
> And soon shall stand on English ground,
> But ere that English land we see,
> We first must fight the Kearsargee."

Three Confederate officers on leave in Paris came out to join the Alabama, but the French authorities would not let them, as they had not previously been attached to the ship. A German baron and a compatriot who were in Paris on leave from the Alabama were permitted to rejoin her.

In the audience were the company of the English steam yacht Deerhound. This boat was the property of Mr. John Lancaster, an Englishman "of ease and fortune." Afterwards a minor controversy arose as to whether he was a "gentleman." Gideon Welles took the position that he was not. Semmes said that Welles lacked capacity to judge. Lancaster had been on the continent and had ordered his Welsh captain, Evan Jones, to pick him up at Cherbourg. Lancaster's family were on board, consisting of his wife, three sons, a daughter and a niece. A family council was called to decide whether they should go out and see the fight or stay in port and go to church. The casting vote was that of the little daughter, Catherine, aged nine, who voted for the battle. She was egged on by her five-year-old brother. We shall see that Captain Semmes and forty-one of his men owed their lives that day to those bloodthirsty children.

Their father owed them a peck of trouble. For months he was kept explaining his actions on that morning. The Deerhound preceded the Alabama out of the harbor and cruised about just out of gunshot.

Two French pilot boats were nosing around offshore, each with one eye cocked on the horizon for incoming customers and the other on the fight.

The ships were as evenly matched as naval antagonists are likely to be. The Kearsarge had an advantage of possibly 20 per cent. The following are the particulars of each:

Dimensions	Kearsarge	Alabama
Length of keel	198'	210'
Length over all	232'	220'
Beam	33'10"	31'8"
Depth	16'	17'
Tonnage	1031	1050
Engines (2 in each ship)	400 hp.	300 hp.

Armament

Kearsarge	Alabama
2 11-in. Dahlgren pivot guns	1 8-in. Blakely gun (rifle, 110 lbs.)
1 30-pounder rifle	1 8-in. shell gun
4 32-pounders	6 32-pounders
Metal in broadside, 430 lbs.	Metal in broadside, 360 lbs.

Personnel

163, nearly all American	149, majority British

Rig

Sloop	Bark

The vessels were approximately the same age. Each had steam and sail power. The Kearsarge had been docked within three months. This gave her an advantage in speed over the Alabama, which had never been docked. The Kearsarge gunners were in better practice than those of the Alabama.

The Kearsarge had two other points of superiority. First, her powder was effective, whereas that of the Alabama had not been replenished in the twenty-two months during which she had been cruising in all climates. Black powder will deteriorate in that length of time when stored in a magazine on shore. The changes in temperature had accelerated the loss of explosive force of the Alabama's stock. The shells from the Kearsarge went off with a bright flash followed by a faint blue vapor that drifted away; whereas those from the Alabama gave out a dull flame and sluggish grey smoke.

Second, the Kearsarge wore a coat of mail. She was protected by 120 fathoms of chain cable hung vertically on her sides, covered with 1-inch deal boards. This was intended to protect her engineroom. It had been in place for a year with no attempt at secrecy. According to Lieutenant Sinclair, the Port Admiral told Semmes about this protective covering some days before the fight and advised him not to engage the Kearsarge on this account. Sinclair remarks that the Alabama could have been protected in the same way. The materials were lying in her chain locker. Semmes said he knew nothing about it. In his bitterness of spirit after he had lost his ship, he magnified it into a grievance. He thought it unfair. He persuaded himself that he had not gone into a battle but into a duel (he used the term) with an opponent who cheated by secretly putting on a bullet-proof shirt. This is a curious misconception of the character of warfare to take possession of the mind of a professional naval officer of lifelong training, whose own vessel was born in deception and who for nearly two years had been disguising her with false colors to decoy unarmed merchantmen. The Alabama "changed shapes with Proteus for advantages." This was the simple duty of her commander. The remarkable thing was that Semmes should have considered that an enemy warship owed him more than he had owed helpless enemy merchants, and that he should have seemed to think of battle as a form of sport.

Yet you cannot blame him. He had loved the Alabama with a sailor's devotion to a ship that had become his home. He had fed, diapered, punished, and cursed the crew as though they had been his own children. More than half of them had been with him from the beginning. His discipline had turned a lawless gang into man-of-war's men. The naval tradition of noblesse, which he always stressed, required him to suppose that he loved them.

Then, in an hour, all was lost.

Semmes was an opinionated, wordy man. Confronted with a problem, he acted with decision. At the same time he was reviewing the circumstances in theological terms, demolishing his handcuffed adversary with language (while burning his ship), justifying actions that needed no warrant and could have none except the ultimate rationale of war. Such a man cannot be denied the rationalization of his grief. His voluble self-defenses, hidden doubts, surface vanities, would interest an analyst. This is a story of the sea, not of the soul.

The Kearsarge was standing on and off beyond the three-mile limit. Ambassador Dayton in Paris had cautioned Winslow to be careful to avoid hostile acts in French water. Winslow had no reason to expect the Alabama at any particular moment. Young Dayton, son of the Ambassador, learned of Semmes' plan in Cherbourg and spent the night trying to get out to Winslow with the information, but the Cherbourg police headed him off.

Aboard the ship the usual Sunday morning routine was observed. The men were inspected at quarters and dismissed for church. The bell was tolling and Winslow was standing, prayerbook in hand, when the officer of the deck shouted, "The Alabama." Winslow laid down the book and picked up the speaking trumpet, ordered the ship about, and started out to sea. It was 10:20 A.M.

After the parties ashore the men of the Alabama were required to turn in early. On Sunday morning they were given an extra good breakfast and not allowed to do any work except fire the boilers until nine o'clock. Semmes called the crew aft and addressed them for the last time:

"Officers and Seamen of the Alabama: You have at length another opportunity of meeting the enemy—the first that has been presented to you since you sunk the Hatteras. In the meantime, you have been all over the world, and it is not too much to say that you have destroyed, and driven for protection under neutral flags, one half of the enemy's commerce, which, at the beginning of the war, covered every sea. This is an achievement of which you may well be proud; and a grateful country will not be unmindful of it. The name of your ship has become a household word wherever civilization extends. Shall that name be tarnished by defeat? The thing is impossible! Remember that you are in the English Channel, the theatre of so much of the naval glory of our race, and that the eyes of all Europe are at this moment upon you. The flag that floats over you is that of a young Republic, who bids defiance to her enemies, whenever, and wherever found. Show the world that you know how to uphold it! Go to your quarters."

The ship was made ready for action; the gun crews stripped to the waist. Semmes put on formal dress for the occasion; frock-coated uniform with three rows of brass buttons, gold-braided epaulettes, and sword. He stood on the horseblock, a platform just forward of the mizzenmast.

The Alabama got under way at 9:45. The harbor was full of French shipping. As the Alabama passed the battleship Napoleon, the French band played a Confederate air, and the rigging was manned with cheering sailors. The ironclad frigate Couronne followed the Alabama to the territorial limit, stopped, and remained precisely on the line throughout the fight. A peculiarity of this battle was that the contestants had a ready-made escape. When either got tired of fighting she could retire (or try to) within the marine league so carefully marked by the vigilance of the Couronne, and thumb her nose at her adversary. Semmes attempted to avail himself of this refuge when it was too late. Winslow was apprehensive of the move, while realizing that it was open to him if his fortune started running the other way.

On the Alabama the movement of the Kearsarge was correctly interpreted not as flight but as a movement to get fighting room outside of French waters. Winslow proceeded to a point between six and seven miles off shore, went about, and steamed straight for the Alabama at full speed, hoping to run her down. The Alabama sheered to port to avoid the collision. The two vessels started to pursue each other clockwise around the perimeter of a circle about half a mile across, gradually diminishing to 400 yards. Round and round they went, broadside to broadside, at opposite ends of the diameter. A 3-knot current drifted the circular field to westward, so that a diagram of the fight shows a spiral movement which is deceptive.

Semmes started the shooting by firing his 100-pound Blakely gun, followed by three broadsides, before the guns of the Kearsarge spoke. This shooting was very wild. Winslow then replied with a broadside. From this time on the fire was incessant until the ships were describing their seventh circle.

The marksmanship of the Kearsarge gunners was better than that shown on the Alabama. Confederate testimony on this point is that of Bulloch, who says, "The result of the action was determined by the superior accuracy of the firing from the Kearsarge."

The Kearsarge gunners had been trained by much target practice. With every opportunity for exercise in shooting at the prizes, Semmes did little of it, in order to conserve his ammunition. It turned out to be false economy.

The superiority of the Kearsarge in gunnery was the more noticeable because she presented a better target than the Alabama. Her bunkers contained only 170 tons of coal, which caused her black sides to ride high; the protective sheathing did not reach the water line; whereas the Alabama, with 320 tons in bunkers, sat low in the water and had a list to starboard caused by the massing of her batteries on that side. The Alabama's aim was too high throughout. Few of her projectiles reached the side of the Kearsarge; none struck the vulnerable belt below the sheathing. Only 14 out of 370 shots hit the hull of the Kearsarge while 25 or 30 went through the rigging. The inexperience in gunnery on the Alabama resulted in shells being fired without removing the "patch," i.e., sealed against explosion. Winslow told his gunners to aim below the water line and make every shot tell. He fired 174 shots, less than half as many as the Alabama. The only way to estimate the number of hits is by their effect. This was terrific. Great holes were torn in the sides of the Alabama by shells exploding after they had entered the ship. She was shot to pieces.

Indifferent as her shooting was, one shell from the Alabama nearly ended the battle in the first ten minutes.[1] Her 8-inch gun sent over a projectile that penetrated the sternpost of the Kearsarge. It was a vital spot. The ship shivered throughout her length with the impact. This shell buried itself in the timber and did not explode. Had it done its work it would have torn out the stern of the corvette, destroyed her steerage, and left her the easy victim of her antagonist. Southern gentlemen, who are sometimes represented in sentimental romances as devoted to mint juleps and classical allusions, may have remarked that Achilles had been wounded in the heel and did not die.

That was the only real chance the Alabama had. Semmes observed that the shells which struck the side of the enemy merely rebounded into the water; so he ordered his 32-

[1] One account says this shell was fired towards the close of the action.

pounders to pour in solid shot alternately with the firing of the rifle.

It did no good. The rigging of the Kearsarge was somewhat damaged. The deal-board sheathing of the chain armor was knocked off. It is useless to speculate whether these hits would have penetrated if the Alabama's powder had been better. Two shots entered gun ports, one passing through the port on the opposite side, the other taking effect in the hammock netting. One shell ignited a fire, which was quickly extinguished. A rifle shot broke the engine-room skylight, another made a hole in the funnel. The men on the Kearsarge were encouraged by a sailor's good omen. An American flag had been sent to the main truck in a stop, i.e., folded and tied. One of the Alabama's shots cut the halyard confining the stop and the Stars and Stripes broke out free.

The tension on the Kearsarge was also relieved by a little comedy. There was a small gun on board, a 12-pound howitzer not listed in the ship's armament. Two elderly quartermasters were assigned to this gun with instructions to do nothing until ordered. Unable to endure the inaction, the two old sea dogs loaded and fired their pea-shooter steadily until their ammunition ran out, meanwhile directing a continuous stream of billingsgate at one another. They accomplished nothing except to add to the noise. The division officer merely grinned at them and the deck crew were greatly amused.

Meanwhile the Alabama was being put out of action. The spanker gaff carrying the colors was broken off and the flag was run up on the mizzenmast. The fire of the after pivot gun on the Kearsarge was deadly. Semmes offered a reward for the silencing of this gun and turned his entire battery upon it. The only effect was to wound three men. These were the only casualties on the Kearsarge. The majority of the Alabama's casualties occurred among Joe Wilson's crew of eighteen men at the pivot gun. All but one were disabled or killed. The deck was cumbered with dismembered bodies. They were replaced by young Dick Armstrong and the crew of one of the 32-pounders which thereafter was not manned.

Each commander said afterwards that he wanted to get to close quarters, board the enemy, and fight across decks in the fashion of the naval classics. Each asserted that the other avoided this. The nearest they came to grips was in the seventh circuit when Winslow got ready to send in grape shot. He was forestalled by the Alabama's white flag.

The ships had about completed their seventh circuit when the engineer of the Alabama came up and reported that his fires were out. Semmes sent Kell below to learn how long the ship could float. The men in the rising water of the engine room were angrily swearing that Old Beeswax was leaving them down there to drown. Nevertheless, they waited there for orders. Kell reported that the ship could last ten minutes. Semmes thereupon tried to right the Alabama by shifting guns to port but only got one over. He struck his colors, ran up a white flag, and attempted to make the French coast under two jibs and the big fore trysail, with a very light wind. John Roberts, the man who went to set the jibs, finished the job and returned to the deck screaming in death. He was completely gutted.

At this point something like a patriotic mutiny occurred on the Alabama. The horseblock was besieged by men protesting against the surrender. There is conflicting evidence as to whether some of the junior officers rushed aft and continued to fire in defiance of orders. It seems certain that after seeing the white flag, Winslow fired five more shots. He said that the Alabama was shooting from under her white flag and he feared a ruse. "Was this a time," wrote Kell, "for a ship to use a ruse, a Yankee trick?" The surgeon of the Kearsarge complained that the Alabama was not waging "Christian warfare." These controversies and alibis are of no interest now. The Alabama was already settling by the stern.

Semmes sent Master's Mate Fullam with a boatload of wounded to the Kearsarge to ask assistance. It then developed that the chief damage done by the Alabama's shooting had been to the boats of the Kearsarge. Only two of them were not disabled. These were sent to pick up men. Semmes complained, with bitter implication, that the help from the Kearsarge came tardily.

Kell gave the order, "Every man to save himself, to jump overboard with a spar, an oar, or a grating, and get out of the vortex." Those who jumped were warm with their work and found the June sea icy. Two of the swimmers carried packets of papers entrusted to them by Semmes, which they restored to him afterwards. The Alabama's only remaining seaworthy boat was put over and filled with wounded and those who could not swim.

As the wounded were being carried over the side, one of them asked for Lieutenant Kell and kissed his hand. Kell knelt and took the man's head in his arms. "God bless you, Mr. Kell," said Seaman King. He died on the Kearsarge.

The survivors never ceased to deplore the needless loss of two lives at this juncture, those of Bartelli, the steward, and Dave, the little black wardroom boy. They were drowned because on Saturday night when the crew were mustered for instructions these two did not mention that they could not swim. Apparently Bartelli remained silent through pride; Dave, because while he stayed near his white folks no harm could come to him. The wonder is he did not walk dry-soled ashore.

The French pilot boats drew in and picked up a few swimmers. Winslow shouted to the Deerhound for help. She already had two boats overboard.

Floating on some empty shell boxes lay the dead body of Llewellyn, assistant surgeon of the Alabama, an English doctor of high station.

Two men pulled off Semmes' boots. He removed his coat because of the weight of the buttons, and put on a lifebelt, but dignity balked at taking off his trousers and he went into the water impeded with clothing, his right arm disabled

The Sinking of the Alabama Off Cherbourg.

The Gun That Sank the Alabama. On Board the U.S.S. Kearsarge. *Courtesy of the Office of the U. S. Naval Records and Library.*

by a slight wound from a fragment of shell. Kell got hold of a grating and went with him. When clear of the Alabama they turned to watch her.

She was down by the stern. The guns and everything loose had slid aft. The inrushing water, surrounding enclosed spaces in the hull, formed immense air bubbles that burst with agonizing sobs on reaching the hatches. As they watched, she upended, pointed her black bow skyward, and disappeared.

The elderly man in the sea averted his face and resumed his left-arm stroke. The time was 12:24.

One of the Deerhound's boats fished out the commander and executive officer of the Alabama. Semmes crouched in the bottom and was covered with a tarpaulin to avoid detection from the Kearsarge. Four years afterwards, when the Kearsarge was on a courtesy visit to New Zealand, her commanding officer, Commander J. F. Thornton, told the Governor of the Colony that Winslow knew Semmes was in that boat and looked the other way. He did not wish to see his old shipmate executed.

Fifth Lieutenant Sinclair was among those picked up by a boat from the Kearsarge. With one of the men he slipped quietly over the gunwale and swam to a Deerhound boat.

The Kearsarge rescued seventy men; the Deerhound forty-two; the pilot boats fifteen. One of the men wounded on the Kearsarge, Seaman Gowin, died. The Alabama's casualty list was nine killed, twenty wounded, twelve drowned.

One of the pilot boats took its guests to Cherbourg; the other to the Kearsarge. Lancaster asked Semmes where he wanted to go and, at his request, took him to Southampton. Winslow took his prisoners to the marine hospital in Cherbourg, where he left the wounded and paroled the others, who returned to England.

The spectators went home. They were in the position of a prize-ring crowd who had seen a lively bout in which the odds-on favorite had been knocked out in the seventh round.

The reader will wish to know what became of the persons of the drama. The Alabama's crew were paid off and given honorable discharges as soon as Semmes could get access to funds and reach the men. Semmes was feted by the United Service Club in London, lionized by English society. The sister of William E. Gladstone, then Chancellor of the Exchequer, besought him to draw on her for money. Schoolboys all over England wrote volunteering to serve in his next command. He toured Europe, returned to Richmond via Mexico, was commissioned a rear admiral and a brigadier general by a government which then had only honors to bestow, and assigned to a flotilla of gunboats in the James, which he blew up with a grand fireworks display when the cause failed. After the war he was imprisoned in Washington for four months. Then he lectured and taught for a few years. On August 30, 1877, he died in Mobile in the Catholic faith, which he had held through life.

And Captain Winslow? Believe it or not, he drew a censure from Washington for paroling his prisoners. Secretary Seward made Mr. Adams try to get them back, fearing that the parole involved a recognition of the Alabama as a belligerent ship. As most of them were British subjects, Lord Russell gave Adams an argument but no prisoners. The opinion of Admiral Farragut was more favorable: "I would rather have fought that battle than any ever fought on the ocean," he wrote. "I go for Winslow's promotion."

The unfortunate Lancaster came in for castigation in official despatches and letters to the press for not turning in Semmes and the other forty-one survivors picked up by the Deerhound. Lancaster had put some old clothes on them and landed them at Southampton, where the principal hotel excluded them because they were not well enough dressed. Lancaster had to explain to government officials and newspapers that he was unable to see how a drowning man picked up out of the open sea could be anybody's prisoner; that when Winslow shouted to him, "For God's sake, save all you can," he took it as an appeal to save life, not a deputization to capture prisoners for the Kearsarge.

The Federal press accused the Deerhound of being a Confederate naval auxiliary and referred to her as a "Royal yacht." Lancaster "begged to observe that he was under the impression" that his yacht was at Cherbourg to suit his own convenience. If he had gone out to join the fight, he posed the rhetorical question, Was it likely he would have taken his wife along?

What of the Kearsarge? In the Naval Museum at Annapolis you may see a large piece of oak timber protected by a casing of chicken wire. In it is embedded an unexploded globular iron shell, 6.96 inches in diameter, weighing 55 pounds. The timber is a section of the sternpost of the Kearsarge. It was sawed out and sent to President Lincoln by his personal request. The dud is the one which, by not exploding, settled the fate of the Alabama.[1] It was Winslow's only trophy.

After the battle, the Kearsarge proceeded homeward via the Virgin Islands. In the harbor of St. Thomas she met the U.S.S. Wachusett escorting the conquered Florida. The Kearsarge continued to serve the navy for thirty years. She broke up on Roncador Reef in the Caribbean, February 2, 1894.

Lastly, the Alabama. Semmes always said that the shell in the sternpost was her only memento. That was an error. With the ship's papers, money, and other treasures sent ashore for safety the night before the battle, he had cached seventy-five chronometers, wound and running.

---

[1] Frank M. Bennett, in *The Steam Navy of the United States,* expresses the opinion, for reasons which he gives in detail, that this shell did not imperil the Kearsarge. The general belief is to the contrary.

CHAPTER VIII

THE GEORGIA
AND THE RAPPAHANNOCK

The pot-bellied merchant, foreboding no wrong,
With headlight and sidelight he lieth along
Till, lightless and lightfoot and lurking, leap we
To force him discover his business at sea.
—Kipling, *The Cruisers*

THE BUILDER'S NAME for the Georgia was the Japan. At her launching she was christened the Virginia. She followed the usual course with respect to ownership. A member of the firm of Fraser, Trenholm & Company had her built for his personal account at Dumbarton on the Clyde. She was registered in his name as a merchantman in April, 1863. She was an iron-framed steam brig 291 feet long and had a gross register tonnage of 427.

Off the French coast she met an ocean tug, the Alar, with five small guns, ammunition, stores, and men. All were easily transferred, except the crew. These men had been engaged in Glasgow. When the Alar met the Virginia, many of them repented of their bargain and refused to proceed. As a solatium to the American Minister for letting the Virginia get away against his protests, the Crown prosecutor charged those who had induced them to enlist with violation of the Foreign Enlistment Act. The accused were fined £50 each, which was a merely nominal amercement of the Confederate treasury.

The ship, renamed the Georgia, under the command of Lieutenant William L. Maury, had to proceed short-handed. She headed south. Below the Canaries she captured and burned the large New York ship Dictator, 1,293 tons, Liverpool to Hong Kong. Many of the Dictator's crew enlisted, augmenting the cruiser's force to a workable number.

Dodging a Union warship off the Cape Verde Islands, the Georgia entered the sea lanes off Brazil. On May 3, 1863, she met the Alabama in Bahia. The Florida was also in these waters.

After exchanging civilities with the officers and crew of the Alabama, the Georgia coasted southward. Almost within the territorial waters of Brazil she captured the 1,280-ton ship George Griswold, Cardiff to Callao with coal, manned by a crew of Negroes. This vessel was bonded, presumably because of neutral cargo.

Veering off into the Atlantic, the Georgia took several more prizes. One of these, on June 22 (1863) was the 436-ton bark Good Hope, Boston to Algoa Bay. The master of this vessel, Captain Gordon, had died, and his young son who was on board had insisted upon carrying his remains crudely preserved in brine. Lieutenant Maury had the remains brought on board, wrapped them in the United States colors, and conducted the service for the Burial of the Dead at Sea, while the Good Hope was standing by in flames, like a fiery chariot awaiting the spirit of her late commander.

This funeral service was probably unique in the manner of its termination. While Maury was reading the prayer book, Midshipman Morgan, in charge of the deck, received a report from the lookout that a sail was approaching. He whispered to Maury, who calmly read on to "We commit his body to the deep." Then, as the shotted shroud slid overboard, he cried the command, "Beat to Quarters!"

The stranger was the 340-ton bark F. W. Seaver, Captain Snow. Not recognizing the character of the Georgia,[1] he put off a boat and went aboard her, full of concern for the burning

[1] Midshipman Morgan says the Seaver had been in the Pacific since 1860 and Snow did not know of the war. *Hunt's Merchant Magazine*, October, 1863, lists the Seaver as bound from Boston to Hong Kong. This list contains a number of errors.

vessel near by. "Can I be of any assistance?" he exclaimed as he stepped on the deck. "How did she catch fire?" Maury said that he "would stand court-martial before he would burn the ship of a man who had come on an errand of mercy to help fellow seamen in distress." Evidently Maury was not indurated with his job. He took a bond, made a cartel of the bark, and sent her away with his prisoners.

Twenty degrees south of the Equator the Georgia came to anchor in the shadow of the barren island of Trinidad, an inaccessible reef-bound mountain peak projecting from the sea, which was to come briefly into the news thirty years later when the son-in-law of the late John H. Flagler attempted to colonize it with himself as king and hundreds of sea turtles as subjects. Its only value in 1863 was to afford a cover from which the Georgia made sallies for prizes pausing there to adjust their chronometers. She bagged two, the ships Constitution, Philadelphia to Valparaiso, burned, and the City of Bath, Callao to Antwerp, bonded. Then she sailed for the Cape of Good Hope, where she learned that the Alabama had departed a few hours previously for the East Indies. The hospitalities of the Cape were extended to the Confederates as usual.

The U.S.S. Vanderbilt was now hunting the hunters on and off the Cape. The Georgia eluded her by joining a British tea fleet running home from the East, a fortunate convoy for the cruiser, as the Vanderbilt had six times her fighting strength. Presently the Georgia captured the square rigger John Watt.

By this time (July, 1863), the hull of the Georgia was so fouled with marine growth that she could not make half her normal speed under steam. She was dragging a crop of grass six inches deep. Maury went to the Canary Islands, where he got fuel and provisions and gave his crew a run on shore. He was not able to clean his hull there and was obliged to seek a drydock. Continuing his northing, he captured the Bold Hunter and thereby nearly made an end of the Georgia.

THE GEORGIA

The Bold Hunter was fired during a gale. With no hand at her helm the flaming prize made straight for the cruiser. As she was bearing down, the Georgia's engines failed. Midshipman Morgan describes the peril:

"In an instant the Bold Hunter was upon us. She recoiled and rushed at us again like a mad bull. This time, plunging from the top of a huge wave, she came down upon our taffrail doing much damage."

The Bold Hunter suddenly sheared off and passed to leeward "the fires seething in her vitals and leaping up her beautiful white sails to her mastheads and then running down her tarry rigging to her body again as she rolled and plunged and seemed to writhe in mortal agony until relief came in one deep dive and she disappeared. Never had a ship without a crew made a more desperate and damaging attack upon her pitiless tormentor."

When the Georgia reached the naval base at Cherbourg late in October (1863) she came into the midst of the entire French ironclad fleet, including the flagship Couronne, which was to be the official witness to the battle between the Alabama and the Kearsarge the following year. There was a wait of four months at Cherbourg before the official permission came to dock the ship. When it was granted, the examination showed her to be unfit for further service. As she was less than a year old, one senses the element of war profits in her construction. Maury was detached, Lieutenant Evans, a junior officer, was placed in command, and the Georgia hastened south to a rendezvous off the coast of Morocco, where she was expected to transfer her battery to the C.S.C. Rappahannock, which had been lying at Calais.

II

The Rappahannock has been mentioned incidentally several times in the preceding chapters. She was originally a decrepit British naval despatch steamer called the Victor. Finding her unseaworthy, the Admiralty put her up at auction in 1863, and one of Bulloch's under-cover agents bought her and turned her over to the Confederate government under the name of the Scylla. As we have seen, British policy in the summer of 1863 had moved to a strict enforcement of neutrality, and when the suspicions of the Ministry were aroused after the sale, the vessel was ordered detained in the Thames estuary. On November 24 she managed to get to sea under pretense of making a trial trip. When she was fairly out in the channel, her engines failed and she went adrift, bringing up off Calais. Lieutenant Charles M. Fauntleroy, C.S.N., was placed in command with orders to dock and repair her and proceed to meet the Georgia. She was named the Rappahannock, though Fauntleroy called her the White Elephant. He was sure that the small guns of the Georgia would be useless to the Rappahannock. "With a battery I could probably do some good in an attack upon the enemy's blockading fleet by taking them by surprise. They certainly would be surprised if the venture were made with the guns which it is proposed I should take, and the result would be a disgrace in all human likelihood." His superior, Commodore Barron, at headquarters in Paris, was of a different opinion. He agreed that the proposed armament was inadequate but thought it would "spread a wholesome alarm amongst the insurance offices to which the United States merchant vessels would apply." He declined to change his order to take the ship out to meet the Georgia.

To add to Fauntleroy's vexations, a French merchant ship, the Nil, attempted to nudge the Rappahannock out of her berth so as to occupy it herself. According to Lieutenant Shryock, executive officer of the Confederate vessel, "this insolent merchant captain" made a "reckless and passionate attempt to compel this vessel to make way for his." The result was that the Nil fouled the Rappahannock and then sued her for damages in a local court. Lieutenant Shryock was a witness for his ship. He complained of the rudeness of the master of the Nil. The court retorted that merchant ships "could

The Rappahannock in the Harbor at Calais.
From Harper's Weekly, *January 16, 1864.*

The Florida and the Rappahannock.
From Harper's Weekly, *August 6, 1864.*

not be expected to exercise the same delicate discrimination that vessels of war do." The court awarded the Nil a judgment of 200 francs. Lieutenant Shryock assured His Honor that this "was the most wanton insult that I had ever known to be offered to a vessel of war by the people of any nation, barbarous or civilized." The court added insult to injury by sending a bailiff, who nailed a handbill to the mainmast of the Rappahannock "in the presence of the flag" and placarded the town with similar bills advertising her for sale at public vendue to satisfy the judgment of 200 francs. The outraged Fauntleroy had to pay it.

These proceedings were not helpful in recommending the Rappahannock to the good will of the French authorities. When she drifted into Calais, the embarrassments of the French government over the Confederate ships under construction at Bordeaux and Nantes were acute and the fortunes of the Confederacy were waning. Fauntleroy was relieved of the necessity of taking her out by a French gunboat which was stationed across her bow, interning her for the duration of the war.

After the war the Rappahannock turned up in Liverpool under the name of the Beatrice and was ultimately condemned and sold for the benefit of the United States. She had no substantial value.

III

Off Mogador the Georgia waited long. Some of the junior officers went ashore and were assailed by a large party of sinister looking Moors armed with their long guns. The Confederates hurriedly retreated to their boat and reported the affair to the commanding officer, who "declared war against Morocco" and shelled the shore for an hour.

The Confederacy's only foreign war was broken up late the same afternoon by an onshore gale, during which the Georgia's engine broke down twice, the anchors would not hold, and the ship got among the rocks. The shore was crowded with hostile Moors. After dark the little cruiser, half disabled, managed to beat to sea.

She made her way back to France, calling at Bordeaux. Then she went on to Liverpool, arriving May 2, 1864. The crew were paid off and the ship decommissioned.

Her subsequent history is curious. Bulloch, the Confederate agent in London, had the armament removed and put the ship up at auction. She was sold June 11, 1864, to Edward Bates, a large Liverpool shipowner and operator. Bates took legal advice, which turned out to be very bad, to the effect that there could be no objection to his purchasing a naval vessel from a belligerent government and putting her to mercantile use. If he had inquired a little further he would have learned that, before the sale, Charles Francis Adams called to the attention of the British government its own long established rule forbidding the purchase of ships of war from belligerents by the subjects of neutral governments.

Bates paid £15,000 into the Confederate treasury, took over the ship, spent £3,000 in reconditioning her, and chartered her to the government of Portugal for a round voyage between Lisbon and the Portuguese possessions in Africa. Minister Adams thereupon notified the commanders of the U.S.S. Kearsarge, Niagara, and Sacramento, which were cruising in the English channel, that the Georgia was lawful prize "whenever and under whatever colors should be found sailing on the high seas." The Kearsarge was destined for larger prey. A week later she went to Cherbourg after the Alabama, with the result we know. The Niagara, Commander Craven, promptly took his ship to Liverpool and kept watch over the Georgia. The latter started for Portugal under her charter on August 8, and on that day Lord Russell notified Mr. Adams that "in future no ship of war of either belligerent shall be allowed to be brought into any of Her Majesty's ports for the purpose of being dismantled and sold."

The Niagara came up with the Georgia off the mouth of the Tagus, put a prize crew on board, and sent her to New

Bedford for adjudication by an American prize court. She was condemned and sold to one J. Rickerson for $44,000; the proceeds were paid into the court. The case made its leisurely way to the Supreme Court of the United States, which on February 15, 1869, held that the prize was good. Half of the fund in court therefore belonged to the officers and crew of the Niagara and half to the United States government.

So Bates lost the £18,000 with which he had gambled, or rather, his insurers lost it, for he had protected his bet against precisely the eventuality that occurred. He had to sue for the insurance in the English courts. The company resisted on the ground that Bates had concealed the previous history of the ship. The jury found for Bates in the full amount.

The Georgia, ex-Japan, ex-Virginia, which had taken eight prizes, now became a seagoing drudge. She was used as a cotton carrier after the war and finally went to pieces on a rock off the coast of Newfoundland.

The Georgia was never a very able ship or an effective commerce destroyer. Her passport to glory is that she was the only vessel of the Confederate Navy to fire a hostile shot against a foreign enemy and the only captor that herself became a prize.

CHAPTER IX

THE TALLAHASSEE
AND THE CHICKAMAUGA

We greet Montauk across the foam,
We work to Vineyard Sound,
The Diamond sees us racing home,
The Georges outward bound.
—Thomas Fleming Day, *The Coaster*

I

THE COMMERCE DESTROYER is not cast for a heroic role. Her business is to hit and run. Her duty is to prey upon the defenseless and avoid the enemy. Her work is as necessary as that of a scavenger and equally admirable. Had it not been for the fight with the Kearsarge, the Alabama would not have reached Valhalla. It is a relief to turn, for a short interlude, to two cruisers whose brief careers were of epic quality.

The first voyage of the Tallahassee lasted only a month; her second, ten days. They occurred in the latter part of the war, when Grant was pounding at Petersburg, Sherman was besieging Atlanta, Georgia was threatening to secede. The Confederacy was declining to its certain end. The Tallahassee began by running a blockade of fifty ships. Thirteen United States naval vessels were specially detailed to catch her and failed. She operated under enemy guns, under fire by night and day. At the end she ran the blockade the second time and came to anchor in the port from which she started, without a casualty, having taken thirty-three prizes in thirty days within or near the territorial waters of the United States. As an exhibition of cold, sustained nerve, her performance challenges any episode in naval history.

Her commander was a Confederate cavalry colonel who

THE TALLAHASSEE

was also a naval officer. John Taylor Wood, grandson of Zachary Taylor and an in-law of Jefferson Davis, was born in 1830 in Iowa Territory. His birthplace is now Fort Snelling, Minnesota. As a youth he was in and out of the newly established Naval Academy twice without graduating and was warranted midshipman. Thereafter he alternated sea service with duty at the Academy. He was instructor in tactics and gunnery there in 1861, when almost simultaneously he resigned and was dismissed. He was aboard the Merrimac during the battle of the ironclads. Placed in command of a flotilla of rowboats, he conducted a series of midnight expeditions, destroying the schooner Frances Elmore in the Potomac River and the ship Alleghanian in Chesapeake Bay. Assigned to the staff of President Davis, he acquired his colonelcy in the cavalry, and then returned to his midnight boat raids in the Chesapeake, capturing two Federal warships, the schooners Satellite and Reliance, after some severe hand-to-hand fighting on the decks; the transports Golden Rod, Coquette, and Two Brothers; and later the gunboat Underwriter, at New Bern, North Carolina.

His reputation for daredevil gallantry won Wood the thanks of the Confederate Congress and, in 1864, the command of the Tallahassee.

This ship was built at Millwall in the Thames, ostensibly for the Chinese opium trade. Through the usual intermediaries she came into the possession of the Confederate government, which used her as a blockade-runner from Bermuda into Wilmington, North Carolina, under the name of the Atlanta.[1] She was a 700-ton vessel, 200 feet long, with twin screws and a speed of 14½ knots. Colonel Wood saw her in Wilmington and suggested that she be converted into a cruiser. Of her three guns, two were cast in Richmond and one had been captured. She operated out of a Confederate port and she had an all-American crew of Confederate vet-

[1] Not to be confused with the Confederate ram Atlanta captured by the U.S.S. Weehawken off Savannah in 1863.

erans. On July 20, 1864, she was commissioned as a cruiser under the name of Tallahassee.

The peculiar geography of the mouth of the Cape Fear River, and the commanding position of Forts Fisher and Caswell at either entrance, gave Wilmington an immunity from effective blockade superior to that of any other Southern port. A strong concentration of blockading ships did not succeed in closing it. They could not get near enough to halt the blockade-runners without coming under the guns of one of the forts. The distance between the two entrances is only six miles in an air line, but, owing to Frying Pan Shoals, which extend ten miles out, they were separated by forty miles of sea. Wilmington remained a favorite nest for blockade-runners long after their other outlets were lost to them.

On the night of August 4 the Tallahassee began her attempt to run the blockade. The first night she ran aground in the darkness. The next night she ran aground again and three steamers were required to float her. That day, while she was being pulled off the bar, Farragut, down in Mobile Bay, was damning the torpedoes and going ahead to close another Southern port, leaving Wilmington as the sole channel for outgoing cotton and incoming supplies upon which the life of the South depended. The third night Wood tried the western inlet to the harbor. After moonset the Tallahassee slowly approached the bar, sounding constantly. She grazed it and then was over and started full speed ahead.

Almost immediately she sighted two steamers of the blockading fleet. She ran between them "so close under the stern of one that a biscuit could have been tossed on board." Shells began to sing over the decks of the Tallahassee from both sides. Wood did not reply, for he wished to preserve the impression that his vessel was merely a blockade-runner. The shooting of the blockaders was too high. The Tallahassee soon outdistanced them and was out of sight in the darkness. She had run the inshore blockade, but the offshore squadron, standing forty or fifty miles out, was more to be feared.

At daylight a Union cruiser appeared in chase. At eight o'clock, another. Steam was crowded into the Tallahassee to the danger point. "Had a screw loosened or a journal heated we should have been lost." By church time—for it was Sunday—the pursuers were losing ground and Wood summoned all hands for divine service. By four o'clock the Union vessels had given up the chase.

Presently another appeared, which was avoided by changing the Tallahassee's course. Just after dark came another, heading straight for the Confederate, shooting as she came. Shells struck the water close to the ship. In half an hour pursuer and pursued had lost each other in the dark.

Wood's objective was New York Harbor. Twenty miles below Long Branch he captured his first prize, the schooner Sarah A. Boice, Boston to Philadelphia in ballast. Her crew and their luggage were taken on board. The schooner was scuttled.

Fire Island Light came in sight, with seven sails intervening. One of them, the James Funk No. 22, was "one of a class of fine weatherly schooners found off New York from 100 to 200 miles out at all seasons, manned by as thorough seamen as ever trod a ship's deck." She at once ran down to the Tallahassee and put off a boat. She was a New York Harbor pilot looking for a job.

The port pilots of New York stood upon dignity and affected formal dress. In a few minutes, "A large well-dressed man in black with a high hat, heavy gold watch guard, a small valise and a bundle of papers under his arm, stepped over the side." At this moment the Confederate colors which had been drooping at the cruiser's peak fluttered in the breeze.

"My God, what's that?" exclaimed the pilot. "What ship is this?"

Wood writes, "A more astonished man never stood on deck of vessel. He turned deadly pale and drops of perspiration broke from every pore; but rapidly bracing himself he took in the situation and prepared to make the best of it. He was told that his vessel was a prize and that I would make a tender of her."

Wood manned the pilot boat with two officers and twenty men. He used her to bring up vessels when several sails were in sight.

Three of the other sails off Fire Island were captured and burned at once, the bark Bay State and brigs Carrie Estelle and A. Richards. Their crews brought the number of prisoners on the Tallahassee to forty. Before night the James Funk No. 22 brought up the schooner Carroll. She was bonded to take prisoners to New York. They were delighted by their capture and release, for, under Federal draft law, the paroles which Wood gave them, proving them to have suffered imprisonment in the Federal cause, exempted them from conscription. The Carroll stopped at Fire Island and telegraphed a warning to New York. The last prize of the day was another pilot boat, the William Bell No. 24. Total bag of the Tallahassee's first day's hunting, seven prizes.

The current New York newspapers which came off the prizes told Wood precisely what vessels were in port. He learned that there was nothing there to oppose an enterprise upon which he had set his heart. This was to take the Tallahassee up the East River, setting fire to the shipping on both sides; shell the Navy Yard; and escape through Hell Gate into Long Island Sound. For this he needed a Hell Gate pilot. As no one on board any of the prizes would admit knowing the road, Wood had to abandon the scheme.

The next day he cruised between Fire Island Light and Montauk Point, burning three craft loaded with lumber, a small schooner, and the packet ship Adriatic,[1] 1,000 tons, London to New York with miscellaneous cargo and 170 German immigrants. When they understood that the Adriatic was to be burned they were panic stricken, supposing they were themselves to be included in a human hecatomb. While the

---

[1] This was not the famous Collins liner Adriatic, the "Queen of the Seas." She had been sold British before the war.

cruiser was busy with the Adriatic, the James Funk No. 22 brought up another prize, the bark Suliote. Wood bonded the Suliote and transferred the company of the Adriatic to her, to their intense relief. It took three hours to get them transshipped, for they carried all their effects with them, first to the Tallahassee and then to the Suliote—broken china, bird cages, straw beds, and miscellaneous household goods. In the course of these proceedings the cruiser and packet came in collision, and the Tallahassee lost her main mast. The Adriatic was fired at sunset, illuminating the sea for miles.

Towing the James Funk No. 22, Wood steamed toward Nantucket. "The neighborhood of New York had been sufficiently worked and the game was already scarce." Sixty miles off Nantucket lightship, a prize worth while was discovered in the large new bark Glenavon of Maine, going from Boston to Glasgow with iron. She was scuttled. "We watched the bark as she slowly settled, strake by strake, until her deck was awash and then her stern sank gradually out of sight until she was in an upright position and one mast after another disappeared with all sails set, as quietly as if human hands were lowering her into the depths. Hardly a ripple broke the quiet water. Her head spars were the last seen. Captain Watt and his wife never took their eyes off their floating home, but side by side with tears in their eyes watched her disappear. 'Poor fellow,' she said afterwards, 'He has been going to sea for thirty years. All our savings were in that ship. We were saving for our children at home, five of them.' " Her grief was genuine, for the Glenavon was not adequately insured. The prisoners were transferred to an inbound Russian bark that came along.

Skirting Cape Cod, the Tallahassee turned into Massachusetts Bay. As the Funk was impeding his movements, Wood regretfully destroyed the trim little pilot craft.

On August 12 and 13 telegrams began pouring into the Navy Department at Washington. They came from officials, newspapers, and insurance underwriters, at Fire Island,

Brooklyn, and New York, reporting depredations of the new "pirate." Following the formula which had become almost a pattern in the cases of the Alabama, the Tacony, and the Florida, orders were at once despatched to the commandants at Boston, New York, Philadelphia, and Hampton Roads to send ships in pursuit. As it was just a month after the raid of the Florida, many of the vessels sent out after her had returned to port. The U.S.S. Mingoe and two armed transports left New York on the 12th, three vessels sailed from Philadelphia, and one—our old acquaintance the Tristram Shandy—from Boston on the 13th; two more from Boston the next day. The pursuing vessels began to pick up charred wreckage and dismasted hulls.

The Tallahassee continued her hunting up the coast, heading for Halifax to replenish her bunkers. After leaving Massachusetts Bay she took twenty-three prizes in five days close inshore, in the mouth of the Penobscot, and off Cape Sable. Three of them were small lumber schooners; three were little craft with loads of firewood. The Lammot duPont, of Wilmington, the Howard, of Bridgeton, and the Neva, of East Machias, were southbound with coal from Cape Breton, and the large ship James Littlefield with Welsh coal. Half a dozen were small fishermen clearly exempt from capture. Others were out in ballast. The weather was foggy and an old sea was running, so that attempts to transfer coal to the cruiser were unsuccessful. Of this group of prizes, nine were scuttled, nine burned, three bonded, and two Canadians from Gaspé released.

On August 16 telegrams began to come into the State Department from the United States Consul at Halifax. At first he reported that six ships had been sunk off Cape Sable the day before. On the 18th and 19th he reported the arrival of the Tallahassee, closing each telegram with, "No Federal warship here yet." He was protesting to the colonial authorities against allowing the cruiser to remain in port and take on coal, and was enticing members of her crew to desert.

Wood wrote that his own reception by the Port Admiral was cold and uncivil and by the Governor not much more cordial. They refused to permit the deserters to be arrested. The war was old and neutrality was being enforced. Wood received strict orders to leave within twenty-four hours, later extended to forty. After getting a new mainmast and a hundred tons of coal, the Tallahassee left Halifax at one o'clock in the morning of August 20. If the port officials had been less exigent she would have encountered the U.S.S. Pontoosuc, which arrived in Halifax before noon of that day.

Notwithstanding the incivility of the Nova Scotians, Wood returned to Halifax after the war and spent the rest of his life there in the insurance business.

Knowing of the hue and cry at his heels, Wood determined to return to Wilmington. He saw none of the pursuit ships until he arrived off the Carolina coast. There he dodged two of the offshore blockaders; then encountered one of the inshore vessels almost in the surf. There was a running fight in the night. Two or three other Union ships came up and joined it. The firing on all sides was wild, for the only targets were the flashes from the guns. At daybreak the blockaders were lying five miles out, and the Tallahassee in the entrance to the harbor was exchanging a 21-gun salute with Fort Fisher (August 26, 1864).

The total captures were thirty-three, of which half were square riggers. Twenty-six were destroyed, five bonded, and two released.

II

On returning to Wilmington the Tallahassee found there a vessel which strongly resembled her, the twin-screw blockade-runner Edith. The Confederate government took this vessel over, renamed her the Chickamauga, equipped her with a light battery of three guns, and commissioned her as a cruiser under the command of Captain John Wilkinson, C.S.N.

On September 26 he began trying to get out. Eleven Yankee blockaders were waiting outside. Swift, light-draft blockade-runners were slipping in and out almost every dark night, but the depth of the Chickamauga limited her to a time when there was plenty of water in the rip. She made several attempts, grounding each time. Then moonlight nights came and she had to wait three weeks for the dark of the moon. During this period yellow fever broke out in Wilmington.

At length on October 28, escorted down the river by the Tallahassee, the Chickamauga approached the bar just after nightfall, grounded, backed off, tried again, and got over.

An unidentified blockader saw her, fired a gun, and sent up a rocket. The U.S.S. Dumbarton, under the command of Lieutenant Brown, responding to the signal, immediately went in chase, believing the outbound ship to be the Tallahassee. The Dumbarton began firing but the water was so rough as to prevent accurate aim and all her shots went high. She was continually sending up rockets to attract the attention of the offshore fleet. Her foul bottom reduced her speed.

Two other blockaders, seeing the rockets, mistook the pursuit ship for the prey and began to chase their own colleague, firing at her repeatedly, notwithstanding attempts to signal them to stop. Wilkinson did no shooting. He improved his trim by shifting coal and the Chickamauga began to draw away. The last Brown saw of the raider she was a mile ahead and rapidly disappearing.

Lieutenant Brown's impression that the raider he had chased was the Tallahassee caused a new search for that vessel to be instituted up and down the coast throughout the ensuing two weeks. When it became known that a new cruiser was abroad, orders were issued to look for both of them.

Heading north the first three days of her hunting, the Chickamauga bagged four prizes within fifty miles of New York, the barks Mark L. Potter, Bangor to Key West with lime, bricks, and lumber, and Emma L. Hall, Cárdenas to New York with sugar, and the ship Shooting Star, New York to Havana with coal. These were burned. The fourth was the bark Abe Lincoln, which was bonded with prisoners and ordered to proceed to Fortress Monroe. Instead she went to New York and gave the alarm. Off Block Island on November 1, Wilkinson scuttled two schooners, the Otter Rock of Boston and the Goodspeed of Philadelphia. These prizes yielded some news. Midshipman Cary noted in his diary:

"Got late Yankee papers which say the enemy have discovered our exit from Wilmington and have sent three steamers after us; so in a few days we are likely to have a lively time. The alarm was just now made that the Yankees were bearing down upon us in a steamer. All lights were put out and everybody ran on deck, when down came a large schooner with both lights set which nearly ran us down."

Running into an adverse gale, Wilkinson abandoned a plan to raid Long Island Sound, and put out to sea, where, on November 2, he captured his last prize, the bark Speedwell. She was an ancient craft with ladies on board. She was bonded to take prisoners from the Otter Rock and the Goodspeed.

The effective cruising of the Chickamauga had lasted four days. Wilkinson ran for St. George, Bermuda, for coal. Here he encountered the same newly-adopted rigidity in the enforcement of the neutrality regulations that had obstructed the Tallahassee at Halifax. Wilkinson sabotaged his own condenser and was allowed a week for repairs. What he wanted was time to take on more coal than the rules permitted. A difficulty was made about the coal, which Wilkinson overcame, in part, by a present of a large supply of liquor to the customs officer, who was thereby "made oblivious" to the quantity of coal going into the Chickamauga's bunkers.

At Bermuda a wholesale desertion occurred. The Governor refused to permit Wilkinson to have the deserters arrested. The alcoholic oblivion of the customs officer served for only a hundred tons of coal, not enough for a cruise. Short-handed and short-bunkered, Wilkinson started back to Wilmington on November 15.

His object was to reach the mouth of the Cape Fear River on the night of November 18 before moonrise, which was at ten o'clock. Both the timing and the position were miscalculated. At ten o'clock the Chickamauga was not yet on soundings. At eleven she was found, unaccountably, to be almost in the breakers. The pilot was sent ashore and returned with the report that he did not recognize the coast at all. Later it was found that the ship was twenty miles north of her supposed position. Wilkinson himself took over the pilot's work. The night was misty, congealing into a thick fog before daybreak. In dangerous proximity to shore and in waters full of shoals the Chickamauga felt her way southerly. While the course was one the commander would not have dared to choose, even by day, much less on a foggy night, it brought the ship down the coast inside the inshore blockade without mishap. A Confederate guardian angel must have had a hand on her wheel that night. Before dawn she was at anchor under the guns of Fort Fisher but outside the bar and under the necessity of awaiting high water to get over.

As daybreak thinned the fog somewhat, four of the inshore guard boats discovered her. They thought she was a blockade-runner that had gone aground. The U.S.S. Clematis, Wilderness, Cherokee, and Kansas drew in, firing through the mist. Fort Fisher returned the fire, and to the surprise of the Union vessels the grounded ship began to send over shot and shells which were identified by their sound as coming from two Whitworth guns and a heavy rifle. Owing to the thick weather accurate shooting was impossible. No shot on either side took effect. By 8:30 A.M. all firing ceased. The Chickamauga was then safely in the river.

III

While the Chickamauga was making her cruise of three weeks, the Tallahassee's name was changed to the Olustee and she went out and back on a second raid, lasting ten days, under the command of Lieutenant Ward, who had served on her under Wood.

She left Wilmington the night after the escape of the Chickamauga, under very similar circumstances. The blockader Dumbarton sighted her as she approached the bar just at dusk and fired a rocket as a signal to the fleet. The cruiser turned back, reversed her course several times and finally stood right out, less than a thousand yards from the Dumbarton, which was firing and throwing up rockets. The U.S.S. Maratanza came up and began to shoot, but was soon lost astern. As the racing ships passed the U.S.S. Vicksburg she fired a shot at the pursuer. The Dumbarton was burning pine wood and salt pork, making a dense, black smoke which obscured her identity. Steadily gaining and churning up a deal of white water, the Olustee was out of sight about two hours after the pursuit started. Brown followed the course until daybreak and then he turned the Dumbarton back to her station.

The Olustee headed once more for Sandy Hook and once more telegrams were flashing up the coast sending out pursuit ships.

On November 1, 1864, off the Delaware capes the Olustee destroyed the bark Empress Theresa, and on November 3, five more prizes, the schooners A. J. Bird, E. F. Lewis, and Vapor, the ship Arcole, and the brig T. D. Wagner. With coal nearly exhausted she turned south. Off Cape Charles the Federal gunboat Sassacuss, out from Philadelphia, chased her for two days. It was an exciting race. The Sassacuss sighted the cruiser at 3:30 P.M. on November 5 in a full gale and a heavy sea, about ninety miles east of the Cape, running south. As long as the wind held, the Union vessel gained, for she was a fast sailer and, like all ships of that day, could make better time under sail than under steam. By the moonlight of early evening the Sassacuss came within range and began to fire a Dahlgren 20-pounder, causing the Confederate to steer wildly from S. by E. to S. by W. "I felt sure he was ours," wrote Lieutenant Commander Davis to Admiral Porter. But at ten o'clock the moon set and, although the ships were less than two miles apart, nothing could be seen. At daybreak the Sassacuss sighted the Olustee twelve miles ahead and resumed the pursuit. The wind failed, but by crowding on steam and trimming ship, Davis diminished the distance to five miles. "Again I congratulated myself and the ship that the Tallahassee would soon be a prize." But Ward lightened his vessel and lost no more distance. In the stokehold of the Sassacuss the firemen were driven to the limit of their endurance. "A number of them gave out entirely." They were raw hands and could not maintain the pressure which repeatedly dropped to 30 pounds, was pushed up to 35 and dropped again. The chase went on all day. At 9:00 P.M. the Sassacuss finally lost sight of the Olustee and Davis had to be content with the knowledge that he had driven her between the offshore and inshore blockaders directly outside Cape Fear, and that she would have to wait until daylight to get inside.

In the morning (November 6) the Olustee was discovered by three Federal cruisers, the U.S.S. Quaker City, Lilian, and Osceola, and by the gunboat Montgomery. All four started in pursuit, the Lilian burning a mixture of coal, fire wood and salt pork which yielded a steam pressure of 10 pounds and "kept it there." The chase continued throughout the day with frequent changes of course as the Confederate dodged about to escape the Montgomery which was the only vessel to get within range. The gunboat fired forty-four shots. The Olustee kept firing her after gun at the Montgomery. Late in the afternoon the Union vessel ran out of ammunition. A thick haze obscured everything. About seven o'clock signal lights were seen along the beach. The Olustee was once more running up the river to Wilmington (November 10, 1864).

This closed the cruising career of the ship which had been known as the Atlanta, the Tallahassee, and the Olustee. She was disarmed and taken off the navy list. Her naval crew was discharged and she shipped civilian seamen. Title was transferred to a private firm, Wm. G. Crenshaw & Company, of Virginia. Upon this transfer she received a new name, her fourth. Appropriately she was christened the Chameleon. She was once more a blockade-runner operating for account of the Confederate government under the command of Captain John Wilkinson, late of the Chickamauga. While the Federal fleet was bombarding Fort Fisher, she slipped out through them with a load of cotton for Bermuda, where she took on supplies for the army.

The Lieutenant Governor of Bermuda was uneasy. It was now December, 1864. Sherman was in Savannah; the long siege of Richmond could end only in one way; the most sanguine friends of the Confederacy knew that its days were numbered. The situation was calculated to trouble a colonial government which had been enjoying extravagant prosperity from the patronage of the moribund Confederacy and might soon be called to account by a victorious and irritated power. The Chameleon had no trace of the warship about her now; her owner was represented to be a "private merchant." After some hesitation the colonial authorities let her load.

She left Bermuda to become for a time an outcast on the sea. She tried to get back into Wilmington. It was in the hands of the Union Army. Then she tried Charleston with no better luck. Next she sailed into Nassau, unloaded her cargo, and cleared for Liverpool, where she arrived April 9, 1865, and was taken in charge by Fraser, Trenholm & Company.

The collapse of the Confederacy moved the United States, as successor to the defunct government, to embark upon a series of lawsuits in English courts to recover various assets of the decedent's estate located in England. The legal questions were threshed out in suits brought against Prioleau, Liverpool manager for Fraser, Trenholm & Company, and McCrea, Confederate fiscal agent in London. The courts sustained the heirship of the Federal government except as to bona fide liens held by individuals. The English courts honored these, while the courts of the United States annulled similar liens as having been created in aid of rebellion. The French court in Arman's case gave the Confederate funds to his French creditors.[1]

On the advice of the most eminent maritime lawyer of his day, Sir Travers Twiss, the United States brought actions of possession in the High Court of Admiralty to recover the Chameleon (Tallahassee), the Shenandoah, and the Rappahannock, all of them in the Mersey. A claim to the Tallahassee was set up by Crenshaw & Company, who abandoned their defense on the eve of trial. A judgment of possession in favor of the United States was given April 24, 1866. The Consul at Liverpool took the ship over and put her up at auction on June 26.

The further history of the ship belongs to another navy. In 1864 the officers of the Mikado, warring against the Shogun, fired upon the foreign shipping in the harbor of Shimoneski. The swift retribution which followed convinced the Imperial government of the value of a navy. We have seen that it purchased from the United States the powerful ex-Confederate ironclad ram Stonewall.[2] A representative of the Mikado's government bid the Tallahassee in for £4,600 and she was commissioned as a cruiser in the Japanese navy.

IV

We left the Chickamauga safely back in Wilmington on November 19, 1864. To stop up the hole there, the only remaining gap in the blockade which, after nearly four years

[1] See Chap. IV, above.
[2] *Ibid.*

Confederate States Steamer 'Tallahassee.'

Courtesy of the Office of the U. S. Naval Records and Library.

C. S. C. Shenandoah.
From Official Records of the Union and Confederate Navies.
Courtesy of the Office of the U. S. Naval Records and Library.

of effort, had been made effective at all other ports, the Federal government sent a combined land and naval expedition in December, 1864. Admiral Porter commanded the largest fleet the Union Navy had yet assembled. General Benjamin F. Butler brought 10,000 troops from the land side, concluded that Fort Fisher was impregnable, and withdrew. He was relieved by General Terry. There was hot fighting in the middle of January, 1865; the fort and the shipping under its shadow were beleaguered by land and sea. On January 15, 1865, the fort was stormed. The last haven of the blockade-runners, and the last Confederate port, was now in Union hands; the Federal government was in a position to win the war by starvation if it had not been won by arms. In this fighting the Chickamauga played a valiant part. She survived only long enough to be taken up the river and burned.

CHAPTER X

THE SHENANDOAH AND THE WHALERS

So is the great and wide sea,... There go the ships, and there is that Leviathan whom thou hast made to play therein.—Psalm 104:25, 26

I

WHEN CAPTAIN SEMMES told his crew, on the last day of the Alabama's life, that they had destroyed or driven under neutral flags one half of the enemy's commerce, he might have added that a great part of the remainder consisted of whaling ships. The Alabama had begun her career by destroying a dozen whalers in mid-Atlantic. Then she turned her attention to merchant ships. The Pacific whale fishery remained undisturbed.

Whaling is one of the oldest forms of American maritime enterprise. By the beginning of the war it had become the most important one. It was an industry in which Americans dominated the world market. This position had been achieved by two hundred years of trial and error and by the superior skill of the Yankee sailor of the sail, which was largely acquired in the hard school of the whale fishery. It was an American whaling captain who demonstrated a method of getting a ship off a lee shore in a full gale with both anchors gone and no room to tack. As phrased by Midshipman Tattnall in his examination, the classic rule in such cases was to "take to the boats and let the damned old tub go to hell where she belongs." Under cross-examination by an insurance adjuster, a whaling master actually showed a way of *backing out* under such conditions.

Whale oil, which was "tried out" of the blubber of all

varieties of whale, was used for making soft soap, for dressing leather, for lubrication, for making coarse paint and varnishes, combined with tar for treating ship cordage, and for illumination. As an illuminant it was burned in lamps and torches. Its unpleasant odor limited its use for this purpose to those who were willing to smell the midnight oil as well as burn it, in preference to replenishing faint, rapidly burning tallow candles.

Sperm oil, which is much less abundant than whale oil, is recovered from the head and body of the sperm whale. It was used as an illuminating oil and in the manufacture of sperm or "store" candles, which give a brighter, steadier flame than tallow and last much longer. Sperm candles are luxuries. The price of sperm oil was from two to three times that of whale oil.

For one type of illumination whale and sperm oil had a monopoly, i.e., lighthouses. The multiplication of lighthouses along the Atlantic coast augmented the demand for oil for heavy consumption in their great lamps. For this purpose there was no substitute before the Civil War.

Whalebone is taken from the mouth of the baleen or right whale. It was used to stiffen women's dresses or "stays," in upholstery, and in making fishing rods, umbrella ribs, and driving whips. At the height of the fashion for corsets and crinolines, in 1853, the whalers brought home 5,652,300 pounds of it. No doubt the style and the supply of whalebone interacted. Ambergris is a lard-like lump sometimes found in the stomach of a sick whale. It intensifies the aroma of perfume. It is rare and of great value.

The requirements of the domestic market are not sufficient to account for the magnitude of the American whaling business before the Civil War. A large part of the crop was exported to England, sometimes exceeding the total take for a current year and encroaching upon reserves from the previous year. The British whale fishery, which was encouraged from time to time by government aid, by import restrictions, and by tariff duties, never was adequate to supply the home demand.

The beginnings of the industry were coeval with the settlement of New England. To engage in commercial fishing was one of the motives of the Pilgrims in emigrating. It was a factor in determining their choice of a site for their settlement. The hundred passengers on the Mayflower were fugitives, not from oppression, but from hunger. In the congested slums of Amsterdam and Leyden and in the London sanctuary where these English country folk found religious freedom, they had no means of livelihood. Food was so inadequate that their children developed rickets. They were reduced to desperation. Their Dutch neighbors were making money from whaling, with an admiral in charge of the fishing fleet. Some thirty-five of the six hundred odd who comprised the Leyden group decided to try it. King James encouraged them by telling them that "fishing was an honest trade, the Apostles' own calling." On board the Mayflower, off the tip of Cape Cod in the bitter November of 1620, they debated for nearly a month whether or not to seek another haven. The question was settled by the fact that "large whales of the best kind for oil and bone came daily alongside and played about the ship." The master and his mates (not members of the Pilgrim group) and others experienced in fishing preferred it to the Greenland whale fishery and said that, were they provided with the proper implements, £300 or £400 worth of oil might be secured.[1] Their first charter granted unrestrained fishing rights.

The colonists began by taking drift whales along shore. By 1650 there was a substantial floating fishery off Long Island and a trade in oil in Massachusetts Bay. By 1700 a beginning had been made of the important whaling fleet which sailed from Nantucket. Most New England and Long Island ports sent out a few vessels. Then about 1765 ships began to sail from the last and greatest of the whaling ports, New Bed-

[1] J. Thacher, *History of the Town of Plymouth*, p. 21.

ford. After the vicissitudes of the Revolution and the War of 1812 the fishery quickly revived. At the outbreak of the Civil War, New Bedford, with about 20,000 permanent inhabitants and a population afloat of about 10,000 more, was the fifth commercial port in the United States and the largest whaling port in the world.

The volume of business varied from year to year with fishermen's luck, with fluctuations in the foreign demand, and with the vagaries of fashion. The price of whale products was highly responsive to supply and was correspondingly unstable. The practice of paying the labor, i.e., the whaling crews, by a share or "lay" of the value of the cargo computed upon prices set up before sailing and well below the market, reduced the risk of loss to the investor by passing some of it on to the men. As profits became more reliable, the "lay" was progressively diminished. In the decade ending with 1861 the business was at its peak. In round figures, the annual crop of sperm oil during that period ranged from 69,000 to 103,000 barrels; whale oil from 84,000 to 328,000 barrels; whalebone from 1,000,000 pounds to 5,500,000. The prices fluctuated from $1.207 per gallon to $1.772 for sperm oil; from 44⅕ to 79½ cents for whale oil, and from 32 cents per pound to 96 cents for whalebone. The whaling fleet showed a steady growth down to 1860. The statistics begin in 1843, when the fleet consisted of 594 ships and barks, 75 brigs, and 6 schooners, with an aggregate tonnage of 199,192. The banner year was 1854, with 668 vessels of 209,000 tons. In 1860 there were 596 craft of 176,848 tons.

A good index of the prosperity of any port is the number of saloons, dives, and brothels it supports. By this test New Bedford qualified for the highest rating. A garland of such resorts adorned its waterfront, whence the flowers of Puritan culture, the venereal diseases, were distributed among the islands of the sea. The Hawaiian aborigines, the handsome, innately genteel Kanakas, were annihilated by these Grecian gifts. Here as elsewhere it was customary to give an outbound sailor an advance against his future wages. In 1858 these advances in New Bedford amounted to $130,000. Add to this the pay-off of the incoming ships, in most instances several multiples of the advance, and you have an idea of the takings of the New Bedford merchants of joy and an exponent of the business of the port.

Back of these *palazzi* were the great warehouses, the counting houses of the ship owners, the insurance offices, and the stores of the ship chandlers, rope makers, and coopers. In 1858 these purveyors received for outfitting ships a sum just under two million dollars. The cruisers were always glad to capture outbound whalers because, by reason of the length of their voyages, averaging forty-five months, they were well supplied with all the commodities needed on board. The completeness of their equipment is illustrated by the merchandise the chandlers of New Bedford sold. The stocks included flour, meal, beef, pork, salt, molasses, rice, beans, dried apples, sugar, butter, cheese, ham, codfish, coffee, tea, raisins, corn, potatoes, onions, vinegar, sperm candles, fresh water, firewood, hardwood, flags, brick and lime for making the try-works, lumber, canvas, cordage, cotton cloth, tobacco, the ingredients of paint, barrels and the material for making them, rum, gunpowder and clothing for the slop chest.

Further uptown, behind rows of maples and elms, were the ample, dignified houses of the shipowners and merchants; the churches and, on a hill top the Whaleman's Chapel so graphically described in *Moby-Dick*. While one does not look for "social work" in the mid-nineteenth century, it is gratifying to record that one of the local clergy, in advance of his time, was used to visit the incoming ships and distribute tracts—on Sabbath observance. He had a counterpart in Honolulu, where one of the missionaries, Rev. Mr. Diel, was accustomed to invite the men of the whaling crews to his home.

It is unlikely that anyone will be reading this book who does not already know *Moby-Dick*. If any such there be, let him turn down the corner of this page and lay it aside until he has subjected himself to the spell of that magic. Whether he comes back or not is relatively unimportant. He will have learned all a landsman need know about the ways of whales and whaling ships; much more than he would get from the learned monographs upon the subject. With that immortal fable at hand it would be a mere impertinence for a pedestrian author to duplicate even the factual information upon which Melville erects the superstructure of his allegory. You will understand how life was lived upon the ships, how whales were harpooned and secured and their oil and bone extracted. Reference need not be made to the thirty-five concluding chapters. Those belong to literature, with their orchestral prose, the apocalyptic grandeur of the catastrophe. They do not belong particularly to this matter of the cruiser Shenandoah and the whaling fleet.

Between the voyage of the Acushnet in 1841, upon which Melville predicated his tale, and that of the Shenandoah, which we are about to rehearse, certain things happened.

For one, Maury's *Whaling Charts of the World* had been issued in 1852, and in 1861 Captain Matthew Fontaine Maury, of Virginia, pioneer oceanographer, had forsworn the United States Navy for that of the Confederacy. For the first time the habitat and migrations of sperm and right whales were scientifically charted so that the whalers knew more surely where and when to hunt their prey and the cruiser knew where and when to hunt the whalers.

Whaling was a commercial sport unhampered by game laws. Pregnant and suckling cows were destroyed without regard to conservation. The season was any weather in which a ship could live. Through the centuries the hunters had been making empirical discoveries about the habits of whales and their feeding grounds.

They had found the right whale, which yields oil and bone, off the coast of Greenland and sometimes off that of Brazil on its way to and from the Antarctic. Its food, known as brit, consists of myriads of tiny yellow marine organisms afloat upon acres of surface, giving the sea the appearance of a wheat field. The brit adhere to the shutter-like bones in the whale's mouth. The right whale is an amiable foolish giant with a soft spot on his nose where a smart blow will finish him.

Not so the sperm whale. This hugest of living creatures, thirty times the bulk of an elephant, yields no bone, but his blubber makes whale oil and his great head is a reservoir of valuable sperm oil. He travels in a herd of his kind, looking for the squid on which he feeds. He is fearless, a terrible antagonist, who prefers battle to flight and more than once has been known to founder a ship by ramming it. Crushing a boat in his 14-foot jaws and swamping it with his flukes is part of his regular technique. He swims from the Brazil grounds to the onshore grounds near the coast of Chile, the offshore grounds between Galapagos and the Marquesas, the Sychelle grounds in the Indian Ocean, the Japan grounds, the Sea of Okhotsk, and Bering Sea.

The Pacific grounds were located by American whalers beginning in 1791. In 1819 the first ships put into the harbor of Honolulu, speedily to become the great rendezvous of the Pacific, where nearly every whaler called at least once during its voyage. By 1844 they were calling there at the rate of four hundred per year. Thence they pressed their explorations through the area of a circle with a radius of more than three thousand miles, east to Payta, south to Vau Vau, west to Yokohama, north to Kamchatka.

With the reports of these experiences and the data compiled by a naval expedition, and by carefully circularizing the captains of the fleet, Maury made up his charts. It seems ironical that they should have shown the way to the destruction of the vessels for whose benefit they had been prepared.

Another development between the days of the Acushnet and those of the Shenandoah was the accelerated deterioration of the quality of the whaling crews, as their "lay," or remuneration, was diminished in order to enhance profits.

From 1/90 for a foremast hand it had been reduced to a proportion ranging from 1/160 to 1/250 of the proceeds of the voyage, calculated as previously explained. This reduction in wages was possible because whalers could use a larger number of unskilled, ill-conditioned hands than a merchant ship could. By 1860 the crews had declined from their high rank as seamen and had become a motley assortment of sorry human castoffs of all races, from the sailortown of every port in the world, plus teen age boys green from New England farms.

The occupation was hazardous. On one voyage Melville spoke thirty ships, each of which had lost a life since leaving home. Some had lost entire boat's crews in contests with whales. In Starbuck's *History of the American Whale Fishery*, which is the bible of all students of the subject, there are many notations to the effect that "Captain died on voyage."

The living conditions on board the whalers were repellent to merchant seamen. Some twenty foremast hands had to bunk in a room about sixteen feet square. The food was seldom appetizing, although usually abundant. The long periods with little occupation and no variety frayed the nerves, sometimes affected the mind. Mr. Foster Rhea Dulles in his delightful book, *Lowered Boats*, quotes from an earlier authority a speech by a whaling agent: "A whaler, gentlemen, is a place of refuge for the distressed and persecuted, a school for the dissipated, an asylum for the needy. There's nothing like it."

Because of the necessity of carrying men to man the boats and try out the oil in addition to navigating the ship, a whaler's crew relative to her size was much larger than that of a merchant ship. It was found to be economical, therefore, for those engaged in the Pacific fishery to transship their oil and bone at Honolulu, San Francisco, or Talcahuano, to be brought home in other vessels belonging to the same owner and sent out for the purpose of replenishing supplies and bringing home cargo, or in large merchantmen, while the whaler continued her work. The practice was followed in the Atlantic by transshipping at Montevideo and St. Helena.

The first whalers to be destroyed during the war were bought by the Federal government for that purpose. In aid of the blockade more than forty old vessels were purchased in 1861, loaded with stones, and sunk in the approaches to Charleston Harbor. These formed the two "stone fleets," the first containing twenty-four whalers, the second fourteen. The other ships of the stone fleets were ancient merchantmen, one of which had been sailing the sea for nearly a hundred years; another was an ex-British naval vessel captured as a prize during the Revolution. The use of some thirty-eight ancient whalers for this purpose subtracted nothing from the efficiency of the whaling fleet and added little to the efficiency of the blockade, for the water immediately excavated new channels through the soft delta.

The destruction wrought by the Alabama, the Georgia, and the Florida upon the merchant marine turned the attention of the Confederate authorities to the whalers. Two officers, Lieutenants John M. Brooke and R. R. Carter of Virginia, while on a United States naval expedition to the Pacific in 1855, had interested themselves in the movements of the whaling fleet. In consultation with Bulloch in London, Carter prepared a comprehensive plan of campaign. This report and a set of Maury's whaling charts formed the sailing directions for the expedition against the Pacific fishery which was now undertaken.

Two cruisers were assigned to this duty, the Florida, which was on her way to the Pacific when she was captured, October 7, 1864, and the Shenandoah, which, as it happened, began her career in London the day after the Florida came to grief in Bahia.

II

Before the loss of the Alabama, one of the Confederate agents had seen a ship called the Sea King at her builder's yard in Glasgow and had noted her as a vessel adaptable for cruising. She was built by A. S. Stephens & Sons for a Bombay company and had made her maiden voyage to New Zealand with British troops. She was a full-rigged ship slightly larger than the Alabama, a long rakish craft of 1,160 tons, with an auxiliary engine of 450 indicated horsepower, capable of steaming 10 knots an hour. Indeed, she proved to be one of the fastest ships afloat and once logged 320 miles in twenty-four hours. She had an iron frame, 6-inch teakwood planking, iron lower masts, a detachable hoisting propeller. In sum, she was in the great tradition of the East Indiaman.

On September 20, 1864, having returned from Bombay and lying at London, the Sea King was purchased by Richard Wright, of Liverpool, a merchant whose son-in-law was Charles K. Prioleau of South Carolina, managing partner of Fraser, Trenholm & Company, Confederate financial agents in England. A group of Confederate officers were secretly assembled in Liverpool to await orders from Commodore Barron in Paris. Among them was Lieutenant James Iredell Waddell, of North Carolina, formerly of the United States Navy. Waddell, who was forty years of age, had been in Europe nineteen months awaiting assignment. In the group were five officers who had served on the Alabama, also a nephew of Robert E. Lee, and two graduates of the Naval Academy at Annapolis, who were classmates of a Union officer destined to distinguish himself in a later war, George Dewey. One officer, Lieutenant Whittle, was sent to London where he met Wright, the owner.

On October 8, 1864, the Sea King cleared from London for Bombay, laden with coal, her British master, Captain Corbett, and her regular crew. She carried a supercargo who was supposed to represent the owners of the coal. This was Whittle under an alias, sent along to familiarize himself with the ship. No other Confederate was on board. Captain Corbett carried an authorization from Wright to sell the ship for £45,000.

On the same day, October 8, the British steamer Laurel cleared from Liverpool, commanded by Lieutenant J. F. Ramsay, C.S.N., loaded with cases marked "general merchandise," which contained guns, ammunition, and ship's stores. As passengers she had Waddell and the other Confederate officers and some five or six men who had served on the Alabama.

The same program was followed as in the case of the other cruisers. The two vessels met at Madeira, withdrew to a nearby uninhabited rock and made the transfer of officers and supplies from the Laurel, which thereupon sailed away to become a blockade-runner under the name of The Confederate States, while title to the Sea King was vested in the Confederate government and her name was changed to the Shenandoah.

Before the two ships parted company on October 20, Waddell attempted to enlist a crew from the sailors of both vessels. Seaman Temple (alias William Jones) described the proceedings in an affidavit after the war:

"We were all called aft by the boatswain of the Sea King; the men from the Laurel were also called on board. As soon as we got aft Captain Corbett came out with the ship's articles in his hands and made a speech to us, something to this effect:—'Men of the Sea King, you signed these articles with me to go to Bombay or any intermediate port, and if the ship should be sold on the voyage you were to sign clear of her! Someone said we did not hear anything about that in London; He replied, Here it is, and read it to them. He then went on to say that he had sold the ship, and that those who wished to join the ship could do so; that they would be paid on their signing a paper clearing from the Sea King two months wages, whilst those who did not want to join her were to take their clothes and go on the steamer alongside, which would take them to Liverpool where they would be paid immediately. Captain Waddell was standing close to Captain Corbett at the time in full Confederate uniform, and as soon as Captain Corbett had finished, stepped forward and took his place by the side of Captain Corbett and said:—Men, I am an officer of the Confederate navy, authorized to take command of this ship. He offered to read his commission but the men said, No, never mind. He then said, Any of you that feel inclined to serve under the Confederate flag will get good wages and good treatment. I do not intend to fight; anyone can see that this vessel was not made to fight; I intend to run away rather than fight unless in a very urgent case. My orders are simply to destroy the federal commerce by burning and destroying all ships that I can find sailing under the federal flag. He said, as each vessel was taken they would be valued and half the value of each would be divided among the ship's company and paid to them at the end of the war. Someone asked what bounty he would give; he replied he would give £15 bounty in gold; to able seamen he would give £7 per month and those that were married could have their wages paid to their wives in Liverpool during the cruise."

Not counting the bounty, the wages offered were four times the rate for able seamen prevailing on merchant ships. This assurance, the high pay and the generous promises attracted only nineteen men. The fate of the Alabama was too vividly in mind. Waddell was seriously disappointed. The chagrin of his officers was expressed by Lieutenant Ramsay, "I never saw such a set of curs in all my experience at sea." Counting the officers, the company of the Shenandoah consisted of forty-three men to handle a ship which normally required a complement of eighty-five.

On Captain Corbett's return to England he was arrested at the instance of Charles Francis Adams and tried for violating the Foreign Enlistment Act. Conflicting evidence was offered as to what he said to the crews of the Sea King and

Laurel. After long deliberation the jury brought in a special verdict equivalent to an acquittal, and Corbett was discharged.[1]

Short-handed as he was, Waddell was inclined to sail for Teneriffe in the Canaries and there endeavor to have a crew sent out to him by Bulloch. His senior officers opposed this, fearing that the Shenandoah might be interned. They advised Waddell to "take the ocean." This counsel prevailed. The inadequate force of the Shenandoah had to convert the merchantman into a cruiser, mounting guns, cutting gun ports, constructing a powder magazine and shell room. When the work was done the battery consisted of four 8-inch smooth bores, two 32-pounder rifles, and two 12-pounder signal guns which had been part of the Sea King's equipment. All this work was done while navigating the ship. The captain took his trick at the wheel, steering the Shenandoah steadily southward.

The orders under which he sailed were as follows:

"A fast vessel with auxiliary steam power leaving the meridian of the Cape of Good Hope (say on the 45th parallel of latitude) on the 1st day of January, would reach Sydney, Australia, in forty days. Adding twenty days for incidental interruptions, and leaving the coast of Australia on the first day of March, passing through the whaling ground between New Zealand and New Holland and the Carolina group, touching at Ascension, and allowing thirty days for incidental delays, would reach the Ladrone Islands by the 1st of June. She would then, visiting the Bonin Islands, Sea of Japan, Okhotsk, and North Pacific, be in a position about the 15th of September, north of the Island of Oahu, distant sixty to a hundred miles, to intercept the North Pacific whaling fleet bound to Oahu with the products of the summer cruise."

The ship was ahead of schedule all the way, reaching the Cape of Good Hope by Christmas; Australia a month later. She was at Ascension Island on April 1 and in the Sea of

---

[1] *Rex v. Corbett*, 4 F. & F. 555.

Okhotsk on May 21. After that, circumstances made it impossible to carry out her orders.

The first prize was taken on October 30 off the Cape Verde Islands. She was the bark Aline from a Welsh port to Buenos Aires with railroad iron. Waddell caused her to be scuttled. With her crew he adopted the practice that he subsequently followed with all his prisoners—that is, he placed the men in irons in the forecastle and accommodated the officers as guests in the ward room.

Seven men from the Aline enlisted in the service of the Shenandoah, an important accession in her undermanned condition. Lieutenant Whittle, the executive officer, had the job of procuring enlistments. His method, which was later described by ten men from the prizes in affidavits, was to threaten the prisoners that they would be "made sorry" and that "it would be worse for them" if they did not join. These threats were addressed only to American citizens. No attempt was made to coerce foreigners. Even after enlisting, some of the men were kept in irons at night, probably a reasonable precaution.

Southerly from Cape Verde the Shenandoah took five more prizes during the first fortnight of November. The first of these, the little schooner Charter Oak, Boston to San Francisco, yielded a consignment of chairs and sofas which the Shenandoah lacked, 2,000 pounds of canned tomatoes, and a large quantity of tinned fruits and vegetables. The schooner was burned. Waddell took $200 from Captain Gilman of the Charter Oak and presented it to Mrs. Gilman, who was among the prisoners, on being told that it was all they had now that the schooner was gone. As the master of the schooner was not one of her owners and as the vessel and her cargo were in any case fully insured against war risks, it would seem that Waddell's gallantry was imposed upon. Then came the big bark D. Godfrey, Boston to Valparaiso with lumber and salt beef. While she was in flames her captain, pacing the quarterdeck of the cruiser, was heard to mutter something about "... her duty for forty years... to be destroyed by men... on a calm night." Six of her men were forced to enlist.

By this time the Shenandoah had twenty or more prisoners. She overhauled the Danish ship Anna Jans and sent several of them on board with a supply of provisions, presenting the commander of the Anna Jans with a chronometer in lieu of passage money.

The next prize was the little brig Susan, Cardiff to Brazil with coal. Sunk.

On November 12 a magnificent ship was overtaken, the Kate Prince of Portsmouth, New Hampshire, Liverpool to Bahia with coal. The coal was proved to be neutral cargo; so Waddell placed her under bond, put on board the prisoners from the Susan and those remaining from the Charter Oak, and released her.

A bark called the Adelaide, Baltimore to the Plate, was picked up the same day. Although disguised with Argentine documents, she was in every respect good prize, but after her crew, papers, and effects had been removed, Waddell became satisfied that she was owned by a citizen of Virginia and let her go.

The last prize above the Equator was the small schooner the Lizzie M. Stacy, Boston to the Sandwich Islands by the Cape of Good Hope with assorted cargo. This shipshape little craft was speedier than the Shenandoah. If the wind had not failed, she would have got clear away. Her sailing qualities and her diminutive size excited admiration on the cruiser. Sailing Master Hunt remarked that no one but a Yankee skipper would have undertaken a voyage half way round the world in such a tiny craft, but Captain Archer appeared to think nothing of it. Waddell would have liked to convert her into an auxiliary but could not spare a crew, and she was burned. She had only seven men on board, four of whom enlisted under compulsion. One of these, John H. Colby, afterwards deposed that he was triced up by the thumbs for refusing to work and joined the crew to escape torture.

Crossing the Equator, the Shenandoah cruised for nearly a month through forty degrees of tropical seas. At the end of the twenty-four hundred miles she sighted simultaneously the island of Tristan da Cunha and her first whaler, the decrepit, fifty-year-old bark Edward, four months out of New Bedford, engaged in cutting the first whale of her voyage. She yielded a quantity of stores and twenty-six prisoners, most of whom were Hawaiians.

By this time forced enlistments had augmented the cruiser's foremast crew to thirty-nine. Since twenty of these were acquisitions from the prizes, they had to be watched to prevent coöperation between them and the prisoners from the Stacy and the Edward, numbering twenty-eight. The latter were in irons, but Waddell thought it very necessary to get rid of them.

In 1864 Tristan da Cunha had not become a recurrent feature of the Sunday supplements. It lies in the South Temperate Zone a little below the latitude of the tip of Africa. The imprisonment of Napoleon on St. Helena, twelve hundred miles to the north, led the British government to forestall the possibility of a rescue from this island by placing a naval garrison upon it. The place is a mountain top seven miles square, rising high above the sea. In 1864 Napoleon had been dead for forty-three years; the naval station, long since discontinued. A remnant of population remained, for Tristan da Cunha is a pleasant, fertile spot. At the time of the Shenandoah's call, there were seven families there, comprising about forty persons, who were contentedly raising cattle, sheep, and chickens, knowing neither money, magistrate, nor priest, and accepting the leadership of the senior inhabitant, old Peter Green. A whaler putting in every few months for water or to barter coffee, tea, sugar, and flour for fresh meat and eggs gave them their only contact with the world of men.

Up to the steep shore of this primitive Eden steamed the Shenandoah, towing the boats of the Edward and flying a flag the islanders had never seen. They were told that some prisoners were to be landed. Let Master's Mate Hunt tell the story:

"'And where the devil did you get your prisoners?' queried one of the mystified natives.

"'From a whaler not far from here,' responded one of the officers.

"'Just so, to be sure, and what became of the whaler?'

"'We burned her up.'

"'Whew! Is that the way you dispose of the vessels you fall in with?'

"'If they belong to the United States; not otherwise.'

"'Well, my hearty, you know your own business, but my notion is that these sort of pranks will get you into the devil's own mess before you are through with it. What your quarrel with the United States is I don't know, but I swear I don't believe they'll stand this sort of work.'"

Thus the population of Tristan da Cunha was nearly doubled in one day by inexplicable and unexpected guests of a strange race who were forced to await the uncertain arrival of the next vagrant vessel calling there.

Waddell gave them rations for six weeks. The U.S.S. Iroquois was hunting for Confederate cruisers in the mouth of the Plate. On December 12 (1864) her commanding officer got a Rio de Janeiro newspaper which told of the existence of the Shenandoah and of her work north of the Equator. Conjecturing that she was en route for the Cape of Good Hope, Commander Rodgers started in that direction at once. As Tristan da Cunha lay in his course he called there for news, arriving three weeks after the Shenandoah had left. The Iroquois took off the prisoners of the Stacy and the Edward and carried them to Cape Town, where they would have no difficulty in finding berths.

Leaving Tristan da Cunha, the Shenandoah spent Christmas in a full gale off the Cape of Good Hope. On December 29 she burned the only prize she took in the Indian Ocean, the bark Delphine of Bangor, Maine, carrying machinery from London to Akyab, with the captain's wife and little boy on board, and a crew of fifteen, bound for Akyab for a cargo of rice. Among the captain's personal effects was a collection of books which were returned to his possession, with one exception; a copy of *Uncle Tom's Cabin* was thrown overboard. The Delphine was the craft that has been mentioned as having come within the orbit of the cruiser through the casual alteration of her course a quarter of a point on the morning of her capture.

New Year's Day, 1865, found the Shenandoah passing St. Paul's Island on her course toward Australia. She paused long enough to take on a boat-load of fresh fish and a penguin that had been marooned by some passing whaler and was suffering from heat and solitude. It brayed like a donkey. The brief stop at Tristan da Cunha, where the crew were not allowed to go ashore, was the only call she made between Madeira and Melbourne, a voyage of three months.

III

About the middle of January, 1865, the November mail from England arrived in Melbourne, bringing news of the departure of the Sea King and the surmise that she was destined for the Confederate Navy. On January 25, the Shenandoah, flying the Stars and Bars, came into the harbor. The United States Consul, J. J. Blanchard, immediately inquired what sort of teaspoons her officers were using. He soon learned that all the table silver and dishes on board were stamped "Sea King."

Blanchard also began to receive calls from the Shenandoah's captives, chiefly prisoners from the Delphine and some men enlisted from earlier prizes, who appeared before him and made affidavits of ill-treatment. Their statements are plausible because they agree with the short-handed condition of the cruiser throughout her career in the North Atlantic. The threat to make the men sorry was enough to produce a number of enlistments. To those who were recalcitrant, Lieutenant Whittle became more definite, threatening to put them in double irons in a room next the boiler. It was not necessary to carry this out. The men either enlisted or expressed a willingness to work. One man was coerced by being bedded in the sheep pen and another by confinement in the chicken coop. One man put up a resolute resistance. This was John Williams, Negro, cook and steward of the D. Godfrey, the Shenandoah's first prize. He deposed that he was triced up by the thumbs on seven occasions "for upholding my country." His affidavit, along with the others, was published by the British government in a dossier on the Shenandoah in 1866. Waddell, who was in England at the time, made no denial. In fairness to him it should be said that the Shenandoah's log book contains no record of these punishments. In usual course it would mention them.

Lieutenant Waddell applied to the Governor of Victoria, Sir Charles Darling, for permission to place his ship in a patent slip which was available, for the purpose of making repairs. He also asked permission to take on fuel and supplies. Blanchard protested that the vessel was a pirate and should be denied the use of the harbor. The proceedings from the arrival of the Shenandoah until her departure on February 18 exhibit the local authorities in an unhappy frame of mind. They did not know what to do. In consequence they did "everything by turns and nothing long." Waddell and Blanchard continually badgered them from opposite sides. Permission to use the patent slip and take on supplies was refused. Then it was granted. Leave to land the seventeen prisoners from the Delphine was denied, and when they were put ashore anyhow, no objection was made. Complaints that the cruiser was enlisting men were ignored; then they were acted upon; then they were shelved again. The provincial legislature debated the case with such animation that a member suggested that all those except the gentlemen having the floor should go out for a drink. In one respect the colonial authorities were consistent. They distributed insults impartially between Waddell and Blanchard. The Crown law officer refused to listen to the Consul because it was dinner time, shouting, "My dinner, my dinner, that is what I want." The Governor sent a detachment of men to search the ship for British subjects illegally on board and elicited from Waddell a threat to bombard the port rather than submit to search. He sent some men ashore and then assured the Governor that he had no one from Victoria on board. At the same time he was inserting advertisements in the newspapers for men "to work up new country." Applicants were enlisted on the Shenandoah. Meantime Blanchard had induced several of the original crew to desert. On the basis of Blanchard's complaints, the Governor finally sent fifty policemen and a squad of soldiers to the slip. Not venturing to go on board, they arrested a man named Charlie, who was frying chops and potatoes on shore, and three other men whom they marched to the lockup. These defendants were charged with violation of the Foreign Enlistment Act. One of them turned out to be a citizen of the United States and one was a young boy. These were discharged. On the trial of the other two their counsel said, "A poor young man, twenty-two years of age, having been found cooking in the patent slip, Inspector Lyttleton with 50 policemen and Major Verdon with all the artillery marched down to take him into custody; and then there had to be a state trial because a man had cooked some chops. Does the jury suppose Her Majesty is trembling on her throne because Charlie was frying potatoes?"

The learned court took the matter seriously:

"Men cannot fight unless they eat and the operations of a vessel of war cannot be carried on unless someone is set aside to perform the necessary cooking. Cooks are therefore useful and necessary persons on board ships."

Charlie and his companion were convicted and received

nominal sentences. That was the net total of the efforts of the colonial authorities to observe neutrality. When the Shenandoah departed on February 18, 1865, after having been in the port of Melbourne for upwards of three weeks, she was fully repaired, provisioned, and fueled, and had among her crew between forty and forty-five men who were not there when she came in. One was an English merchant master. A number of them were covered with grime and nearly suffocated. They had "eluded the search of the ships officers" by hiding in the coal and by crawling into the hollow bowsprit. Consul Blanchard wrote in his report to the State Department on the attitude of the Victoria officials, "They have eyes that see not; ears that do not hear."

The Shenandoah was now fully manned and equipped to start her search for Pacific whalers. She turned northward, sighted Drummond's Island, Strong's Island, and McAskill Island with no luck. Waddell concluded that the South Pacific whalers had been warned from Melbourne. The cruiser entered the Caroline archipelago on April 1, 1865. She anchored off Ascension Island (now known as Ponape) and found Thomas Horrocks, an escaped convict of Yorkshire, who had lived there for thirteen years and knew nothing of the war. This old rascal piloted the ship into the harbor where four whalers were lying: the Edward Carey, of San Francisco, the Hector, of New Bedford, the Pearl, of New London, and the Harvest, which hailed from Honolulu. All four masters were absent. They had gone ashore to visit the local missionary, according to one account, for a convivial party, according to another. The prizes were taken outside the harbor and burned. The crews and the returning captains were made prisoners, 130 in all. One of the captains was confined in double irons and gagged for disrespect. The Shenandoah's men were convinced that the natives were cannibals; so they were relieved when King Ish-y-Paw, who at first was inclined to be disagreeable, thawed out and showed a friendly disposition. Waddell sent a delegation to pay respects. These diplomats, accompanied by Horrocks as interpreter, scrambled up a long rocky path under the tropic sun to a large bamboo hut, where they were received in state by a wizened old man clad in a coating of cocoanut oil. He signified his royal pleasure to visit the ship. This he did, shining with a fresh coat of oil and with the stems of tobacco pipes through the lobes of his ears, escorted by more than one hundred canoes which surrounded the Shenandoah, somewhat to the dismay of her crew who had learned that Melanesian natives can throw stones with the accuracy of gunfire.

Arriving on board, His Majesty preceded his suite up the ladder and seated himself at the top, blocking the way of those behind him and leaving the Crown Prince dangling against the side by a manrope. Escorted to the cabin, the king "drank freely of Schiedam Schnapps," became extremely courteous and displayed a certain social grace. "I wish to spit," he said through the interpreter, "but don't like to spit on the carpet." He accepted a present of muskets, ammunition, and tobacco. Previously there had been no firearms on the island. The gift may have been a dubious courtesy.

With the exception of eight men who enlisted on the Shenandoah, the prisoners asked to be left on the island. With the king's consent, Waddell put them ashore with a stock of provisions.

In destroying a Hawaiian ship, the Harvest, in the belief that she was American-owned, Waddell paved the way for the rescue of all the marooned prisoners. By some conveyance, presumably a small Pacific trading craft, they got a message to Hawaii. A ship bearing the name of the reigning monarch, Kehamaha V, was sent out and took them to Honolulu, which, as the great Pacific whaling center, was as good as home to all these men. Waddell was mistaken in assuming that the Harvest was really an American vessel. Her principal owner was one Henry Stackfield, who claimed to be a citizen of Hawaii by denization. He was probably one of those expatriated Englishmen who had acquired dominating influence in Hawaiian business affairs. We shall hear of him again.

The Shenandoah remained at Ascension Island for thirteen days. Her men were given shore leave after their six weeks' confinement on board. They disported themselves after the standard pattern of white sailors in a native port. On Palm Sunday, while they were enjoying these tropical amusements, two grave, constrained soldiers were meeting in a hamlet a third of the world away. One remarked that his army had been subsisting on parched corn for three days. The other inquired, "Will 25,000 rations be enough?" General Lee replied, "Plenty, plenty," and rode away from Appomattox to parole the Army of Northern Virginia.

There was no thought of any such thing on Ascension Island. The Shenandoah sailed on April 13. Two nights later —allowing for the difference in time—while her crew were adjusting themselves to naval discipline, Miss Laura Keene's dramatic performance of "Our American Cousin" was interrupted by a pistol shot. But that, again, was 120 degrees of longitude away and awoke no echo on the Tropic of Cancer.

The cruiser headed north across the track of vessels bound for Hong Kong but found none; she weathered a typhoon and, on May 21, passed through Amphitrite Strait between two of the Kuril Islands and entered the Okhotsk Sea.

Only one whaler was found there, the fifty-year-old Abigail, twenty-three months out of New Bedford. She was burned on May 27 with a small quantity of oil she had in her hold. She had previously sent home a good catch. Captain Nye managed to man two boats and sent them to warn the rest of the fleet. Her remaining crew of thirty-five were taken on board and, in the course of the ensuing three weeks, fourteen of them enlisted in the Confederate Navy. One of these, a Sandwich Islander, died during the cruise. This was one of two deaths aboard the Shenandoah, the other being a man who enlisted at Melbourne. Among the stores of the Abigail was a quantity of whiskey which her captain had brought out for trading purposes. When transferred to the Shenandoah it was broached by the crew, who indulged in a stupendous orgy that gave the officers serious concern for a time.

In the Okhotsk Sea Lieutenant Whittle records a vivid impression:

"The most beautiful optical illusions I ever witnessed were in the mirage in this latitude about Kamchatka. When not foggy the atmosphere was a perfect reflector. We saw prominent points seventy miles distant. We would see a snow-clad peak direct, and above it, inverted, the reflection, peak to peak, with perfect delineation; or we would see a ship direct, and above it the reflection of the same ship inverted, mast-head to mast-head. . . . It was most interesting as we went north toward the pole to mark the days grow longer . . . until finally we went so far that the sun did not go out of sight at all, but would go down to the lowest point, and without disappearing, would rise again. In short it was all day."

Although there were many whaling craft in the Okhotsk at the time, the warnings sent out by the master of the Abigail enabled them to keep out of the way. The Shenandoah cruised about for three weeks, encountering only ice and fog. Twice she was jammed among floes. She was not constructed for such work. None of her company had any experience in Arctic navigation. On June 14 Waddell took her out into the Pacific and turned her head north again, past the westerly Aleutian Islands and into Bering Sea, steering toward Cape Navarin. It had become apparent that he was in urgent need of a pilot. The want was unexpectedly supplied. Master's Mate Hunt tells of it:

"About this time the second mate of the Abigail began to express a desire to join us and of course claimed to be a strong Southern sympathizer. He was a Baltimorean by birth, anything by profession, and a reprobate by nature. He had last shipped in San Francisco where, I was informed, he had been hired to vote for Lincoln by a drink of whiskey, and he now proposed, after a little backing and filling, not only to cast in his lot with us but to pilot the Shenandoah to the spot where the whaling fleet, which contained more than one vessel upon which he had served, was pursuing its bold laborious calling."

Accordingly Thomas S. Manning was enrolled as ship's corporal. He proved to be a thoroughly competent pilot.

The apparition of an armed steamer in Bering Sea was discovered by the whaling craft there with incredulous amazement. The first to be burned was the 405-ton ship William Thornton, largest of the whaling fleet, a year out of New Bedford. The next victim, on June 23, was not a whaler but a trader, the Susan and Abigail of San Francisco, loaded with miscellaneous articles to be bartered with the Eskimos for fur. An old gun and some ammunition were worth fifteen sables. A good knife would fetch almost anything.

The capture of the Susan and Abigail was heartbreaking to her captain and hardly less so to Waddell, for she had on board San Francisco newspapers of the second week in April, with telegraphic news sent over the wire which the Western Union Company had strung across the continent in 1862. The despatches reported verbatim Lee's letter of acceptance of Grant's terms of surrender on April 9. They also contained this item:

"New York, April 14.—The *Express* has information from one of its editors in Richmond that Jeff Davis on the 5th penned a proclamation at Danville saying that Virginia had been reoccupied by the federal forces and that the war would be continued." [1]

And the following which appeared in the *Evening Despatch* of April 14:

"Guerilla Moseby says that he does not care for Lee's surrender but will fight so long as he has a man left."

The news confronted Waddell with a serious problem. If

---

[1] *Daily American Flag* (San Francisco), April 15, 1865.

the war had indeed ended, any subsequent captures by the Shenandoah would be acts of piracy for which he and his crew might be hanged in any civilized country. Yet he was loath to believe that the cause was lost. The reader must be left to conjecture the workings of his mind. What he did was to burn the Susan and Abigail in spite of the pleadings of her captain, and take a score more vessels in the next five days, or nearly two-thirds of his total number of prizes.

The 400-ton ship Milo, nineteen months out, was bonded to transport prisoners to San Francisco. She did not return to her home port of New Bedford until May 7, 1869, when she arrived with a good cargo of sperm oil.

Then came the 424-ton ship Sophia Thornton and the 454-ton bark Jireh Swift of New Bedford. The latter had been out two years and ten months, had sent home large shipments of oil and bone, and had four hundred barrels of whale oil when taken. She was a fast sailer and tried to escape to the protection of the marine league off Siberia. The chase consumed three hours. Both prizes were burned.

The ship General Williams, thirty-two months out of New London, yielded $400 in specie. She was burned. Next came two New Bedford barks; burned; and the ship William C. Nye of San Francisco, which had sailed from San Pedro March 27 and had a hundred and fifty barrels of oil on board. Burned. Her owners made a prompt and vigorous protest as soon as they learned of her loss. It reached Charles Francis Adams in London before the Shenandoah got back. The General Pike, a 313-ton bark, of New Bedford, whose captain had died during the voyage, was bonded to receive prisoners for San Francisco. The crews of seven vessels were herded on board her, and by the time she reached San Francisco on August 1, all were suffering from the crowded condition of the ship.

The captain of the Gipsey, a 360-ton bark three years and one month out of New Bedford, had a library of two hundred volumes, a tastefully furnished cabin, and a selection of choice wines. Burned. Fate dealt the owner of this vessel a double blow. The Gipsey had shipped home 174 barrels of sperm and 670 barrels of whale oil, and 9,200 pounds of bone by the tender Golconda, which was caught and burned in the Atlantic by the C.S.C. Florida July 8, 1864.

Although the Shenandoah carried a condenser, its operation consumed coal; so she was glad to get a supply of fresh water before firing her next prize, the bark Isabelle of New Bedford, which had sent home good takings of oil and bone during the twenty-one months she had been out.

These activities bring us to June 28, the last day of the Shenandoah's hunting and the day of her best bag, eleven whalers in seven hours. The 327-ton bark Waverly, of New Bedford, with five hundred gallons of oil was caught at ten o'clock. The Waverly was an ill-fated vessel. Her third mate and an entire boat's crew had been lost while made fast to a whale. Now, after nineteen months of fishing she was burned in Bering Sea.

At noon the Shenandoah sighted a fleet of ten whalers. The ship Brunswick, of New Bedford, after thirty-two months at sea, sending good shipments home, had been stove by ice and all the neighboring craft were standing by. The Shenandoah stood in, showing United States colors. The astonished whalers thought her arrival a providential blessing. A boat was sent from the Brunswick to ask the loan of a carpenter. While the visitors were on board, the Confederate flag was run up and a blank cartridge fired. At this juncture the wind failed, leaving the whole flotilla at the mercy of the steamer.

Captain Young of the Favorite offered a brief defiance. He assembled his men with muskets and a bomb gun and threatened slaughter to the boarding party. His officers, however, had taken the precaution to unload the guns, and an armed boat's crew from the Shenandoah soon disposed of the annoyance. Captain Young had special reason to resent the loss of the Favorite, for she was a famous vessel. A bark of

298 tons, she was fifty-three years of age and had once made a banner voyage, bringing in $116,000 in a three-year cruise. When news of Young's resistance reached her home port of Fairhaven, it was celebrated as heroic. On the Shenandoah, however, it was observed that his courage was of the Dutch variety.

The ship James Maury, of New Bedford, was found to have on board a woman and three children. Captain Gray had sailed with his wife and family. He died in Guam in March and Mrs. Gray with the three little boys continued with the ship. She implored Lieutenant Waddell to spare the vessel, which had been her husband's home and hearse. Waddell yielded and placed the James Maury under bond to carry prisoners to San Francisco. The Maury finally got home in May, 1868. The bark Nile, of New London, was also bonded as a cartel.

Prisoners had been removed and all the rest of the fleet was in flames by five o'clock. Hunt describes the unearthly phantasmagoria of ice and fire while the sun revolved around the rim of the hyperborean sky:

"We hauled off a little distance and anchored with a kedge, to watch the mighty conflagration our hands had lighted... The red glare from the eight burning vessels shone far and wide over the drifting ice of those savage seas; the crackling of the fire as it made its devouring way through each doomed ship fell on the still air like upbraiding voices. The sea was filled with boats driving hither and thither with no hand to guide them and with yards, sails, and cordage, remnants of the stupendous ruin there progressing. In the distance, but where the light fell strong and red upon them, were the two ransomed vessels, the Noah's Arks that were to bear away the human life which in a few hours would be all that was left of the gallant whaling fleet."

So it seemed to the master's mate of the Shenandoah. The commanding officer of that ship wrote that the consternation of the officers and crews of the whalers was "a source of amusement," and that the scene of destruction was one of "indescribable grandeur."

Upon the completion of the holocaust, Waddell continued his northing into the Arctic Ocean, where he knew there were more whalers. He got as far as latitude 66° 14′ on June 29. This was the Confederacy's Farthest North, fifteen miles below the hem of the Arctic Circle, two months after Appomattox. Here heavy ice floes blocked the Shenandoah. Waddell turned her head southerly to try for trans-Pacific vessels and the steamers on the San Francisco-Panama run.

On the second of August she came up with the British bark Baracouta, fourteen days and twenty degrees due south of San Francisco, whence she was bound for Liverpool. Her English master told the boarding officer of the surrender of all the Confederate forces, the capture of President Davis, and the complete collapse of the Confederacy. The news, while hardly unexpected, had a dreadful finality. The entry in the log book is: "Having received by the Br. Barque Baracouta the sad intelligence of the overthrow of the Confederate government all attempts to destroy the shipping or the property of the United States will cease from this date."

"We were bereft of country," wrote Lieutenant Whittle, "bereft of ground for hope or aspiration, bereft of a cause for which to struggle and to suffer." This was perhaps somewhat exaggerated since the Shenandoah's company had neither struggled nor suffered beyond the ordinary lot of seafaring men. Still the experience was poignant enough and was accentuated by the immediate practical problem of where to go in order to avoid being hanged for the piracies of the closing days of June.

The obvious thing was done without delay. The guns were dismounted and stowed in the hold and the cruiser, so far as possible, converted into a merchantman.

Waddell determined to sail for Liverpool by way of Cape Horn. After rounding the Cape and emerging into the South Atlantic sixteen officers petitioned to be taken to Cape Town;

five were for England or France; seventy-two petty officers and enlisted men signed an expression of confidence in the commander. Waddell, having determined upon England, regarded all contrary advice as equivalent to mutiny. The strain of apprehension and disappointment created an unhappy condition in the ward room of the ship. In his anxiety Waddell avoided such sails as he saw, and in the entire three months of the voyage after speaking the Baracouta no ship was spoken. The whole distance was traversed under sail because the coal had run out.

Completing the circumnavigation of the globe, the Shenandoah entered St. George's Channel on November 5. The English were celebrating their national festival with the alarming rites customary among them, setting up grotesque effigies called "Guys," upon which they inflict indignities while their priests chant a tale of ancient wrongs—doubtless a form of homeopathic magic.

A pilot was secured and the ship proceeded up the Mersey anchoring next day. The cruise had extended over a year, had traversed fifty-eight thousand miles of sea without any sort of mishap or contact with a combatant enemy, and had netted thirty-eight prizes of which thirty were whalers, and 1,058 prisoners.

Waddell surrendered his command to H.M. Guard Ship Donegal. He sent a report to Lord Russell, who honored a demand by Charles Francis Adams to turn the vessel over to the United States.

The problem of the disposition of the crew was deliberated by the law officers of the Crown. They came to the conclusion that only those who were known to be British subjects could be prosecuted for piracy. Accordingly the men were mustered and asked their nationality. In the accents of the Clyde, the Shannon, and the Thames, one and all claimed to hail from Georgia, Alabama, Mississippi and other Southern states. Their word was accepted and the men were enlarged.

Bulloch, the Confederate naval agent in London, still had

some money in his hands and saw to it that they were paid. An obscure controversy arose out of an accusation that Waddell was withholding funds. Many of the Confederate officials in Europe were involved in similar contentions with one another over alleged misappropriation of funds, while seamen from the Tallahassee and the Rappahannock made futile efforts to collect their unpaid wages. It is impossible to unravel these disputes. They are of no interest to anyone now. Waddell's spiritual reward is recorded in the bitter boast, "I made New England suffer."

Waddell lived in Europe for some years until he got a job as a master for the Pacific Mail Steamship Company. After that company came to grief,[1] he retired to join the little company of ancient mariners clustering outside the gates of the Naval Academy at Annapolis, where he died in 1886.

On March 22, 1866, the Shenandoah was put up at auction by the American Consul at Liverpool. The Liverpool *Courier* reported the sale.

The auctioneer "begged gentlemen to give her a start, to put her up at their own price. A voice, 'You put a price on her.' The auctioneer said that if they would permit he would conduct the business in his own way. Would some gentleman be good enough to put a price on her? Mr. Lamport, 'Ten thousand pounds.' The auctioneer, 'Thank you, sir; any other bid?' Eleven thousand; going for eleven thousand. Twelve thousand; thank you; any more? Thirteen thousand; much obliged to you; she is now at thirteen thousand; thirteen thousand. Fourteen thousand (the bidding very brisk); fourteen thousand five hundred; fifteen thousand (bid by Mr. Bates we believe). The auctioneer repeated this advance two or three times and then proceeded: 'Any advance? Fifteen thousand once; fifteen thousand twice; if there is no advance on fifteen thousand pounds she is to be sold. Any advance on fifteen thousand? Once; twice,—' A voice, 'Five hundred.' The auctioneer, 'Thank you, sir, fifteen thousand five hun-

[1] See p. 258, below.

dred. Sixteen thousand? Oh very well, sir' (turning to another); 'Then fifteen thousand seven hundred fifty is your bid? Thank you, sir. Any advance? Once; twice; the third and last time. She is sold in a moment should there be no more bidding. Once. Twice,—' and down went the hammer announcing that the vessel was sold."

The purchaser was Nathaniel I. Wilson, who got the ship for about one-third her original cost. He resold her immediately at a profit of £1000 to an agent of the Sultan of Zanzibar who was extending the commerce of his sultanate in ivory, gum, coral, and cloves. The vessel did not operate profitably in this trade and was laid up at Zanzibar most of the time until the autumn of 1879, when she was sent to Bombay for repairs. On the way she foundered on a reef in the Arabian Sea.

The publicity of the sale attracted the notice of the owner of the brig Harvest, the Hawaiian ship destroyed at Ascension Island. Mr. Henry Stackfield was domiciled at Bremen. The day after the auction the Hawaiian Consul at Liverpool wrote to Mr. Dudley, the American Consul, that Stackfield had a claim on the proceeds of the Shenandoah for the value of the Harvest and the expense of getting her crew back to Honolulu. He conceived his rights against the cruiser to be superior to those of the United States as successor to the belligerent government which had destroyed his ship. By a remarkable coincidence, the loss sustained by the owner of the Harvest was $75,000, which was just under the sum the Shenandoah had fetched at auction the previous day. Mr. Dudley referred the matter to the State Department. The claim was not paid.

There was never a time after the war when the whaling tonnage afloat was more than half that of 1860. The Shenandoah merely accelerated a decline which began with the discovery of petroleum in Pennsylvania in 1859. Kerosene and its derivatives rapidly supplanted whale and sperm oil; umbrella ribs and fishing rods were made of steel or bamboo; corsets later went out of style. What remained of the Pacific fleet was obliterated by Arctic ice in 1871 and 1876. Whales are still hunted, with steam and dynamite; indeed, the kill for 1939 was the largest in history. Friends of the whale fear his extermination is in sight. The oil is used in oleomargarine and has a military use as constituent of glycerin. But the industry is not peculiarly American. The air of Nantucket and New Bedford is no longer fortified with the tang of tried-out blubber. At Round Hills an old Pacific whaler has actually been dragged ashore and enshrined in concrete by a cushioned descendant of a man who owned her when she was alive. You can go on board and mourn the dead for the modest fee of fifty cents.

In 1939 two American travelers, Dane and Mary Coolidge, visited a forlorn remnant of the Seris Indians on the Island of Tiburon in the Gulf of California, a race gone to seed and nearly extinct. These Indians were found to be cherishing a legend of gigantic white whale hunters who long ago visited Tiburon in a great ship and stayed a year and four months, trying-out oil. The Indians commemorated them in a song, perhaps the last living tradition of the New Bedford fleet:

> Far off in the sea a whale spouts.
> The giants follow him in their boat.
> The whale goes deep to the bottom.
> They spear him in the head,
> And the seas are red with blood.

The Whaling Ship Charles W. Morgan.
Courtesy of the Estate of Edward H. R. Green.

"A Still Bigger Claimant."
From Punch (London), Reproduced by permission of the proprietors of Punch.

CHAPTER XI

GENEVA

Reparation for our rights at home and security against the like future violations.—William Pitt, 1770

THE COLLAPSE OF the Confederacy placed England in a dilemma. As Lord Salisbury said ruefully, English capital and English officials "had backed the wrong horse." The victors were in an angry mood. England had given them a great deal of trouble. They considered that her early proclamation of neutrality and her persistent disregard of it, as they contended, in favor of the South during the first fifteen months of the conflict had heartened the insurgents to make twice as much war as they would have made without this encouragement. In reply, the English pointed out that the declaration of neutrality followed Lincoln's recognition of Confederate belligerence by giving notice of blockade. On the alleged British violation of neutrality they raised an issue of fact.

Throughout the war Charles Francis Adams had been industriously laying a foundation for pecuniary claims. The United States now began to assert them.

The Chairman of the Senate Committee on Foreign Relations, Charles Sumner, with a large Irish constituency in Boston, asserted that England owed the United States half the cost of the war. He computed the figure at two and one-half billion dollars. He proposed that the claim be liquidated by the abandonment of British dominion over "all parts of the Western Hemisphere including all provinces and islands." This would have included Canada, Newfoundland, Bermuda, and the British West Indies.

Diplomatic representatives were appointed to negotiate a treaty. Mr. Sumner's suggestion, having been asserted in the

Senate by the responsible spokesman of American foreign policy, was presented to the negotiators and rejected.

A flood of controversy overspread the world. The newspapers of India and China were inundated with it. The Hong Kong daily press championed the cruisers and gave space to a long series of letters in rebuttal by "E.P.U.," who at last announced that the argument was ended, threw aside his incognito, and stood confessed to the incredulous Orient as E Pluribus Unum. The Library of Congress contains 135 titles on the subject in various languages, not including its treatment in general texts on international law.

The matter was argued pro and con with much diplomatic correspondence and many assurances of distinguished consideration, getting nowhere until 1871, when the victorious armies of the new Germany, encircling Paris, made British statesmen bethink themselves of the value of American good will. Another factor that entered into British calculations was the increase in the fighting strength of the United States Navy. In the last year of the war the Navy Department began to build a number of warships faster and more powerfully armed than anything the Royal Navy possessed. Among these were the Ammonosuc and the Wampanoag, already mentioned as the fastest ships afloat. In view of this naval equipment and of the vast reserve of "human material" trained in four years of war, the Ministry found it desirable to adopt a conciliatory attitude toward the United States. There was also the possibility that Britain, with her enhanced merchant marine, might desire in future to assert against some other nation the principles propounded in this instance by the United States.

With these things in mind Great Britain proposed an arbitral tribunal. The Treaty of Washington, dated May 8 and proclaimed on the Fourth of July, 1871, expressed "in a friendly spirit the regret felt by Her Majesty's Government for the escape under whatever circumstances of the Alabama and other vessels from British ports and the depredations committed by those vessels." A tribunal was set up, to consist of one arbitrator to be named by each contracting party and three to be named by the Emperor of Brazil, the King of Italy, and the President of the Swiss Republic, respectively. The nominees were Charles Francis Adams, American; Sir Alexander Cockburn, British; ex-President Staemfli of Switzerland; Count Sclopis, Italian; and Baron Itajuba of Brazil. They were given jurisdiction to hear and determine "claims growing out of the acts committed by the aforesaid vessels (i.e., 'The Alabama and other vessels') and generally known as the Alabama claims." The principles by which the arbitrators were to be guided were laid down. They have been quoted in the first chapter of this book.[1]

The United States was represented by J. C. Bancroft-Davis, as American agent, and William M. Evarts, Caleb Cushing, and Morrison R. Waite, as counsel. The case for the United States was prepared by Mr. Bancroft-Davis and President Woolsey of Yale. For Great Britain Lord Tenterden appeared as agent, with Sir Roundell Palmer as counsel, assisted by Montague Bernard and Mr. Cohen. The Commission sat at Geneva from time to time through the summer of 1871 and until September 14, 1872.

The United States demanded a sum in gross to cover (1) the claims for direct losses growing out of the destruction of vessels and their cargoes by the cruisers; (2) the national expenditures in pursuit of the cruisers; (3) the loss by the transfer of the American commercial marine to the British flag; (4) the enhanced payments for insurance; (5) the prolongation of the war after Gettysburg and the addition of a large sum to the cost of the war. This last item Lord Granville computed at nine billion and ninety-five million dollars, or four times what Sumner thought it was. Granville's purpose, of course, was to magnify to absurdity the American claim.

When these claims were presented an agitation arose in England for the repudiation of the treaty. The British market

[1] See p. 25, above.

for American securities disappeared. The tension was relieved on June 19, 1872, when Count Sclopis announced that the commissioners had reached the conclusion that the indirect claims could not be considered under the terms of the treaty.

Thus limited, the American agent presented the claims for the depredations of the Sumter, the Alabama, the Florida and her brood, the Georgia, the Shenandoah, the Tallahassee, and some lesser cruisers; also for the damage done early in the war by several privateers.

The British contested all the claims on the facts and on the law. With regard to the Florida, the British agent contended that she had been delivered to a Confederate port, Mobile; also that she was virtually a new ship when she left there. In either event he argued that no responsibility could attach to the construction in England.

A singular circumstance of this arbitration was that one of the commissioners, Sir Alexander Cockburn, Chief Justice of the Queen's Bench, declared in advance of hearing any evidence or arguments that he conceived it to be his duty to give judgment for Great Britain. He complained of the precipitancy of the proceedings. They consumed only a little over a year. "We are judges," he said, "and therefore should proceed slowly." In the end the judgment of the tribunal was given by a vote of four to one. On the day set for the announcement of the final decision (September 14, 1872) the British arbitrator delayed the meeting by being forty-five minutes late. He then hurried in; handed the Umpire a printed dissent nearly three hundred pages in length, which he had not previously communicated to his colleagues as the custom is; reached for his hat and rushed away without greeting his fellow arbitrators, who were shaking hands with one another and with counsel while all the bells of Geneva were ringing to celebrate the amicable termination of the controversy which had led the two powers to the verge of war. The dissenting opinion, four times as long as that of the majority, was a bitter, confused tirade. The London press unanimously condemned it. Their champion had been guilty of a cardinal sin in the British catalog, bad sportsmanship. Caleb Cushing had another explanation. He said the Lord Chief Justice of England had "gone clean daft."

The tribunal held Great Britain in fault for the Alabama and the Tuscaloosa, and for the Florida and her three offspring, finding that she was the same ship before she went into Mobile as when she came out. With reference to the Shenandoah, Britain was adjudged in fault for the damage done after leaving Melbourne. Great Britain was exonerated in the cases of the Sumter, the Georgia, the Tallahassee, and minor cruisers. The circumstances of their acquisition by the Confederacy were not proved to have cast responsibility upon England and the assistance they received in British ports was held not to have been shown to exceed permissible limits. The claims on account of smaller craft, some of which were privateers, were unsupported by evidence and were dismissed. The tribunal adjudged the British Government to pay to the United States the flat sum of $15,500,000. This is substantially the sum at which Mr. Cobden had computed the direct losses in May, 1864.[1] Payment was duly made. An eminent authority, Sir Travers Twiss, endorsed the view that England had purchased a valuable precedent for a bargain price.

The last word was with Bismarck. In behalf of Germany he repudiated the rules of neutrality laid down in the Treaty of Washington and the decision of the Geneva Tribunal. These principles were finally incorporated in the body of international law by The Hague Conference of 1907. In substance they were enacted by Congress as the municipal law of the United States in 1917.

The United States was confronted with the problem of disposing of the indemnity. A court was set up which heard evidence in support of claims for direct losses by owners and shippers, and by insurers who had suffered a net loss on war

[1] See p. 244, below.

risks. The court made awards totaling $9,416,120.25, leaving an undistributed balance of $6,083,879.75. This was increased by accumulation of interest on the bonds in which the fund was invested and by profits on the sales of some of them, to the sum of $10,089,004.90. Some sentiment developed in Congress in favor of giving this balance back to England. After much debate, a second claims court was created, which was authorized to pay claims for losses inflicted by the cruisers other than those for which the Geneva Tribunal had cast responsibility upon England. If there was anything left after indemnifying those claimants, it was to be used to refund the premiums paid for war risk insurance. The direct losses were paid in full, the premium claims were prorated against the balance of the fund, and the books were finally closed.

By this time twenty-five years had elapsed since the damage had been done. The payments of indemnity were helpful to those who got the money. They were of no value in resuscitating the merchant marine. The irreparable injury which it had sustained was complete in 1865. The reimbursement of individual sufferers many years later could not restore the American flag to the sea.

CHAPTER XII

THE FLIGHT FROM THE FLAG

We have been informed that sundry of Our subjects, Masters and owners of Ships, respecting more their private Gain and Advantage than the public good and safety of Us and our Dominions, do daily sell or otherwise dispose to Strangers and Foreigners their Ships and other vessels, to the great disservice of Us and of the State, in weakening the Navigation of this Kingdom.—Proclamation of Charles I, 1629

To the prosecution of the Civil War the Confederate cruisers made only a minor contribution, worth no more than an incidental chapter in a military or political history of the conflict. If the fifteen and one half million dollars at which the Geneva Tribunal reckoned the value of the prizes and cargoes captured by three of them were the measure of the damage they did, their story would be a closed episode of subordinate importance in history. Fifteen million dollars' worth of ships and goods was no great matter even then. The loss of two hundred sailing craft, nearly one-fourth of them old whalers, would have had no permanent effect upon the merchant marine. The indirect claims which the tribunal excluded from its jurisdiction could not have been computed by it unless the commissioners had been gifted with second sight. The future that was veiled to them is now the past and we can count the cost, though not in dollars.

During the war the United States Navy blockaders, numbering perhaps as many as three hundred,[1] captured or de-

---

[1] The exact number cannot be estimated as ships assigned to a station had other duties than blockading. Three hundred is certainly not an excessive estimate.

stroyed over fifteen hundred blockade runners of various nationalities, valued approximately at thirty-one million. A documented comparison of the commercial effect of the blockaders with that of the cruisers is impossible. Professor Owsley guesses that the blockade was run more than eight thousand times. At the peak of its stringency it was full of holes through which cotton and munitions bootleggers were passing. Yet the cost of making use of this instrumentality was backbreaking, because the blockade runners, like the prohibition bootleggers, charged their customers for a real risk plus a fictitious one, thus adding to the economic drain on the South and putting a prohibitive price on Southern staples abroad. What we cannot compute is the volume of trade the Southern ports would have had if open to legitimate trade after Northern outlets became inaccessible to the South. No one can guess the total tonnage that abstained from entering those ports or the quantity of goods the Southern producers refrained from attempting to export, or the weight of the burden of the excessive freights on the commerce that did move.

While these things must remain conjectural, the broad conclusion can be defended (and also debated) that the eight commerce destroyers, with their few captures, did greater and more permanent damage to the entire nation than the blockaders inflicted on the South.

On November 17, 1864, Commander Bulloch wrote to Secretary Mallory, "The announcement that another Confederate cruiser (the Shenandoah) is at sea cannot fail to have a depressing effect upon the foreign commerce of the United States by increasing the rate of insurance in and upon American bottoms." That is what a lawyer would call a monument in the evidence. The cruisers wielded a weapon more deadly than their guns, namely, fear, the fear with which they inspired the shipping industry. This quickly made itself apparent in the insurance market. The idea that the government should pay the premiums on war risk insurance had not been thought of. In 1861 the extra premiums for war risks on American ships were from 1 to 3 per cent of the insured value. The rate increased steadily until the careers of the Alabama and the Florida came to an end. In 1862 it was 4 per cent; in 1863, the banner year for the cruisers, there were instances in which 9 per cent was paid. That means that if you shipped $100.00 worth of goods you paid $9.00 in addition to the regular marine insurance rate and the freight. In 1864 the rate was 6 per cent. On June 24, 1863, the New York Chamber of Commerce advised the Secretary of the Navy that "the war premium alone on American vessels carrying neutral cargoes exceeds the whole freight in neutral ships."

In November, 1863, Frederick M. Edge, an Englishman who had traveled and resided in the United States, published a pamphlet addressed to Lord Russell, entitled *The Destruction of the American Carrying Trade,* in which he said:

"As a natural result of these unlooked-for depredations upon American commerce, the war risks on insurance policies rose to an exorbitant figure; five, seven and one-half, and even ten per centum being demanded by insurance companies, over and above the ordinary risks. No wonder that American merchants complain of this state of affairs or that the commerce of the country languishes, since the exaction of such exorbitant, although necessary, premiums must cancel the profits of almost any venture."

These heavy charges were enough to keep cargoes out of American bottoms. Why should a shipper pay them and impair his competitive position in the market for his goods, when he could escape them by sending his cargo under a foreign flag?

In order to hold the business, the American shipowner had to pay the shipper's insurance premium for him, in addition to paying the enormously increased rate of insurance on the vessel itself.

Insurance against war risks, even when carried at the excessive rates, did not assuage the disastrous effect of the depredations of the cruisers. The insurance on the prizes, their cargoes and freights, was carried for the most part by American marine underwriters, so that the indemnification of the owners did not diminish the loss. It was merely transferred from the American owner to the American insurer and remained a burden upon the commerce of the country. The premiums paid for the insurance also came out of American pockets. The destruction of floating property was a total loss to American shipping.

In only a few cases was there anything approaching complete coverage against war risks. This was due to the system of vessel ownership. Corporations have been slow to go to sea. Of all the prizes destroyed by the Confederate cruisers, totaling some two hundred, only one had a corporate owner. Each ship was owned by a group of part-owners in unequal proportions. The owners of the larger shares usually insured their interests. The smaller participants sometimes did not. Cargo and freight insurance were similarly unequal and inadequate. Large consignments of goods were likely to be insured either by the shipper or by the vessel, whereas in a ship laden with miscellaneous merchandise, the owners of the smaller individual consignments seldom took out policies, preferring to rely on the legal responsibility of the vessel as a carrier as we do today. Some prudent shipowners carried insurance against the loss of freight and charter hire for the voyage; many more did not, preferring to carry their own risk rather than have their profits absorbed in high premiums. In no case did insurance indemnify the owner for the most serious element of his loss, that of the future use of the ship.

The carrying by a vessel of full insurance coverage on a cargo was not enough to hold the trade. A shipper would rather have his goods delivered than collect a claim against an insurance company. He is speculating on the commodity market at the place of destination, or else he has sold the cargo at a profit contingent upon delivery. Whether the insurance would indemnify him or not, he is in trade and wishes to continue.

So, in order to attract cargoes, the American shipowner had not only to pay the increased premium on both ship and cargo; he had also to reduce the freight. The New York Shipping and Commercial List tells the story. In 1861 it notes, "Neutral flags command 15 to 20 per cent over American vessels." On October 18, 1862, "Vessels under foreign flags command higher rates in consequence of the reported seizure and destruction of American vessels by rebel cruiser 290." Again, on October 25, "Shipments making almost entire in foreign bottoms, American vessels being in disfavor." On October 29, "Shipments to Liverpool and London by American vessels small and rates on grain lower, but by foreign bottoms there is a fair business at full previous rates."

The next year the condition was the same. August 1, "American vessels are in but little request and chiefly for coastwise voyages." November 4, "Neutral vessels continue to receive the lion's share as may be inferred from the fact that of some 150 vessels loaded for foreign ports, only 20 were covered by the American flag."

In 1864 the report was, "The discrimination against American bottoms is so great that neutrals are almost monopolizing European trade." And in January, 1865, "Neutral flags continue to monopolize the bulk of the business to foreign ports and the fact that two more rebel cruisers, the Shenandoah and Olustee (Tallahassee) are depredating upon our commerce is not likely to help matters."

Collating the advanced insurance rates with the reduced freights, it appears that during the last half of the war neutral vessels had an advantage of about 25 per cent over American bottoms. The only business the latter got consisted of evil-smelling, offensive cargoes that the neutral vessels did not want.

The condition is dramatized when we observe the destinations of the prizes. Captures on north trans-Atlantic voyages became progressively fewer. Increasingly the prizes became coasters, whalers, ships homewardbound from long trips to the Far East, vessels in the South American, West Indian, and California runs. The absence of quarry worth the chase on the northern routes was what sent the Alabama into southern waters in the spring of '63; thence to the Indian Ocean and the China Sea. The Stars and Stripes were no longer afloat in the northern ocean.

Although the American flag disappeared from the sea, the ships which had flown it (except the destroyed prizes) did not. They were sold to foreign owners and became part of the merchant marine of other nations. There was then no legal obstacle to the transfer of the flag.

At first these transfers were merely colorable. An American ship would be sold to a foreigner, who gave the former owner a mortgage for the purchase price so that the American retained a hold on the ship. Satisfied that these transfers were subterfuges, Judah P. Benjamin published a list of the mortgages taken from the custom house records and advised the commanders of the cruisers that the vessels listed were good prize notwithstanding their apparent foreign ownership. It was fortunate for the Confederacy that none of the listed vessels was captured, for the sham sales soon became genuine. As soon as British operators understood that they could buy American tonnage at panic prices, they began to make bona fide purchases. In the one instance in which a cruiser took an ex-American ship, that of the capture of the Martaban by the Alabama—a case in which the transfer was actually bogus—we have seen how quick England was to sustain the British registration.

As early as November, 1861, the *Baltimore Sun* reported, "The shipments of grain from this port during the past week have been almost entirely in foreign bottoms, the American flag for the moment being in disfavor in consequence of the raid of the rebel steamer Alabama."

On March 21, 1862, Bulloch wrote to Mallory, "American ships are fast being put under the British flag."

On July 8, 1863, R. B. Forbes, a Boston financier, wrote Secretary Welles that of 180 vessels in New York, 146 were under foreign flags. "Our commerce will soon be entirely in the hands of foreigners unless our trade is protected by every means within the power of the government."

On October 22, 1863, Commander McDougal of the U.S.S. Wyoming reported, ". . . nearly all of the American vessels in the China seas have changed flags, otherwise get no employment. While at Macao three fine American vessels were put under Portuguese colors," and the *Singapore Times* of December 9, 1863 (as quoted by Semmes) said:

"From our today's shipping-list it will be seen that there are no fewer than seventeen American merchantmen at present in our harbor, and that they include some of the largest ships at present riding there. Their gross tonnage may be roughly set down at 12,000 tons. Some of these have been lying here now for upward of three months, and most of them for at least half that period. And all this, at a time when there is no dullness in the freight market; but, on the contrary, an active demand for tonnage to all parts of the world. It is, indeed, to us, a home picture—the only one we trust to have for many years to come—of the wide spread evils of war in these modern days."

On February 18, 1864, Commander Bulloch reported to Secretary Mallory: "There really seems to be little for our ships to do now upon the open sea. Lieutenant-Commanding Low of the Tuscaloosa reports that in a cruise of several months, during which he spoke over one hundred vessels, only one proved to be American; and she being loaded entirely on neutral account, he felt forced to release her after taking a bond. The Alabama also only picks up a vessel at intervals, although she is in the East Indies, heretofore rich in American traffic."

Speaking in the House of Commons on May 13, 1864, Cobden, one of the champions of the North, said,

"You have been carrying on hostilities from these shores against the people of the United States and have been inflicting an amount of damage on that country greater than would be produced by many ordinary wars. It is estimated that the loss sustained by the capture and burning of American vessels has been about $15,000,000 or nearly £3,000,000 sterling. But that is a small part of the injury that has been inflicted upon the American marine. We have rendered the rest of her vast mercantile property for the present valueless. Under the system of free trade by which the commerce of the world is now so largely carried on, if you raise the rate of insurance on the flag of any maritime power you throw the trade into the hands of its competitors because it is no longer profitable for merchants or manufacturers to employ ships to carry freights when those vessels become liable to war risks. ... I hold in my hand an account of the foreign trade of New York for the quarter ending June 30, 1860, and also for the quarter ending June 30, 1863, which is the last date up to which a comparison is made. I find that the total amount of the foreign trade of New York for the first mentioned period was $92,000,000 of which $62,000,000 were carried in American bottoms and $30,000,000 in foreign. This state of things rapidly changed as the war continued, for it appears that for the quarter ending June 30, 1863, the total amount of the foreign trade of New York was $88,000,000, of which amount $23,000,000 was carried in American vessels and $65,000,000 in foreign, the change brought about being that while in 1860 two-thirds of the commerce of New York was carried on in American bottoms, in 1863 three-fourths was carried on in foreign bottoms. You see, therefore, what a complete revolution must have taken place in the value of American shipping; and what has been the consequence? That a very large transfer has been made of American shipping to English owners, because the proprietors no longer found it profitable to carry on their business. A document has been laid on the table which gives us some important information on this subject. I refer to an account of the number and tonnage of United States vessels which have been registered in the United Kingdom and in the ports of British North America between the years 1858 and 1863 both inclusive. It shows that the transfer of United States shipping to English capitalists in each of the years comprised in that period was as follows:

Year	Number of ships	Tonnage
1858	33	12,684
1859	49	21,308
1860	41	13,638
1861	126	71,673
1862	135	64,578
1863	348	252,579

"I am told that this operation is now going on as fast as ever.[1] ... What with the high rate of insurance, what with these captures, and what with the rapid transfer of tonnage to British capitalists, you have virtually made valueless that vast property. Why, if you had gone and helped the Confederates by bombarding all the accessible seaport towns of America, a few lives might have been lost which, as it is, have not been sacrificed, but you could hardly have done more injury in destroying property than you have done by these few cruisers."

On January 20, 1864, when the Sumter and the Georgia had finished their work, the Alabama had gone to the eastern seas, the Florida was refitting at Brest, and the Tallahassee, and the Shenandoah had not started, T. M. Gibson, President of the British Board of Trade, made a speech in which he said, "We find that the tonnage of British ships entering and clearing out with cargoes in the United Kingdom has increased in

[1] During 1864, an additional 400,865 tons were sold British and in 1865, 133,832 tons.

the present year to an amount of something like 14,000,000 tons and upwards against 7,000,000 tons of foreign shipping. ... But it would not be fair to take credit for this improvement in shipping as due to any policy of this country. I am afraid that some of it is due to the transference from American ships to British ships. And why this transference from American ships to British ships? No doubt partly in consequence of the war that prevails in America. There is the fear among the American merchant shipping of attacks by certain armed vessels that are careering over the ocean and which are burning and destroying all United States merchant ships which they find upon the high seas. The fear therefore of destruction by these cruisers has caused a large transfer of American carrying trade to British ships. Now the decrease in the employment of American shipping is very great. In the trade between England and the United States it is something like 46 or 47 per cent." [1]

The *New York World* of July 7, 1864, listed by name 608 vessels transferred to the British flag since 1860 and gave the reduction in tonnage as from 5,219,181 to 1,674,516. About 300 others were transferred to other flags. Being an opposition newspaper, the *World* attributed the losses to the "imbecility" of the Secretary of the Navy. On October 22, 1864, Reverdy Johnson, speaking in support of McClellan's candidacy for the presidency, asserted:

"More than 1,000 of our ships we have been compelled to sell to foreigners because our flag furnished no protection but on the contrary is but an incentive to the pirate's torch. They are now travelling the ocean with American freemen and property under the shelter of foreign banners. The insurance against war risks is now as high as it was in the war with England in 1812 and much higher than in that with Mexico."

On April 7, 1865, Mr. Adams wrote to Lord Russell complaining of the British policy with reference to the cruisers. He said, "That policy, I trust I need not point out to your

[1] *London Times,* January 21, 1864.

Lordship, is substantially the destruction of the whole mercantile navigation belonging to the people of the United States.... It may thus be fairly assumed as true that Great Britain as a national power is in point of fact fast acquiring the entire maritime commerce of the United States." Adams adverted to this again in a letter to Russell on May 29, 1865: "In addition to this direct injury, the action of these British built, manned and armed vessels has had the indirect effect of driving from the sea a large portion of the commercial marine of the United States." He commented upon the figures, which showed that during the war ten times as many tons and six times as many ships had been transferred from American to British ownership as during 1858, 1859, and 1860.

Secretary Fish wrote to Mr. Motley September 25, 1869, "The number of ships thus destroyed amounts to nearly 200 and the value of the property destroyed to many millions. Indirectly the effect was to increase the rate of insurance in the United States and to take away from the United States its immense foreign commerce and transfer this to the merchant vessels of Great Britain."

More than half of the total American merchant fleet was lost to the flag during the Civil War. The cruisers burned or sank 110,000 tons of it; 800,000 tons were sold to foreign owners. In addition, there was a considerable loss of tonnage, for which figures are not available, by reason of the fact that some foreign powers, notably Portugal, issued licenses to American owners by which vessels were placed under the registry and protection of the foreign government under an arrangement which was intended to be temporary but in fact became permanent. The ships that were left under the American flag were the ones the foreigners did not want—old, obsolete, and nearly worthless craft.

These losses to the carrying trade of the nation occurred at a time when the foreign commerce of the United States was steadily and largely increasing. Throughout the war the North enjoyed a high degree of prosperity not attributable to wartime inflation. Bumper crops of wheat, augmented by immigrant field labor of both sexes and the introduction of agricultural machinery, doubled the previous output of the Western states. Crop failures in Europe during the same period provided a favorable market. The mounting population of immigrants stimulated the market for imports in step with that for exports. American trade was booming in both directions while the flag was being driven from the sea and English ships were acquiring the supremacy of the ocean.

The effect upon British shipping is dramatically summed up in a report submitted to the Statistical Society of London by Mr. John Glover, relating to the decade 1860-1870.

"Cargoes were brought to and carried from our [British] ports under the American flag in 1860 to the extent of nearly 2¾ million tons but in 1870 the quantity was little over one million; the decrease between the first and last year of the decade being 1,600,116 tons.

"While the American flag so decreased in our ports, British tonnage in the direct trades between the United States and the United Kingdom alone, doubled between 1860 and 1866. ... In the same direct trade alone, American tonnage in 1860 attained the unparalleled quantity of 2,245,234 tons; by 1865 it had fallen to less than half a million. It seems to be clear from these facts that the great bulk of the trade thus lost by the American flag was gained by ours. Prior to 1860 in the India and China trade, as well as in the direct trade between the United States and the United Kingdom, the American flag had been gaining on ours. The Civil War not only stopped but reversed that process and gave a great impetus to our flag. From no quarter was such a result less likely when the decade began."

II

Thus the flag was driven from the sea. We have now to inquire why it did not return.

The ships that had been sold foreign or licensed under

foreign flags were not restored, because of legal impediments. Under an act passed in 1797 and still in force, an expatriated ship is denied repatriation. Application was made to Congress for the removal of this ban, but the proposal was rejected and, instead, Congress passed an act (February 10, 1866) excluding the group of ships which were still American-owned and were sailing by license under foreign flags. In the debates on these measures the cleavage was between the East and the West, the opposing factions being led by James A. Garfield of Ohio and James G. Blaine of Maine, who was later to become President Garfield's secretary of state. Blaine tried to secure an opportunity for the New England shipowners to resume their vessels. Garfield asserted that the American Merchant Marine was of no value to the West so long as foreign ships were available to carry the wheat. The Western votes closed the door against the return of any of the ships which had fled from the flag.

This is the reason the renegade ships did not come back. It does not explain why they were not replaced.

When the United States began to function under the Constitution in 1789, there were no national ships. Eight years later, when Washington delivered his warning against entangling foreign alliances, the nation possessed the largest merchant fleet afloat relative to the volume of its commerce. Twenty years after that, as the result of the Napoleonic Wars, including the War of 1812, American shipping, like that of Great Britain, had been reduced to low estate by privateering; yet it was immediately restored. Notwithstanding the competition of the greatly augmented British fleet after Waterloo, our ships were carrying about 70 per cent of our commerce during the three decades preceding the Civil War.

Why was there no similar recovery after 1865? There were a number of reasons.

1. Great weight is usually assigned to the diversion of capital and enterprise to the development of the West. The United States entered upon an era of railway building, min-

ing and manufacturing. S. E. Morrison has noted in the ledgers of New England investors, the change in assets from ships to railway and mining shares. Between 1860 and 1870 upwards of 30,000 miles of railway were laid in the United States, or twice the mileage built in the preceding decade. The following ten-year period added a like amount. Much of this construction was heavily subsidized by local, state, and federal governments. "The epic of the railroad builders, the vast machinery of enterprise that was required to equip new settlement across a continent,—those activities sufficed to occupy the growing energies of the United States."[1] Nevertheless there was an abundance of reserve capital which could have been invested in ships. English money flowed into American investments in such a tide as to place the United States in the category of debtor nations, so to continue until the first World War. This inflow of foreign money left American capital looking for work. Some weight must be accorded to internal development, but it cannot be regarded as a preponderating cause of the failure of the flag to return to the sea.

2. A more potent reason why capital did not go into new ships was the system of vessel ownership which has been mentioned. By the practice and tradition of many generations, long antedating the use of business corporations, ships were owned by groups of part-owners in varying proportions; in effect, a tenure in common. The individual part owner dealt with his share independently, insured it for his own account, took his profit or loss through the medium of the ship's husband or managing owner, who acted as agent for each of the several owners. The rapid internal development of the country introduced the modern industrial and commercial corporation starting from scratch. A number of states promptly adopted quick and easy corporation laws, to facilitate the use of this instrumentality, and authorized one corporation to own stock in another, a thing theretofore unlawful. It was a

[1] Philip Guedalla, *New York Times,* June 4, 1939.

revolutionary step upon which no restraint was placed until the adoption of the Sherman anti-trust law in 1890. Industrial corporations and holding companies burst into full bloom over night in the decade after the war. Corporate ownership of ships proceeded more slowly, having to overcome an established usage in an ancient industry. Investment in shares of stock is simpler, easier, and safer than part ownership of a vessel. Although protected by various legal immunities, there were circumstances in which a part owner might find himself liable for obligations of the vessel beyond his investment and beyond the value of the ship. A stockholder does not run this risk. Thus the simplicity and safety of industrial shares tended to deflect capital from shipbuilding during the appreciable period that intervened before the corporate ownership of vessels supplanted the ancient traditional system of part ownership.

3. The diversion of labor was a more serious factor than that of capital. The factories and the Western country offered greater opportunities than the forecastles of ships. The result was a progressive deterioration in the quality of marine labor. Increasingly the seamen on American ships ceased to be citizens of the United States. Vessels were able to recruit their crews only from the least desirable foreign habitués of sailortowns, including many orientals. It became impossible to obtain men, even for the navy, who could speak English. Serious disasters resulted from the inability of the crews to understand the language in which orders were given. This impairment of the quality of labor made a real contribution to the decline of American shipping.

4. The labor shortage interrelated with another cause, that is, the enlargement of the Navy. We have seen that during the war the number of vessels in the naval establishment was increased more than ten-fold. Secretary Welles boasted that he had acquired the best ships in the merchant service. With demobilization, the Navy list was reduced from 700 ships to 200. Few of the converted merchantmen had proved

efficient as naval vessels and when those the Navy did not want were returned to civil life, they were no longer fit for competitive trade. The new jerry-built naval vessels were equally ill adapted to private employment. Many of both classes were scrapped. The Navy also enlisted the best men. The enlisted personnel increased from 7,600 to 51,000. This exhausted the supply of native seamen. Twenty years after the war it was impossible to man a naval vessel with a crew half of whom understood English.

5. Another obstacle to the return of the flag was a change in tariff policy. Beginning with the organization of our national government, Congress passed fifty tariff laws in forty years, all directed to the protection of the shipbuilding industry. American ships were at first favored by discriminating duties on their cargoes, protective duties on building materials, and discriminating tonnage and lighthouse taxes; later, by reciprocity arrangements. These indirect aids ceased in 1830. By that time the United States was established in the carriage of her own commerce. Shipbuilding was a major industry from the Mystic to the Delaware. It was supposed that government support was no longer needed. The coasting monopoly was of course maintained.

The opening of the war marked the beginning of a long series of ever-mounting protective tariffs upon commodities. A recent English writer remarks, "The Americans as the country advanced, became more and more committed to a high tariff policy. Any country which imposes import tariffs high enough to raise its internal prices substantially above world levels, may as well say goodbye to its mercantile marine, and the Americans were no exception."[1] This statement needs qualification. The protective tariffs in the years following the Civil War did not diminish our foreign trade. The needs of a population increasing upon a floodtide of immigration and the unlimited European markets for American surpluses augmented the exchange of commodities over the tariff wall,

[1] R. H. Thornton, *British Shipping*, p. 76.

sometimes even to the point at which imports exceeded exports. That this commerce was carried on in foreign bottoms is not altogether attributable to the tariff on foreign commodities. It is partly due to a heavy duty on iron, which retarded the construction of iron hulls by increasing the price of the domestic product. Duties on shipbuilding materials were repealed in 1871. This belated aid was insufficient to restore the industry. The adverse effect of the protective tariff policy upon American shipping arose chiefly from the increase in domestic prices for the necessities and conveniences of life, which made a higher wage scale necessary in the construction and operation of ships. The portion of this disadvantage assignable to the high cost of shipbuilding could have been overcome if we had followed the English example of 1849 and permitted American owners to build or buy ships abroad when destined for foreign trade. We did not do this until 1914. By protecting the monopoly of our shipyards we contributed to the discrimination against our ships. The part of the disadvantage attributable to increased cost of operation could have been overcome only by direct government aid sufficient to offset the handicaps which the government had created. In sum, the protective tariff operated directly and indirectly to discriminate against American ships.

6. A number of writers, particularly the English, have ascribed the retreat of commerce from the American flag to another cause, namely, English leadership in the construction of iron hulls. They arrive at this conclusion by treating as a continuous process the British experience in the application of steam to ocean navigation. This line of reasoning loses sight of an important distinction. It is true that the abundant supply of timber in the United States, which was replenished by the acquisition of Florida in 1819, created a predilection for wooden sailing ships and a skill in their design and navigation unapproached in the history of commerce. American superiority at sea was that of sail and began to decline before the war. American sailing ships were confronted with com-

petition from British steam at a time when the success of the clipper ships was at its peak. The clippers were bringing in fortunes with every round voyage to China and California. Since steamers could not carry fuel for these long voyages it is undoubtedly true that American shipowners continued to be preoccupied with their success in sail and that this retarded the establishment of rolling mills and machine shops adjacent to deep water. Unquestionably also the scarcity of wood in England, the plentiful supply of iron, and the invention of the rolling mill in the late eighteenth century, directed English attention to the construction of iron hulls, which were lighter, cheaper, and more durable than wooden ones. But all the early English experiments were with sidewheel propulsion, which contributed little to the conquest of the ocean by steam and was merely a step in the wrong direction, which wasted nearly a quarter of a century of effort. The first paddle wheels installed on an ocean-going ship were mounted upon the Savannah in 1819 and were driven by a wood and coal burning engine. They were used for about one-third of her voyage as auxiliary to her sails. British builders, following this example, began to turn out auxiliary sidewheelers from 1823 on. Twenty years of trial and error proved that they could not compete with sail. They wore out so rapidly as to require replacement every four years. They were slower than sailers, noisy, sooty, and, most serious of all, unmanageable in a high sea. It was not until the invention and practical application of the screw propeller and the multiple expansion engine, installed in an iron hull, that steam began seriously to compete with sail. The first propeller was a British ship which arrived in New York in 1845. Then followed ten years of experimentation. The first iron, screw-propelled Cunarder was placed in service in 1855. Then, and not until then, British steam began to challenge American sail. That was only six years before the war. Lloyd's insurance rates did not begin to favor iron hulls until 1860. In the decade 1860-1870 the tonnage of steamers in and out of Great Britain trebled.

Nearly 95 per cent of these were under the Union Jack. Long before that the United States had rolling mills, machine shops, and engine builders. It is true that they were less efficient than those that had been developed over a longer period in Great Britain, that the cost of iron hulls was increased by the tariff, and that, in the words of Charles Cramp, a leading American shipbuilder, "The first iron steamers built here were fearful specimens of naval architecture." Yet by the time the war was over American mills were turning out plates, rails, locomotives, and marine engines, and had built a number of iron hulls. The English experience was available to Americans. Undoubtedly Great Britain had a head start in the application of steam to ocean transportation and this advantage contributed to the failure of the American flag to return to the sea. The handicap would have been overcome, however, if this had been the only obstacle in the way of American shipping.

7. The surplus of foreign tonnage at the close of the war was a deterrent to the construction of new American ships to compete under the handicaps which have been enumerated. When trade is thriving there are always more ships than are needed. A paradox of commerce is that there are never enough ships unless there are too many. This is because the seas are so wide. There can be no nice adjustment of schedules whereby a ship discharges one full cargo and immediately loads another for her next port. To pick up and deliver goods in accordance with seasonal or spasmodic production and consumption, the variation of markets, and the innumerable factors that enter into distribution, some ships will sail full, many partly full, some in ballast, and some will be tied up. It is only thus that the world can be served. An adequate mercantile marine means one that is too large. This was the condition of British shipping in 1865. It was brought about by a series of acts of Parliament in the late 1840's, after nearly a quarter of a century of debate. Under pressure of increased population and insufficient supplies, England reversed her

commercial policy, repealed nearly a thousand old restrictive laws, and adopted free trade in 1845. The sweeping nature of this innovation, which now seems so natural a policy for England, can be measured by the opposition it aroused. It was new; it was doctrinaire. Entrenched privilege was solidly against it. Adopted by a radical House of Commons, the Lords, contrary to all expectation, passed the bill by the votes of the bishops. The intervention of the spiritual arm brought in an element of the miraculous, of which the immediate stimulation of British industry is cumulative proof. Britain's foreign trade jumped from nine million tons in 1840 to fourteen million in 1850, and to twenty-four million in 1860. It was, indeed, as a contemporary statistician reported, a "grand march of millions."

Then in 1849 the British navigation laws were revised by permitting foreign-built vessels, when owned by British subjects, to be registered in Great Britain, and by abolishing the coasting monopoly of British ships. This liberalization was the logical corollary of free trade. The theory was that the advantage of free goods might be nullified by the high freights charged by protected ships. The ship operators lamented that the new legislation was "the last straw" and supposed that they were about to be bankrupted. What actually happened was that, while free trade and free ships, coming together, created a large increase in tonnage trading to the United Kingdom, there was no immediate lowering of ocean freights. Ships continued to prosper. The enhancement of British commerce absorbed much of the new tonnage; the gold rushes to Australia and California and the transport requirements of the Crimean war took up the surplus. When these temporary stimuli subsided, there was indeed an unemployable surplus of shipping—something like 1,700,000 tons according to a report to the London Statistical Society—and a corresponding depression of ocean freights. This condition, which was acute at the close of the Civil War, was one of the elements operating against the return of the United States flag to the sea.

III

As we have seen, some of the causes of the failure to recover were in operation before the war and had begun to send American shipping into a decline. The work of the cruisers was to accomplish by catastrophe what might otherwise have come about through a long decrepitude. The havoc wrought within the space of two years presented the United States with an opportunity to forestall the gradual atrophy of its mercantile marine by the construction of a new and modern replacing fleet. Looking backward with the proverbial advantage of retrospect it is easy to see that this was the moment when government aid promptly bestowed could have saved the American carrying trade to our national ships. It would not have been necessary to replace the losses ship for ship or ton for ton, since a steamer which is twice as fast as a sailing vessel of the same size can make two trips to the sailing ship's one and therefore has a potential carrying capacity twice as great, while a steamer which is double the size as well as twice as fast, is equal to four sailers, whereas the difference in cost of construction is less than four times the price of the sailing vessel.

What is true of construction is also true of operation. It does not require double power to propel a ship twice the size of another. The progressive improvement in marine engines increased cargo capacity with less than an equivalent increase in running cost. A steamer twice as large and twice as fast as a sailer had an operating advantage more than four times as great and, in most trades, the shipper finds it economical to pay increased freight for speed and reliability in reaching the market. The United States could have regained its former position with fewer ships than it had before and at less cost.

Unfortunately it was a time when government aid was politically impossible. The political fortunes of the West were rising, and, so long as the grain moved to market, shortsighted Western politicians thought they had nothing to gain from spending public money to fly the Stars and Stripes instead of the Union Jack over the cargoes.

England has been more solicitous for her shipping. As early as 1837 she began to grant postal subventions, at first to the Peninsular Line to Spain, then to the Cunard, the Royal Mail, and the Pacific Steam Navigation Company. This was the beginning of a British policy which has been pursued consistently. No other nation granted subsidies until ten years after England began to do so. In that time Britain acquired a lead she has never lost. England and her colonies and dominions have continuously favored the Union Jack with grants in aid, operating and postal subsidies, preferences and discriminations. In addition, England has been generous with low-interest construction loans of government money.

In the 1840's and 1850's the United States countered the British subventions with several grants to steamship lines for carrying mail. Postal contracts were let for trans-Atlantic and southbound services. They were local stimulants set up to meet particular conditions under pressure of interested groups, not in pursuance of a general policy, and all were withdrawn in 1859. Their only lasting effect was to help drive out the clippers in favor of foreign steamers.

Immediately after the war, some abortive gestures were made toward repairing the losses to our shipping, while at the same time the return of the turncoat ships was forbidden. A line was briefly subsidized between New York and Rio de Janeiro, another from San Francisco to the Orient. The latter became entangled in the meshes of political corruption and the aid was withdrawn in 1877.

The scandal that engulfed the Pacific Mail Steamship Company put a long quietus on attempts to aid the merchant marine. There remained a brief sunset glow for American sailing ships. They could still operate in the Pacific though steam had begun to invade even those broad lonely seas. These havens began to be lost to sail when steamers began to increase in size.

With the American fleet out of competition, a field for ships of a new design was opened on a single day, a Wednesday, in 1869. On November 17 of that year, in the presence of Eugenie, Empress of the French, the Emperor of Austria, the Crown Prince of Prussia, and the Khedive of Egypt, the Suez Canal was opened. It rendered obsolescent a large proportion of the shipping trading to the East, leaving for existing bottoms only such cargoes as gain no value from speed in delivery. The building of the canal had been attended with so many mishaps that the skeptical shipping world had not prepared vessels of suitable design for using it. Existing ships were not adapted to the new route. There is some difference of opinion among the experts as to the extent and immediacy of the effect. Coaling stations had to be set up along the way before full use of the new facility could be made. But the leading British company trading to the East was in no doubt. Apprehending competition from other nations, it promptly scrapped one hundred thousand tons of ships and replaced them with others suitable for transiting the canal. The United States lost another golden opportunity.

No further effort to restore our overseas shipping was made by the government until 1891. In that year, and again in 1928, Congress enacted postal subvention laws, which proved to be half measures, inadequate to accomplish the intended result. In 1914, following England's lead sixty-five years late, it exempted our ships in foreign trade from the requirement of American build, but in the following year increased the heavy operating differential against American vessels by passing the Seamen's Act, which undoubtedly guarantees better working conditions to American seamen but has so greatly increased the labor factor in the operating bill as to put unaided American ships out of competition in the world freight market.

During the American participation in the World War, the government built as many ships as possible in frantic haste—concrete ships, wooden ships, and some very good ships. All are now obsolete. The life of a cargo carrier is about twenty years. An effort was made to keep the war-built vessels in operation and use them as a basis for building up the overseas services. The story of this attempt is a painful chapter in our maritime history, now fortunately closed and best forgotten.

In 1936 the present building and operating subsidies were set up and, for the first time in our history, the United States has a comprehensive policy of general application, not motivated by "pressure groups." The purpose of the law is to make government funds available to equalize the building and operating costs of American ships with those of foreigners. Theoretically, American and foreign vessels are to be placed on a parity of cost to build and run. Whatever profit the American builders and operators get is to be derived from their ability to trade in a highly competitive market. The government does not pay or guarantee a profit or insure against loss. The government aid is to be refunded out of profits in excess of 10 per cent. Provision is made for long-term, low-interest loans for ship construction, and for construction of vessels by the government for sale or charter to operators. The system, which is too complex to be described here (the legislation contains about 40,000 words), is administered by the United States Maritime Commission. It is designed to accommodate the age-old conflict of interest between shipbuilders and shipowners; to permit American seamen to enjoy their superior wages and working conditions without ruining their employers; and to exclude favoritism to particular lines to the prejudice of unsubsidized ships in the same trade. This is important, because a subsidized ship will run an unaided ship off a competing route, as has always been true in fact as well as in obvious theory.

At this writing (May, 1940) the program of the Maritime Commission contemplates the construction of fifty new ships each year for ten years, chiefly moderate sized cargo vessels for foreign trade, and for such replacements of coastwise tonnage as may be warranted. The effect upon this program of the war in Europe is impossible to forecast. World tonnage is diminishing by the destruction of belligerent vessels thus far in a somewhat lower ratio than was the case during the first World War. North European trade routes have been closed to a relatively small number of United States ships, though sufficiently to release a large body of marine labor for employment in other services if the withdrawal of foreign ships warrants their development. The expanding naval program calls for more auxiliaries than the United States now possesses, and this may offset the diminution, if any, in trade requirements. The trade requirements are themselves affected by the withdrawal of foreign tonnage, foreign markets, and foreign purchasing power, and the probable opening of other markets for carrying trade hitherto largely monopolized by foreign ships. The naval program has the effect of absorbing American shipbuilding facilities, which have been diminished by the long depression in the industry. With all these factors pro and con in a state of rapid flux, it is impossible to forecast the effect of the war even during the period that must intervene between the writing and publishing of anything on the subject. What emerges as a certainty is that the commercial and military position of the United States after the war cannot be otherwise than improved by the possession of an adequate mercantile fleet, for, whatever may happen, such a fleet would have the great advantage of newness; in this respect it would have world superiority.

The principal maritime states of Europe belatedly followed England's lead in the policy of government aid. Some of them have bettered the instruction. By means of subsidies, reduced rail rates on goods transported in national ships, burdens placed upon competitors, and other aids, they have improved their position without serious challenge to that of Great Britain. Foreign countries have invented and applied upwards of one hundred and thirty methods of direct and indirect financial aid to their national ships, in many instances highly complex and cleverly concealed. A comparison made before the outbreak of war in 1939, based on gross tonnage, speed, and age of ships throughout the world, shows that the ocean carrying resources of the United Kingdom on all seas exceed those of her next four competitors combined. The United States is fourth in total tonnage, sixth in speed, and seventh in newness. Japan and Germany stand second, each with a little less than one-fourth of the British tonnage. Then come the United States and Italy, neck and neck in tonnage, but behind France in speed, while in modernization we lag behind all the nations which have been named, plus Norway and the Netherlands. Our ships carry about 30 per cent of our goods, as against 90 per cent a century ago.

Labor afloat and ashore has suffered severely from the decline in American shipping. The hope is that the new system will provide more jobs. For the first time in history American sailors are required to be American nationals. There is a time-tested maxim of the sea that was old when the Castor & Pollux shipped Saint Paul as a workaway, namely, that Freight is the Mother of Wages. Since one-fifth of our population get their living from our foreign commerce, it will be well to ponder this ancient truism.

What has been said of the decline of overseas trade does not apply to coastwise shipping, which is reserved to national vessels. That is another story, containing some grief but more joy than the lamentable tale of our foreign-bound freighters. In 1939 Congress enacted legislation extending government aid in the construction of new coasters to replace those which have become obsolete. This may be expected to provide a modern coasting fleet capable of caring for the demands of coastwise and intercoastal commerce.

CHAPTER XIII

THE LESSON

*Lose not the opportunity; by the forelock take
That subtle power of never-halting time,
Lest the mere moment's putting off should make
Mischance almost as grave as crime.*
—Lord Brougham

THE CAUSES OF the decline of the merchant service enumerated in the preceding chapter are but incidents illustrating a cycle as ancient as the partnership between conquest and commerce, the metamorphosis of the Maritime into the Territorial State. We can trace the age-old pattern through the coastal settlement of our country and its maritime development, the progressive enlargement of the hinterland, the westward recession of the frontier, the subjugation of our native peoples, the exploitation of the interior land, the suppression of the attempt at geographic integration in the Civil War, the final imposition upon economically disparate regions of central political supremacy.

In the course of this process it is curious to notice the way in which the Territorial State, in asserting its new sovereignty, has taken over the vocabulary of its predecessor. The fine old marine adjective "merchant" has been divorced from its substantive, "adventurer," and is actually used to mean a shopkeeper. "Freight" is used as though it meant the goods on which the freight is paid. We even hear of "a freight" meaning a train of goods vans. The word "ton" has come ashore and become a measure of weight. We "ship" goods by rail and motor-truck. Railways issue bills of "lading." Bills of exchange are used to finance all sorts of inland transactions, while the court of admiralty, which formerly had exclusive jurisdiction of suits on negotiable instruments, is now forbidden to entertain them. The naturalization of these terms shows how thoroughly the Territorial State took over the Maritime. It is sometimes said that our people ceased to be "ship minded." This is profoundly true.

"Almighty wisdom made the land subject to man's improving hand
But differently devised the sea unto an unlike destiny."

If there is a trace of mysticism in all this, it inheres in the nature of change itself. Men "run across the sea," as Horace warned the Romans, and then busy themselves ashore, while Ocean, the burden bearer, merely waits—ominously.

How ominously appears in the headlines of the daily press. Wars, recent, current, and prospective, are the foreground and background against which we are living as this is written. They are said to represent conflicting "ideologies." More realistically, we are witnessing a renewal of the contest between land and sea. Maritime and landlocked powers of East and West seek, each with its special military and economic weapons, to capture the admiralty of one or the dominion of another. Like any generalization in a world of accidents, it is easy to press this one to the point of fantasy and, while pursuing a theory of history (or riding a hobby if you prefer), to lose contact with the Facts of Life. Discounting that, enough remains to point the moral for the United States if we will but learn our geography as well as our history lesson.

Postulating the continuance of nationalist states with national interests, and making no postulate with respect to internal organization and economy, it appears that this country, perhaps alone, possesses the elements required for the durable fusion of the Maritime and the Territorial states. Flanked by long seacoasts well furnished with harbors, with three thousand miles of productive domain between, we are in a favorable position to work out our internal problems, if we will but keep a diligent and enlightened watch over our commercial ramparts.

It seems to be generally agreed that most of the stresses and distresses of the world are attributable to the faulty distribution of goods and people. Self-appointed doctors propose various remedies, reading from left to right. When the ideal order, whatever it is, shall have been established, and at all times from now until then, the mechanism of distribution of goods and people must still include the use of ships. The question for us is whether American commerce should be carried on in American ships, protected by an American navy.

Many years ago a member of Congress posed a famous question, "What have we to do with abroad?" The question is being repeated with all the emphasis of fear during the rapid changes of the second modern European war. The answer is to be found in the words of Secretary of State Hull, "Isolation dooms a people to inescapable impoverishment. No single nation holds a monopoly of material resources needed by all to maintain the modern level of civilized existence.... None is or can be self-sufficing within its frontiers except at the price of a disastrous decline in the level of satisfaction of its people's wants.... No nation can prosper without adequate access to the resources of the entire world, rather than only to those contained within its own frontiers."

If the United States were to isolate itself, those of our people whose living is derived from international trade—upwards of twenty million—would be thrown into competition with the unemployed.

These considerations are the case for foreign commerce. The next step is to inquire whether carrying it on in American ships is worth the price. We have seen that their building and operating costs are greater than those of foreign vessels for reasons which have been mentioned. The only ways by which the handicap can be overcome in the world freight market are by government ownership and operation, or by grants in aid such as those provided by the Merchant Marine Act, which have been described.

Government ownership is moot, and requires no comment. If it were adopted in substitution for the present system, it would impose upon the government a heavy unnecessary burden—the risk of loss on operation, which is now borne by the private operator. Our inquiry is limited to the question whether the existing system of government aid is warranted.

In tranquil times no widespread harm is done to our internal economy by carrying on commerce in foreign bottoms. It is when the nation upon whose ships we rely withdraws them to serve her navy or transport her army and its supplies, or loses them to her enemy, that we receive light on a lesson which then we have little time to learn.

The United States has had some instruction in this lesson and has learned a little of it. In 1908-1909, our Navy made a demonstration cruise around the world under the command of Rear Admiral Robley D. Evans. The sensational show demonstrated one thing to the public, another to the sharp-eyed observers from foreign admiralties. They saw something that the American officers would gladly have concealed, namely, that the fleet depended on foreign auxiliaries for fuel and supplies. A flag-trimmed battle cruiser, her band playing, her crew in whites marshaled on deck and grouped on her turrets and guns, is a brave sight. Her commander would feel a more ardent pride if he were not conscious that the shabby craft wallowing astern, which he is trying to conceal, is a foreign tramp which he has been obliged to bring along so that his men and engines may eat.

The lesson was driven home during the World War by America's dependence upon England for transport. Our own efforts in hasty construction have been mentioned. In many cases they bordered on the bizarre.

The effect of the decline in American carrying trade and its absorption by British ships has been to link our foreign policy closely to that of Great Britain. For example, the Open Door in China, while unquestionably advantageous to the United States, is more so to the British Empire. Its adoption in 1898-1902 extricated England from a serious controversy with the northern European powers. It may be doubted whether Secretary Hay would have initiated the policy but for the pressure from Downing Street, moved by the preponderant power of British shipping interests.

Aside from the menace to our markets, which is serious enough, our dependent position holds the continuing threat of unpredictable precipitation into war notwithstanding acts of Congress and proclamations of neutrality. So long as we continue to rely upon the British Navy to guard our commerce in British merchantmen, we must accept the consequences when the protection is withdrawn. Much is said about the economic power of the United States as an insurance against war. That power can be exercised only as it is channeled through the narrow sides of ships.

Here the doctors of philosophy are entitled to their day in court. From Dr. Royal Meeker in 1905 to Dr. Paul Zeis in 1938 they have opposed government aid to shipping upon economic grounds, pointing to the surplus of world tonnage and to the supposed fallacy of the argument that national ships will develop national markets when there is abundant foreign tonnage available for the same purpose. And Mr. Harlan Trott in 1940 holds the same view.

The opposing argument is best stated in the words of Mr. Alfred H. Haag, now Director of Research of the Maritime Commission, addressed to the American Merchant Marine Conference in 1935:

"A German economist once remarked that America without her own merchant marine would be like a bird without wings or a fish without fins. The truth of that statement was brought home with force in 1914, when we found ourselves in a helpless position due to our lack of ships. To compute the price America paid for her weakness upon the seas we must refer to the years immediately following the Civil War when our shipping in the foreign trade began its decline. Had we maintained a strong merchant fleet in the foreign carrying trade for the half century preceding the World War, it is reasonable to assume that we would have carried at least half of our commerce in our own ships, and the revenues derived therefrom would have increased our national income by nearly three billion dollars. Allowing ten million dollars annually for government aid to American ships, which would have been ample for those years, the cost to the government for the entire fifty year period would have totaled 500 million dollars. Thus, the possession of such a merchant marine would have brought us an additional national income six times greater than the sum that would have been spent to establish and maintain it. Furthermore, with the long intrenchment resulting from this program, the cost to the government would probably not have exceeded 700 million dollars up to the present day.

"From 1914 to the time of our entry into the World War we paid over a billion dollars to foreign shipowners, most of which would have gone to American ships had we possessed an adequate merchant marine.

"Our shipbuilding program and related activities cost us over three billion dollars. Interest upon that expenditure has totaled another billion and a half dollars.

"A hundred million dollars was paid for the transportation of American troops in foreign ships, all of which could have been carried on American ships had we possessed an adequate merchant marine.

"After making an allowance for the earnings of our government fleet since the war, it is plainly evident that our weakness upon the seas has cost us from the time of the Civil War nearly seven billion dollars—or an amount ten times that which would have been required by a fair and uniform system of government aid. . . .

"The primary purpose of government financial aid to Amercan shipping is to place American services on an economic parity with our foreign competitors, whose capital and operating costs are on a lower level. The rendering of such aid will not accomplish the purpose for which it is intended unless our ships are on a parity, in both speed and economy of operation, with those of our competitors. As a penalty for obsolescence our ships operating in the foreign trade are paying five million dollars annually in excessive fuel costs alone.

"In conclusion, let me state that in spite of the rapidly growing obsolescence of our merchant fleet and the vicissitudes through which it has passed since the war, our maritime position today is better than it has been for seventy years. We have no desire to monopolize the trade routes of the world, but only to occupy a position commensurate with our place in the family of nations."

The theorists point out that national ships are not needed to develop new avenues of commerce so long as foreign vessels are under the same inducement. As this book is on its way to press the cables bring the news of the acquisition by Germany of fifty-two shipbuilding ways in Denmark and Norway and seventy-nine in Holland. At the moment of writing, the idea that these facilities will be used to promote American trade seems rather implausible.

In some respects the arguments of the theorists are untimely rather than unsound. In that millennial dawn when a free economy shall have leveled all trade barriers and the movement of goods, money, and people is unhampered, the profits resulting from the increased volume of business may be expected in theory (and economic theory is what the doctors are discussing) to eliminate the subsidies. The year 1940 is not the time, the United States is not the place, the American people are not the guinea pigs, and ships are not the apparatus for an experiment in commercial non-resistance. On April 12, 1940, the chairman of the Committee on Merchant Marine (Congressman Bland) told the House of Representatives:

"A combination of world circumstances gives America a great opportunity to reëstablish its merchant marine.... It is inconceivable that, in the light of world conditions, any delay in the building program will be permitted now. There never has been at any time in the past as great a need and as great an opportunity for a modern, up-to-date, fully equipped, economical merchant marine as at present."

Something was said in the preceding chapter about the matter of surplus tonnage. The rate at which belligerent cargo carriers are being destroyed by enemy raiders in this spring of 1940 answers the philosophers on this head. An excess of ships, when they belong to one's own nation and not to another, is essential to the national defense. On this point an English historian, Mr. C. Ernest Fayle, in *The War and the Shipping Industry*, is emphatic:

"It is no exaggeration to say that the possession by Great Britain of a mercantile fleet much larger than was required for her minimum essential needs was, *above all else,* the decisive factor in the [World] war.... Whether we look at the magnitude of the achievement or at the appalling waste involved in the diversion from productive to destructive activities there is no more significant fact in the history of the war."

Allowing for the greater dependence of Britain upon shipping, the residual truth of that statement is applicable to the United States.

There is also a theological objection to government aid to shipping, namely, that it is immoral to take money from the common purse and give it to a favored group to enable them to make a profit—or sustain a loss. This may be conceded as a counsel of perfection. The ideal commonwealth in a world of similar states will not subsidize any enterprise. Meanwhile, the historians have neglected to point out a nation that has been able to avoid doing so. From first to last the United States and the state and local governments have subsidized the railroads to the extent of one and one-half billion dollars in money and property. The tariff subsidies to manufacturers between 1920 and 1930 and the agricultural subsidies of the New Deal are too recent to need more than citation. The greater part of the internal economy of the United States has been subsidized by tariffs and by more direct aids.

It is difficult to set up comparative costs. In its former attempts to aid the merchant service by the various plans adopted during the century prior to and including 1936, the grand total from first to last was about the present cost of four first-class battleships. The operation of the present system is too new to judge of its long-run cost. In theory the operating subsidies are to be recaptured out of profits and should cost the Treasury nothing. There is no immediate prospect of complete indemnification through this channel. In addition, as indicated in the quotation from Mr. Haag, the result should be a large net gain to the whole nation, with resultant increase in tax revenue. The extension of the naval requirements as this is written tends to transfer the burden of the differential subsidies from commerce to the national defense to an extent which diminishes their commercial cost to zero.

So long as producers are protected by tariffs and other aids, and seamen are subsidized by sumptuary laws, it is difficult to perceive a reason for laying the burden of these subventions upon the shoulders of ship operators without some countervailing aid, when we consider that the alternative is the loss of the merchant marine and its value to the national defense, and the abandonment of our commerce to the vessels of foreign nations. Ships are part of the mechanism of the commercial system, not its basis, and should not be the first object of attack in a basic reform. It may strike the reader that the whole system of government aid, if carried through logically, moves in an expanding spiral, in which all purses except the longest (that of the United States) must be exhausted. If that be true, the way to reform it is first to reform the foreigner by abolishing his aids to shipping and leveling his tariff walls; then to withdraw protection from the

American seaman and place his wages and working conditions on a par with those of the foreigner; and to repeal our protective and retaliatory tariffs, upon which, at bottom, the whole edifice rests. This alternative is likely to be adopted by the parliament of man in the federation of the world. Until then, the economical course for the United States would seem to be to continue to extend sufficient aid to merchant shipping to countervail the foreign discrimination against it and enable our ships to earn money enough to restore the government grubstake.

If the case for a national merchant marine be regarded as established, we are near the end of our lesson but not quite there. In order to operate, ships must have something to carry both ways. This is the very core of any discussion of shipping policies. The subject cannot be pursued here, beyond what had been said, because it opens the whole field of the tariff, reciprocal trade agreements, and inland transport. The reader must carry on for himself.

In considering the problem, citizens living west of the Alleghenies, whose lives are spent far from the sea, should commit to memory the importance of the merchant marine to their own interests and to the entire nation. It is of no consequence that they may not know the gunwale from the garboard strake; it is of vital importance to themselves and to the entire nation that they should realize the effect of ocean commerce on their own lives and upon the national economy as a whole.

The building of ships calls for capital goods on a large scale. Their operation uses labor in a service employment. Freights on American ships bring in money that would otherwise go abroad. Wages paid on American ships and in American shipyards increase purchasing power within the United States. When goods are shipped in foreign bottoms the wages go into the freight bill to increase purchasing power in foreign lands and diminish it at home.

A merchant marine is needed to keep us out of wars other

than our own; to implement our Navy; to promote our foreign markets and increase our trade; to provide employment and wages for labor in the many industries that contribute to the building and operation of ships and the production, inland transportation, and distribution of the goods that come and go in them; to put idle capital as well as idle men to work in productive industry; in sum, to contribute to the safety and welfare of the United States.

POSTSCRIPT: As the proof of this last page goes irrevocably to the printer, the French surrender is announced. The events that may occur before this book reaches its readers can have no other effect upon it than to underline in blood the positions contended for in its concluding chapter.

BIBLIOGRAPHY

(See Preface for Sources not listed here)

Adams, Charles Francis. *Charles Francis Adams,* by his son. Boston, 1900.
Adams, Ephraim Douglass. *Great Britain and the American Civil War.* New York, 1925.
Adams, James Truslow. *The Adams Family.* Boston, 1930.
Bankers Trust Company. *America's Merchant Marine.* New York, 1920.
Bates, William W. *American Marine.* Boston, 1897.
———. *American Navigation.* Boston, 1902.
Bemis, Samuel Flagg. *A Diplomatic History of the United States.* New York, 1936.
Bennett, Frank M., Engineer, U.S.N. *The Steam Navy of the United States.* Pittsburgh, 1896.
Benstead, Charles R. *Atlantic Ferry.* London, 1936.
Boynton, Rev. Charles R. *History of the Navy during the War of the Rebellion,* 1868.
Bradlee, F. B. C. *The Kearsarge—Alabama Battle, the story as told to the writer by James Magee of Marblehead, Seaman on the Kearsage.* Salem (Mass.), 1921.
Bulloch, James D. *The Secret Service of the Confederate States in Europe.* 2 vols. New York and London, 1884.
Callahan, James Morton. *Diplomatic History of the Southern Confederacy.* Baltimore, 1901.
Canfield, H. S. "Aboard a Semmes Prize," *Magazine of History,* 1908.
The Career of the Alabama. Anonymous. London, Dorrell & Son, 1864.
Chamber of Commerce, State of New York. *Proceedings on Burning of Ship Brilliant.* 1862.
Cushing, Caleb. *The Treaty of Washington, Its Negotiation, Execution, and the Discussions Relating Thereto.* New York, 1873.
Dollar, Robert. *One Hundred and Thirty Years of Steam Navigation.* San Francisco, 1931.
Dunmore, Walter T. *Ship Subsidies.* Boston, 1907.

Edge, Frederick M. *An Englishman's View of the Battle Between the Alabama and the Kearsarge.* New York, 1864.
——. *Destruction of the American Carrying Trade.* London, 1863.
Fayle, Charles Ernest. *The War and the Shipping Industry.* New Haven, 1927.
Federal Coördinator of Transportation, *Public Aids to Transportation.* Washington, 1940.
Fullam, George T. *Cruise of the Alabama.* Liverpool, 1863.
Goodrich, Albert M. *Cruise and Captures of the Alabama.* Minneapolis, 1906.
"Haywood, P. D." *The Cruise of the Alabama.* Boston, 1886.
Hendrick, Burton J. *Statesmen of the Lost Cause.* New York, 1939.
Hill, Charles E. *Leading American Treaties.* New York, 1922.
Hunt, Cornelius E. *The Shenandoah; or the Last Confederate Cruiser.* New York, 1867.
Jones, Grosvenor M. *Government Aid to Merchant Shipping.* Washington, 1916.
Jordan, Donaldson, and Pratt, Edwin J. *Europe and the American Civil War.* New York, 1931.
Kell, John McIntosh. *Recollections of a Naval Life including the cruises of the Confederate Steamers "Sumter" and "Alabama."* Washington, 1900.
Kirkaldy, Adam W. *British Shipping.* London and New York, 1914.
Knox, Dudley W. *History of the United States Navy.* New York, 1936.
Maclay, Edgar Stanton. *History of the United States Navy.* New York, 1901.
Marvin, Winthrop L. *The American Merchant Marine.* New York, 1902.
Mason, John Thomas R. "The Last Confederate Cruiser," *Century Magazine,* August, 1898.
Meeker, Royal. *History of Shipping Subsidies.* New York, 1905.
Meloney, William Brown. *Heritage of Tyre.* New York, 1916.
Meriwether, Colyer. *Raphael Semmes.* Philadelphia, 1913.
Morgan, James Morris. "The Confederacy's Only Foreign War," *Century Magazine,* August, 1898.
—— *Recollections of a Rebel Reefer.* Boston, 1917.
Morison, Samuel E. *The Maritime History of Massachusetts, 1783-1860.* Boston and New York, 1921.
Owsley, Frank L. *King Cotton Diplomacy.* Chicago, 1931.

Porter, Admiral David D. *The Naval History of the Civil War.* New York, 1886.
Pratt, Fletcher. *The Navy, A History.* Garden City, 1938.
Preble, Commander Geo. H. *The Chase of the Rebel Steamer of War Oreto . . . into the Bay of Mobile,* etc. Cambridge, 1862.
Rhodes, James Ford. *History of the Civil War, 1861-1865.* New York, 1917.
Roberts, W. Adolphe. *Semmes of the Alabama.* Indianapolis, 1938.
Robinson, William M., Jr. *The Confederate Privateers.* New Haven, 1929.
Sanderson, Albert H. *Control of Ocean Freight Rates in Foreign Trade.* Washington, Government Printing Office, 1938.
Saugstad, Jesse E. *Shipping and Shipbuilding Subsidies.* Washington, 1932.
Scharf, J. Thomas. *History of the Confederate States Navy from Its Organization to the Surrender of Its Last Vessel.* San Francisco and New York, 1887.
Schwab, John Christopher. *The Confederate States of America, 1861-1865.* New York, 1901.
Scott, Ernest. "The Shenandoah Incident," *Victoria Historical Magazine,* Vol. XI, No. 2.
Semmes, Raphael. *Memoirs of Service Afloat, During the War Between the States.* London and Baltimore, 1869.
Sinclair, Arthur. *Two Years on the Alabama.* Boston, 1895.
Sinclair, G. Terry. "The Eventful Cruise of the Florida," *Century Magazine,* July, 1898.
Soley, James R. *The Blockade and the Cruisers (The Navy in the Civil War,* Vol. I). New York, 1883.
Spears, John R. *The Story of the American Merchant Marine.* New York, 1910.
Sprout, Harold and Margaret. *The Rise of American Naval Power.* Princeton, 1939.
Starbuck, Alexander. *History of the American Whale Fishery.* Waltham (Mass.), 1878.
Statistical Society of London. *Journal, 1863; Journal, 1872.*
Strout, Captain. "Account of the Capture of the Cuba," *Magazine of History,* Extra No. 2 (1908), p. 137.
Thacher, J. *History of the Town of Plymouth.* Boston, 1832.
Thornton, R. H. *British Shipping.* New York, 1939.
Tower, Walter S. *A History of the American Whale Fishery.* Philadelphia, 1907.

Trott, Harlan. *Ships for What?* United States Naval Institute Proceedings. Washington, March, 1940.

Upton, I. H. "Alphabetical List of Vessels Captured by Rebel Privateers," *Hunt's Merchant Magazine*, October, 1863. (Very inaccurate.)

Villiers, Brougham (pseud. for Frederick J. Shaw), and Chesson, W. H. *Anglo-American Relations, 1861-1865.* London, 1919.

Welles, Gideon. *Diary of Gideon Welles.* 3 vols. Boston, 1916.

Whittle, William C. *Cruises of the Confederate States Steamers "Shenandoah" and "Nashville."* [Norfolk? Va.], 1910.

Wood, John Taylor. "The Tallahassee's Dash into New York Waters," *Century Magazine,* July, 1898.

Zeis, Paul M. *American Shipping Policy.* Princeton, 1938.

INDEX

ABBY Bradford, schooner, captured, 42
Abe Lincoln, bark, captured, 191
Abigail, whaler, captured, 220
Adams, Charles Francis, United States Minister to England, arbitrator at Geneva, 233; protests to Foreign Office, 95, 131, 174, 180, 231, 246-47, and *passim*
Adderly & Company, Nassau, consignees of Florida, 96
Adelaide, bark, captured, 212
Adriatic, ship, captured, 186-87
Advance wages of seamen, 132-33
Agrippina, bark, tender to Alabama, 131, 135-36, 141, 143, 146
A. J. Bird, ship, captured, 193
Alabama, C. S. Cruiser, career of, 128-73; duplicate name of, 91; and U.S.S. Hatteras, 143-44; and U.S.S. Kearsarge, 158-73; particulars of, 162; pursuit of, 92; and *passim*
Alabama Claims. See Geneva Arbitration
Alar, tender to C.S.C. Georgia, 174
Albert Adams, ship, captured, 41
Albert H. Partridge, ship, captured, 106
Albion Trading Co., 77
Aldebaran, ship, captured, 104
Alexandra, case of, 79, 81
Aline, bark, captured, 211
Alliance, U.S.S., collision of with Florida, 127

Ambergris, nature and use of, 199
America, tug, reports movements of Florida, 119-20
A. M. Schindler, ship, captured, 107
Andrew, John A., Governor of Massachusetts, requests protection, 108
Anglo Saxon, ship, captured, 117
Antietam, battle of, 102
Arabella, ship, captured, 110
Arbitration. See Geneva Arbitration
Arcade, ship, captured, 48
Archer, subsidiary cruiser of Florida, q.v.
Arcole, ship, captured, 193
A. Richards, ship, captured, 186
Ariel, ship, captured, 142-43
Arman, L. French shipbuilder, 84-89
Ascension Island, Shenandoah at, 218-20
Atlanta, C.S.N., duplicate name, 91
Atlanta, original name of Tallahassee, q.v.
Austria, war of with Denmark, 14
Auxiliaries, naval, 261, 266
Avon, ship, captured, 118
Azores, Islands, 3, 135
Azuma, S.S. See Stonewall

BAHAMA, S.S., tender to Florida, 96, 131, 132
Bahamas, Islands, neutrality rules applicable to, 16
Bahia, Brazil, capture of Florida at, 122-24; visit of Alabama to, 147-48

279

Balance of Power, effect of upon British foreign policy, 20
Baldwin, C. S., Commander U.S.N., 92-93
Bananas, cargoes of, 4
Bancroft-Davis, J. C., American agent at Geneva, 233
Bangkok, American ships at, 155
Baracouta, British bark, informs Shenandoah of end of war, 226
Bark, definition of, 7
Baron de Castine, ship, captured, 140-41
Barron, Samuel, Commander C.S.N., ranking Confederate naval officer in Europe, 72, 160
Bates, Edward, purchaser of Georgia, 180-81
Bay State, ship, captured, 186
Ben Dunning, ship, captured, 41
Beaufort, N. C., port, 70
Beecher, Rev. Henry Ward, advocates Union cause in England, 18
Belligerency, definition of, 8
Benjamin, Judah P., lists ship transfers, 212; protests French delay on Alabama, 159
Bering Sea, Shenandoah in, 222-26
Bermuda, neutrality of, 191, 195
Bernard, Montague, British counsel at Geneva Tribunal, 233
B. F. Hoxie, ship, captured, 115-16
Bigelow, John, U. S. Consul General at Paris, 85
Bismarck, Prince Otto von, repudiates Geneva rule, 235
Blaine, James G., champion of merchant marine, 249
Blanchard, J. J., U. S. Consul at Melbourne, Australia, 215-18
Bland, Schuyler O., Congressman, quoted, 269
Blanquilla, Venezuela, coaling of Alabama at, 142

Blockade, effect of, compared with cruisers, 237-38; effect of proclamation of, 17
Bold Hunter, ship, captured, 176-77
Bombay, trade with, 4
Bonds, Confederate. *See* Erlanger loan
Bonds, ransom, explained, 23
Borneo, Alabama at, 154
Boston Chamber of Commerce, request of for protection, 108-40
Boston Marine Society, request of for protection, 140
Bravay A. et Cie, agents for Khedive of Egypt, 85, 86
Brazil, trade with, 4; attitude of, 43; Emperor of, names Geneva arbitrator, 233; neutrality of. *See* Neutrality
Brest, French port, 105; neutrality of, 15, 117
Brig, definition of, 7
Bright, John, English statesman, 17, 18, 135
Brilliant, ship, captured, 138, 140
British foreign policy, 21
Brooke, John M., Lieut. U.S.N., C.S.N., 206
Brooklyn, U.S.S., blockader, 35
Brown, George, Commander U.S.N., 88
Brunswick, whaler, captured, 224
Bulloch, James D., Commander C.S.N., activities during construction of Alabama, 130-34; contracts for Alabama, 129; summary of French policy by, 15; and *passim*
Butcher, Matthew J., Captain, master of Enrica (Alabama), 130, 134
Byzantium, ship, captured, 110

CADIZ, Spanish port, 50, 51
Calcutta, trade with, 4

INDEX

Calderon, Spanish Minister, 50-52
Caleb Cushing, revenue cutter, 113-15
Caleb Cushing. *See* Cushing
California, trade with, 4
Camouflage, use of during Civil War, 90, 100
Canton, American ships at, 155
Cape Fear River, geography of, 184; Chickamauga at, 192
Cape Town, S. A., First visit of Alabama to, 148-52; second visit of Alabama to, 156. *See* Good Hope, Cape of
Cardenas, Cuban port, 98
Cargoes. *See* Carrying Trade
Carrie Estelle, ship, captured by Tallahassee, 186
Carroll, schooner, captured by Tallahassee, 186
Carrying trade, American before the war, 3-5; effect of cruisers on, 237-48
Cartel ships, definition of, 24
Carter, R. R., Lieut., U.S.N., C.S.N., plans expedition against whalers, 206
Cayenne, French penal colony, 43
Ceuta, Spain, 52
Chameleon, formerly Olustee, 195
Chancellorsville, battle of, 102
"Charlie," seaman, trial of at Melbourne, 217-18
Charter Oak, schooner, captured, 211
Cherbourg, engagement between Alabama and Kearsarge at, 158-73
Cherokee, U.S.S., blockader, 192
Chickamauga, C.S.C., career of, 189-92
China trade, 4
Cienfuegos, Cuban port, 41, 42
Citizenship of seamen, 7
City of Bath, ship, captured, 176

City of Flint, S.S., restored to her American crew, 41-42
Claims courts, Alabama claims, 235-36
Clarence, C.S.C., subsidiary cruiser to Florida, career of, 105
Clematis, U.S.S., blockader, 192
Clipper ship, definition of, 8; adverse effect on merchant marine, 254
Coal, bunker, supplies of, 53
Coastwise shipping, 6, 262
Cobden, Richard, mentioned, 18; on transfers of flag, 244-45
Cochin China, 154
Cockburn, Sir Alexander, Arbitrator at Geneva, 233; dissent of, 234-35
Codfish, cargoes of, 4, 5, 110
Codrington, Gen. Sir William, Governor of Gibraltar, 60
Coffee, cargoes of, 4
Cohen, David, Capt. U.S.M.C., captured by Alabama, 142
Collins, Napoleon, Commander, U.S.N., commanding U.S.S. Wachusett, 122-24
Commerce. *See* Carrying Trade
Commerce destroyers, status of, 11
Commodore Jones, U.S.S. pursuit ship, 108
Commonwealth, ship, captured, 105
Conrad (later C.S.C. Tuscaloosa), captured, 148
Constitution, ship, captured, 176
Consuls, U. S., activities and duties of, 21, 22, 43, 44; at Bahia, 122, 123; Cadiz, 40, 41; Cape Town, 149, 151; Halifax, 188; Liverpool, 129, 229; Maranham, 43; Melbourne, 215-18; Pernambuco, 147; Tangier, 54-61
Contest, ship, captured, 154

Contraband, 9
Convoys, requests for and effect of, 109
Corbett, G. H., Captain, Commander of Sea King, 207-8; trial of, 209-10
Corporations, industrial, supplant maritime investments after Civil War, 250-51
Corris Ann, captured, 101
Cotton, shortage in England, effect of, 16-18; Southern policy with respect to, 2; speculation in, 77
Couronne, French frigate, 165-66, 177
Craven, T. A. M., Commander U.S.N., Commanding U.S.S. Tuscarora, 57, 60; mentioned, 66, 68, 69
Craven, T. T., Commander U.S.N., Commanding U.S.S. Niagara, fails to engage C.S.S. Stonewall, 88
Creesy, Josiah P., Acting Vol. Lieut., U.S.N., Commanding U.S.S. Ino, 59-60
Crenshaw, Wm. G. & Co., purchasers of Olustee, 195
Crew, of Alabama, character of, 149, 154; of Shenandoah, enlistment of, 211, 212-13, 215-16
Crimps, character and function of, 132-33
Crown Point, ship, captured, 115
Cruisers, legal status of, 11; For particular cruisers, *see* their names
Cuba, brig, captured, 38-40
Cunard Line, British subsidy to, 258; screw propeller adopted by, 254
Curaçao, W. I. port, 42
Currants, cargoes of, 3
Cushing, Caleb, American counsel at Geneva Arbitration, 233

DAKOTAH, U.S.S., pursuit ship, 45, 92, 93
Daniel Trowbridge, ship, captured, 45
Darling, Sir Charles, Governor of Victoria, 216
Dauntless, H.M. Frigate, 68
"Dave," servant on Alabama, 139, 170
Dayton, William L., U. S. Minister to France, 164, and *passim*
Deerhound, yacht, activities of during Alabama-Kearsarge engagement, 161 *ff*.
De Long, James, U. S. Consul at Tangier, 54-61
Delphine, bark, captured, 215
Denmark, war of Austria and Prussia with, 14, 88; protests discharge of prisoners at St. Thomas, 125
D. Godfrey, bark, captured, 211
Dicey, Edward, 19
Dictator, ship, captured, 175
Dona Januaria, Brazilian corvette, 122-24
Donegal, H.M. Guardship, receives surrender of Shenandoah, 227
Dudley, Thomas H., U. S. Consul at Liverpool, 129, 229
Dumbarton, U.S.S., pursuit of Chickamauga, 190; pursuit of Olustee, 193
Dunkirk, ship, captured, 139

EAST INDIA traders, 4
Eben Dodge, ship, captured, 49-50
Edith, original name of Chickamauga, q.v.
Edward Carey, whaler, captured, 218
E. F. Lewis, schooner, captured, 193
Eggleston, S. E., U. S. Consul at Cadiz, 51

Electric Spark, ship, captured, 120-21
Emancipation, effect of upon British policy, 19; effect of upon fishery, 113
Emily Farnham, ship, captured, 138-40
Emma L. Hall, ship, captured, 191
Empress Theresa, ship, captured, 193
England. See Great Britain
Enrica. See Alabama
Ericsson U.S.S., chased by Florida 116
Erlanger, Emile. See Erlanger loan
Erlanger loan, 76-78, 86
Estella, ship, captured, 101
Evans, W. E., Lieut., C.S.N., in command of Georgia, 177
Evarts, William M. American counsel at Geneva, 233

FABRICS, cargoes of, 4
Fauntleroy, Charles M., Lieut., C.S.N., in command of Rappahannock, 178-79
Favorite, bark, captured, 224-25
Fawcett, Preston & Co., engine builders, Liverpool, 95
Fernando de Noronha, Brazilian penal colony, Florida at, 104, 105; Alabama at, 145-47
Figs, cargoes of, 3
Finance, Confederate external, 73-78
Fire Island, N. Y., Tallahassee at, 185-86
Fish, Hamilton, Secretary of State, quoted on transfers of flag, 247
Fisher, Fort, Wilmington, N. C., 184; captured by Union forces, 197
Fishing industry, 5, 108, 110-11. See also Whaling

Fishing vessels, legal status of, 112
Flag, transfer of, 242-47
Florida, C.S.C., career of, 95-127, and *passim*
Florida, duplicate name, 91
Foreign Enlistment Act, British, 12, 26, 79, 80
Foreign policy, effect of ships upon, 266-67
Fort de France, Martinique, 45
France, Confederate naval construction in, 84-88; foreign policy of, 14-15
Franco-Prussian war, effect of on Alabama claims, 232
Fraser, Trenholm & Co., bankers, 62, 70, 74, 81; construction of Georgia by, 174; suits against, 196
Free trade, effect of adoption in England, 255-56
Freight, definition of, 8; insurance against loss of, 240; reduction of, by American vessels, 241
Furnivall, F. J., 19
F. W. Seaver, ship, captured, 175

GALAPAGOS ISLAND, whaling grounds off, 204
Garfield, James A, opposition of to merchant marine, 249
General Barry, ship, captured, 119
General Pike, whaler, captured, 223
General Williams, whaler, captured, 223
Geneva Arbitration, 231-36
Geneva award, significance of, 237
George Griswold, ship, captured, 175
George Latimer, ship, captured, 118
Georgetown, S. C., port, Nashville delivered at, 71

Georgia, C.S. Cruiser, career of, 174-81, and *passim*
Georgiana, C.S. Cruiser, 82, 84
Germany, not bound by submarine rules, 14; repudiates Geneva neutrality rule, 235
Gettysburg, battle of, 1, 102, 116
Gibraltar, 52, 53, 54, 60
Gibson, T. M., Pres. Board of Trade, on transfers of flag, 245-46
Gipsey, whaler, capture of, 223-24
Gladstone, Wm. E., 78, 84, 172
Glenavon, ship, captured, 187
Gloucester, Mass., fishing industry. See Fishing industry
Glover, John, on transfer of flag, 248
Golconda, ship, captured, 119, 224
Gold, discovery of, 5; export of from South, 75
Golden Rocket, ship, captured, 36-38
Good Hope, Cape of, Georgia off, 176. See Cape Town
Good Hope, ship, captured, 175
Goodspeed, ship, captured, 110, 191
Great Britain. See Neutrality; names of statesmen, ships, etc.
Great Ogeechee River, Ga., 71
Greenland, ship, captured, 119

HAAG, Alfred H., Director of Research, Maritime Commission, quoted, 267-69
Habana, S.S., later C.S.C. Sumter, q.v.
Hague Conference of 1907, adoption of Geneva rule, 235; convention, 22
Halibut, fish, 110
Hamlin, Vice-Pres. U. S., 108
Harding, Sir John, Queen's advocate, insanity of, 135

Harriet Stevens, ship, captured, 118-19
Harrison, Frederic, 19
Harvest, Hawaiian ship, capture of, 218-19; claim for, 229
Harvest Home, ship, 61
Harvey Birch, ship, captured, 65, 70
Hatteras, U.S.S., engagement of with Alabama, 144
Hawaii, whaling center, 204
Hector, whaler, capture of, 218
Hemp, cargoes of, 3
Henrietta, ship, captured, 105
Hides, cargoes of, 4
Honduran logwood, cargoes of, 3
Honolulu, whaling center, 204
Hope, Sir James, Vice-Admiral, orders with respect to capture of British vessels, 155
Horrocks, Thos., guide at Ascension Island, 218-19
Howard, ship, captured, 188

ICE, cargoes of, 4
Ino, U.S.S., 53
Insurance, marine, effect of cruisers on rates, 238-41
Iron, cargoes of, 3
Ironclads, Confederate, 82-89
Iron ship construction, effect on merchant marine, 253, 255
Iroquois, U.S.S., at Martinique, 46, 47; pursuit of Florida, 121
Isaac Webb, ship, captured, 110
Isabella, bark, captured, 224
Isabella, Queen of Spain, 49
Ish-y-Paw, King of Ascension Island, 218-19
Isolation, views on, 265
Itajuba, Baron, Arbitrator at Geneva, 233
Italy, King of, names Geneva arbitrator, 233

JACOB BELL, ship, captured, 103

James Funk, No. 22, ship, captured, 185
James Littlefield, ship, captured, 188
James Maury, ship, captured, 225
Japan, C.S.C., later Georgia, q.v.
Japan whaling grounds, 204
Java Head, 154
Jireh Swift, whaler, capture of, 223
Johnson, Reverdy, on transfer of flag, 246
John Watt, ship, captured, 176
Joseph Maxwell, ship, captured, 42
Joseph Parke, ship, captured, 44
Jute, cargoes of, 4

KAMCHATKA, Shenandoah at, 221
Kansas, U.S.S., blockader, 192
Kate Dyer, ship, captured, 104
Kate Prince, ship, captured, 212
Kate Stewart, schooner, captured, 107
Kearsarge, U.S.S., engagement of with Alabama, 158-73; particulars of, 162
Kehamaha V, Hawaiian ship, 219
Kell, John M., Lieut., C.S.N., 33, and *passim*
Keystone State, U.S.S., 45
Klingender, Melchior F., purchaser of Sumter, 62, 63
Kotetsu. *See* Stonewall

LABOR, diversion of, effect on merchant marine, 251; marine, absorption by Navy, 251
La Guayra, Venezuelan port, 42
Laird Bros., shipbuilders of Liverpool, 85
Lamar, C. A. L., quoted, 73
Lammot du Pont, ship, captured, 188
Lapwing, C.S.C., 104

Lancaster, John, activities of Yacht Deerhound in Alabama-Kearsarge engagement, 161 *ff*.
Laurel, S.S., tender to Shenandoah, 208-10
Lee, Robert E., 29, 30
Lemons, cargoes of, 3
Letters of marque. *See* Marque; Privateers
Liability, limitation of, as inducement to maritime investment, 251
Lighthouses, illumination of, 199
Lilian, U.S.S., pursuit of Olustee, 194
Linseed, cargoes of, 4
Lizzie N. Stacy, schooner, captured, 212
Logwood, cargoes of, 3, 4
Lookout Mountain, battle of, 102
Louisa Hatch, ship, captured, 145-46
Louisa Kilham, ship, captured, 41
Louis Napoleon. *See* Napoleon
Low, John, provisional master of Florida, 96
Lumber, cargoes of, 44
Lyons, Lord, British Minister at Washington, 66

McALLISTER, Fort, 71
McCrea, C. J., agent for Erlanger loan, 78; suit against, 196
Macebo, Gervasio, commanding Brazilian corvette, 124
Machias, ship, captured, 38, 41
Mackerel fishery, 5, 110
Maffitt, John N., Lieut., C.S.N., Commander of Florida, 96-106; 115-18
Mahan, A. T., Capt., U.S.N., author, 127
Malacca Strait, as hunting ground, 154
Mallory, Stephen R., Confederate Secretary of Navy, 26, 27, and *passim*

Manassas. *See* Florida
Manchester, ship, captured, 139
Mann, A. Dudley, Confederate Commissioner, 68
Manning, Thos. S., pilot Shenandoah, 221-22
Maranham, Brazilian port, 43
Maratanza, U.S.S., pursuit of Olustee, 193
Margaret Y. Davis, ship, captured, 119
Marion, U.S.S. schoolship, pursuit ship, 108
Maritime Commission, functions, 260-61; program, 260-61
Maritime state, change to territorial, 263
Mark L. Potter, ship, captured, 190
Marque, letters of, Confederate, 27; Federal, 83
Marquesas Islands, whaling ground, 204
Martaban (ex-Texan Star), captured, 155
Martinique, escape of Alabama from, 141-42; Sumter at, 45, 46, 47
Mary Alvina, ship, captured, 106
Mason, James M., Confederate Commissioner at London, 64, 66, 72
Massachusetts, requests for protection, 108
Maury, Matthew Fontaine, U.S.N., C.S.N., oceanographer, 203, 204
Maury, William L., Lieut., C.S.N., commanding Georgia, 174-81
Mayflower, Pilgrim ship, 200
Meeker, Dr. Royal, economist, cited, 267
Melbourne, Australia, Shenandoah at, 216-18
Melville, George W., Engineer, U.S.N., aboard Wachusett, 123-24

Melville, Herman. *See Moby-Dick*
Memminger, Christopher G., Confederate Secretary of Treasury, 76
Merchant Marine, causes of decline, 249-56; comparison of American and foreign, 261-62; definition, 6; growth, 249; and *passim*
Mexico, French and Spanish designs in, 50
Mill, John Stuart, 19
Miller, Wm. C. & Sons, shipbuilders, Liverpool, 95
Milo, whaler, captured, 223
Mingoe, U.S.S., pursuit of Tallahassee, 188
Mirage at Kamchatka, 221
Missionary Ridge, battle of, 102
M. J. Colcord, ship, captured, 105
Mobile, Ala., Florida at, 99-101
Mogador, Morocco, Georgia at, 177, 179-80
Moby-Dick, by Melville, 202-3
Mohamed Bargash, Governor of Tangier, 54, 55-56
Mohican, U.S.S. pursuit ship in South Atlantic, 147
Molasses, cargoes of, 3, 4
Mondamin, ship, captured, 122
Monroe Doctrine, 14
Montauk, Monitor, U.S.N., 71
Montauk Point, Tallahassee at, 186
Montgomery, Ala., Confederate capital, 31
Montgomery, U.S.S., pursuit of Olustee, 194
Montmorency, ship, captured, 48
Morehead City, N. C., port, 70
Morocco. *See* Tangier; Mogador
Morris, Charles Manigault, Lieut., C.S.N., Commander of Florida, 118-25
Multiple expansion engine, 254
Munitions, right to supply belligerents with, 11

Myers, Henry, C.S.N., paymaster of Sumter, 54-61

NAIAD, ship, captured, 41
Nantucket, whaling industry at, 200
Napoleon III, policy toward belligerents in Civil War, 14, 16, 21, 84, 85, 86
Nashville, C.S. Cruiser, career of, 64-71, 90
Nassau Bahamas, visits of Florida to, 97, 101, 102
Nationalist states, continuance of, 264
Naval Academy, U.S., establishment of, 28
Naval officers, training of, 28
Naval policy, U.S., modern, 1, 90-91
Navigation Laws, British revision of, 256
Navy, U.S., composition of, 90; enlargement of, effect on merchant marine, 251-52
Negro, emancipation, effect on fishery, 113
Neopolitan, ship, captured, 52
Neutrality, definition, 8; laws, American and British, 12, 13, 79; proclamation, American, 1939, 26; proclamation, British, 1861, 11, 231; rules with respect to prizes, 22-23; rules with respect to warship construction, 25; rules, British, 16, 68, 69; of Brazil, 43, 125, 146; of Spain, 50
Neva, ship, captured, 188
New Bedford, Mass., whaling industry, 201-02
Newcastle, Duke of, ruling in case of Tuscaloosa, 151-52
New Haven, Conn., Common Council of, request for protection, 108
New York Chamber of Commerce, request for protection, 109; proceedings on ship Brilliant, 140
Niagara, U.S.S., capture of Georgia by, 180-81; failure of to engage Stonewall, 88
North, James H., Commander C.S.N., 72, 130
Notions, cargoes of, 4
Nuts, cargoes of, 3

OKHOTSK Sea, Shenandoah in, 220-21
Olive oil, cargoes of, 3
Olustee, C.S.C., formerly Tallahassee, 193-96
Oneida, U.S.S., pursuit of Florida by, 99, 101
Oranges, cargoes of, 3
Oreto. See Florida
Osceola, U.S.S., pursuit of Olustee, 194
Otter Rock, ship, captured, 191
Ownership of ships, government, 266; system of vessel ownership, 250-51

PACIFIC Mail Steamship Co., subsidy to, 258; James I. Waddell employed by, 228
Pacific Steam Navigation Co., British subsidy to, 258
Page, T. J., Capt., C.S.N., commanding Stonewall, 88
Palmas, Cape, 103
Palmer, Capt. J. S., U.S.N., commanding U.S.S. Iroquois, 46-47
Palmer, Sir Roundell, British counsel at Geneva, 233
Palmerston, Lord, 67, 84
Pampero, C.S.S., 83, 87
Panama Canal, 5
Panama Railway, revenue of, 142
Paris, Declaration of, 10
Part ownership of vessels. See Ownership
Pass-à-L'Outre, La., 35

Paymaster of Alabama, discharge of, 145
Pearl, whaler, captured, 218
Pegram, R. B., Capt., C.S.N., Commander of C.S.C. Nashville, 64-71
Peninsular Line, British subsidy to, 258
Penobscot River, Tallahassee at, 188
Pernambuco, activity of Consul at, 147
Perry, Horatio G., U.S. Chargé d'Affaires at Madrid, 49-54, *passim*
Peterhoff, British steamer, 93
Pirates, cruisers not, 10; federal treatment of Confederate seamen as, 46
Policy, foreign. See Foreign policy
Policy, U.S. Naval, 1, 90-91
Pollock, Sir Frederick, opinion on warship construction, 79, 81
Potomac, U.S.S., pursuit of Tallahassee, 189
Portland, Maine, mayor requests protection, 108; destruction of revenue cutter at, 113-15
Port-of-Spain, Trinidad, port, 43
Port Royal, Jamaica, hospitality to federal prisoners refused, 144
Powhattan, U.S.S., 45
Pratique, definition of, 8
Preble, Geo. H., Commander, U.S.N., commanding U.S.S. Oneida, 99-100
Premiums, insurance. See insurance
Prince Albert (Prince Consort), death of, 66
Prince Albert, schooner, tender to C.S.C. Florida, 97
Prioleau, Charles K., manager, Fraser, Trenholm & Co., 74; suit against, 196

Prisoners of war, status of, 9
Prisoners, treatment of on cruisers, 45-46, 48, 49, 140-41
Privateers, privateering, definition, 9, 10; Confederate, 34; Federal, 83, 84
Prize, prizes, definition, 9; disposition of, 22; method of destroying, 37; money, 22-23
Propellers, screw, effect on merchant marine, 254-55
Provincetown, Mass., request of for protection, 109
Prussia, sale of vessels to, 15; war with Denmark, 14
Puerto Cabello, Venezuelan port, 42
Pulo Condore, French Cochin China, 154
Pursuit of Confederate Cruisers, policy with respect to, 89-94

QUAKER CITY, U.S.S., pursuit of Olustee, 194

R. R. CUYLER, U.S.N., pursuit of Florida, 101
Railroads, subsidies to. See Subsidies
Raisins, cargoes of, 3
Rams, Confederate. See Ironclads
Ramsay, J. F., Lieut., C.S.N., Commander of Laurel, 208
Ransom bonds. See bonds
Rappahannock, C.S. Cruiser, career of, 177-79, and *passim*
Rattlesnake, ex-Nashville, q.v.
Read, Charles W., Lieut., CSN., Commanding C.S.S. Clarence, Tacony and Archer, 106-13
Red Gauntlet, ship, captured, 115
Revenue cutters as pursuit ships, 94
Rickerson, J., purchaser of Florida, 181
Rienzi, ship, captured, 117

INDEX 289

Riga, port, 3
Rio de Janeiro, trade with, 4
Rockingham, ship, captured, 157
Ronckendorff, William, Commander U.S.N., Commanding San Jacinto, 142
Rost, Pierre A., Confederate Commissioner, 49, 50
Royal Mail Line, British subsidy to, 258
Rum, cargoes of, 3, 4
Rupert Gilfillan, ship, captured, 70
Russell, Lord John, 83; attitude during construction of Alabama, 129; responsibility for escape of Alabama, 135

SABLE, Cape, Tallahassee off, 188
Sacassus, U.S.S., pursuit of Olustee, 193-94
St. Lawrence, Gulf of, protection of fishery, 109
St. Paul's Island, Shenandoah at, 215
St. Pierre, Martinique, 46
St. Thomas, W. I., 48
Sales of American vessels. See Flag, transfers of
Saltpeter, cargoes of, 4
San Jacinto, U.S.S., stops Str. Trent, 65; blockade of Alabama at Martinique, 141-42
San Roque, Cape, 103
Santo Domingo, 50
Sarah A. Boice, ship, captured, 185
Schleswig and Holstein, 14, 88
Schooner, definition of, 8
Sclopis, Count Frederick, Arbitrator at Geneva, 233
Scorpion, H.M.S., 86
Screw propeller. See Propeller
Scurvy, disease, 33, 45
Sea Bride, captured by Alabama, 149-50

Sea King, later C.S.C. Shenandoah, q.v.
Seamen, advances against wages, 132-33; citizenship of, 7; deterioration in quality, 251. See Labor
Seminole, U.S.S., pursuit ship, 108
Semmes, Raphael, Capt. C.S.N., early life of, 30; career of on Sumter. See Sumter; career of on Alabama. See Alabama
Seward, William M., Secretary of State, apology to Brazil, 124; apology in Trent affair, 67; foreign policy, 83
Shanghai, American ships at, 155
Shatemuc, ship, captured, 113
Shellac, cargoes of, 4
Shenandoah, C.S. Cruiser, career of, 198-230, and *passim*
Shenandoah, U.S.S., pursuit ship, 121
Ship, definition of, 7
Shipbuilding, effect of tariff upon, 252
Shooting Star, ship, captured, 191
Shryock, Geo. W., Lieut., C.S.N., Witness for Georgia, 178-79
Side wheelers, retard development of steam navigation, 254
Sinclair, Geo. T., Lieut., C.S.N., 72
Sinclair, Terry, Midshipman, C.S.N., 103
Singapore, desertions from Alabama and recruits obtained at, 155
Slavery, effect of emancipation on British policy, 19
Slidell, John, Confederate Commissioner at Paris, 64, 66, 72
Somerset, Duke of, Pegram's protest to, 69
Sonoma, U.S.S., chase of Florida by, 103
Sophia Thornton, whaler, captured, 223

Southern Cross, ship, captured, 115
Spain, attitude of, 41, 50-51
Speedwell, ship, captured, 191
Sperm oil, uses, 199
Sprague, H. J., Consul at Gibraltar, 53, 54, 55
Spurgeon, Rev. Charles, supports Union cause, 19
Stackfield, Henry, owner of ship Harvest, 219-20; claim of proceeds, 229
Staemfli, Jacques, Arbitrator at Geneva, 233
Star of Peace, ship, captured, 103
State. *See* Maritime, Territorial, and Nationalist States
State of Georgia, U.S.S., 91
Steam navigation, development of, 254-55
Stone fleets in Charleston harbor, 206
Stonewall, Confederate ram, 88. *See also* Ironclads
Strout, Captain, of brig Cuba, 38-40
Submarines, rules governing, 13, 14
Subsidies, conflicting views on, 267-71; hidden, 261; marine, history and effect, 258-62; to railroads, 270; tariffs as, 270-71
Suez Canal, effect of on merchant marine, 5, 259
Sugar, cargoes of, 3, 4
Suliote, ship, captured, 187
Sumner, Charles, assertion of American claims by, 231
Sumter, C.S.C., career of, 30-63
Sunda Strait, as hunting ground, 154
Sunrise, ship, captured, 116
Surplus tonnage, effect of, 255, 270
Surrender of Confederate Army, 220, 222
Susan, brig, captured, 212

Susan and Abigail, trading ship, captured, 222
Susquehanna, U.S.F.S., blockader at Mobile, 101
Swedish ports, 3
Switzerland, President of, names Geneva arbitrator, 233
Sychelle whaling grounds, Indian Ocean, 204

TACONY, C.S. Cruiser, career of, 107-13
Tallahassee, C.S. Cruiser, career of, 182-89; 193-97
Tangier, Morocco, 54-61
Tariff, effect on commerce, 272; effect on merchant marine, 252-53; British policy. *See* Free Trade
T. D. Wagner, ship, captured, 193
Tea, cargoes of, 4
Temple, William A., describes affidavit proceedings on enlistments on Shenandoah, 208
Tennessee, C.S.S., duplicate name, 91
Tenterden, Lord, British agent at Geneva, 233
Territorial state, succeeds maritime, 263
Texan Star. *See* Martaban
Thomas, Gen. Geo. H., U.S.A., 29
Thomas L. Wragg, C.S.S., ex Nashville, q.v.
"Thompson ram." *See* Ironclads
Ticonderoga, U.S.S., pursuit of Florida, 122
Tonawanda, captured by Alabama, 139
Tonnage, definition of, 7; surplus. *See* Surplus tonnage
Trade. *See* Carrying trade
Trade winds, 4
Transfers of Flag. *See* Flag, transfers of

Treaty of Washington. *See* Washington, treaty of
"Trent Affair," 18, 21, 64-68, 126
Trinidad, West Indies, 43
Trinidad, Island in South Atlantic, Georgia at, 176
Tristan da Cunha, Shenandoah at, 213-14
Tristram Shandy, U.S.S., pursuit of Florida, 121; pursuit of Tallahassee, 188
Tuscaloosa, C.S.C., ex Conrad, 148; conflicting decisions with respect to, 150-52
Tuscarora, U.S.S., at Southampton, 53 *ff.;* search for Alabama, 131, 134
Twenty-four-hour rule for belligerent ships, 14
Twiss, Sir Travers, advice of, 196
Tycoon, ship, captured, 157

UMPIRE, ship, captured, 110
United States Maritime Commission. *See* Maritime Commission

VANDERBILT, Cornelius, 91, 109
Vanderbilt, U.S.S., at Cape Town, 152-53; off Halifax, 121; orders for cruise, 152; pursuit of Alabama, 147; and *passim*
Vapor, ship, captured, 193
Venezuelan ports, 42
V. H. Hill, ship, captured, 116
Vicksburg, Miss., 102, 116
Vicksburg, U.S.S., blockader, 193
Victor, S.S. *See* Rappahannock
Vigilant, ship, captured, 48
Ville de Malaga, S.S., 54
Virginia. *See* Georgia C.S.C.
Voruz, J., French ironfounder, 84, 85

WACHUSETT, U.S.S., 92, 93; capture of Florida by, 122-26; decommissioned, 127

Waddell, James Iredell, Lieut., C.S.N., Commander of Shenandoah, 207-28
Wages of seamen. *See* Advance wages
Waite, Morrison R., American counsel at Geneva, 233
Wampanoag, U.S.S., 20
War, definition of, 8
Ward, Wm. H., C.S.N., Commander of Olustee, 193
Warsaw Sound, Ga., 71
Washington, Treaty of, 25-26, 232
Wave Crest, captured by Alabama, 138-39
Waverly, whaler, captured by Shenandoah, 224
W. B. Nash, brig, captured, 117
W. C. Clark, brig, captured, 118
Welles, Gideon, Secretary of Navy, 70, 108, 161, and *passim*
Western development as cause of decline in merchant marine, 249-50
West Indian trade, 4
West Wind, ship, captured, 41
Whalebone, uses of, 199
Whale oil, uses of, 199
Whalers, captured by Alabama, 137
Whaling, methods of, 202-3
Whaling crews, character of, 204-5; compensation of, 204-5
Whaling industry, 198-206
Wheat, movement of, 138; supply of, 14
Whistling Wind, bark, captured, 106
Whittle, William C., Lieut., C.S.N., on Shenandoah, 207 *ff.*
Wilderness, U.S.S., blockader, 192
Wilkes, Charles, Capt., U.S.N., 65-67, 140, 147; insubordination of, 92; popularity of, 92; relieved of command, 93

Wilkinson, John, Capt., C.S.N., Commander of Chameleon, 195; Commander of Chickamauga, 189-92
William C. Nye, whaler, captured, 223
Williams, John, seaman, affidavit relative to treatment on Shenandoah, 216
William Thornton, whaler, captured, 222
Wilmington, N. C., Chickamauga at, 189-90, 192; Olustee escapes from, 193; Tallahassee at, 183-84, 189, 193-95
Wilson, Nathaniel I., purchaser of Shenandoah, 229
Wilson, Thomas F., U. S. Consul at Bahia, 123
Wine, cargoes of, 3
Winona, U.S.S., at Mobile, 99
Winslow, John A., Capt., U.S.N., Commander of Kearsarge, q.v.
Wood, John Taylor, C.S.A., C.S.N., Commander of Tallahassee, 182-89
Woolsey, Theodore D., American consul at Geneva, 233
Worden, John L., Commander U.S.N., 71
World War, effect on shipbuilding, 259-60
Wright, Richard, purchaser of Shenandoah, 207
Wyoming, U.S.S., 93; pursuit of Florida, 121; search for Alabama, 155
Wyvern, H.M.S., 86

YANCEY, Wm. L., Confederate Commissioner, 68
Yellow fever on Florida, 97-100

ZANZIBAR, Sultan of, purchaser of Shenandoah, 229
Zeis, Paul, economist, cited, 267
Zelinda, ship, captured, 119